# Best Hikes Anchorage

The Greatest Views, Wildlife, and Forest Strolls

Second Edition

## John Tyson

**FALCON**GUIDES

GUILFORD, CONNECTICUT

## FALCONGUIDES®

An imprint of The Rowman & Littlefield Publishing Group, Inc.
4501 Forbes Blvd., Ste. 200
Lanham, MD 20706
www.rowman.com
Falcon and FalconGuides are registered trademarks and Make Adventure Your Story is a trademark of The Rowman & Littlefield Publishing Group, Inc.

Distributed by NATIONAL BOOK NETWORK

Photos by John Tyson unless otherwise noted
Maps by The Rowman & Littlefield Publishing Group, Inc.

British Library Cataloguing in Publication Information available

**Library of Congress Cataloging-in-Publication Data available**

ISBN 978-1-4930-3434-5 (paperback)
ISBN 978-1-4930-3435-2 (e-book)

∞™ The paper used in this publication meets the minimum requirements of American National Standard for Information Sciences—Permanence of Paper for Printed Library Materials, ANSI/NISO Z39.48-1992.

Printed in the United States of America

# Contents

Acknowledgments ............................................................... vii
Introduction ..................................................................... ix
    Weather ..................................................................... x
    Flora and Fauna ......................................................... x
    Wilderness Restrictions and Regulations.................. xiv
    Alaska's Public Lands .............................................. xvi
How to Use This Guide........................................................ xvii
Trail Finder........................................................................ xviii
Map Legend ...................................................................... xx

**North of Anchorage**.................................................................1
  1. Albert Loop Trail ........................................................ 2
  2. Rodak Nature Trail ..................................................... 7
  3. Dew Mound Trail ...................................................... 11
  4. River Trail at North Fork Eagle River......................... 18
  5. Lower Eagle River Trail and Barbara Falls ................. 22
  6. Mount Baldy ............................................................ 27
  7. Rendezvous Peak Trail .............................................. 32
  8  South Fork Eagle River Valley Trail............................ 36
  9. Hanging Valley Trail.................................................. 41
 10. Eklutna Lakeside Trail ............................................... 46
 11. Twin Peaks Trail ....................................................... 52
 12. Eydlu Bena Loop Trail .............................................. 57
 13. Bold Ridge Trail ....................................................... 61
 14. East Fork Trail to Tulchina Falls ................................ 66
 15. Thunderbird Falls Trail ............................................. 72
 16. Ptarmigan Valley Trail .............................................. 77

**East of Anchorage** .................................................................. 82
 17. Hillside Trail System (Overview) ............................... 83
 18. Powerline Trail ......................................................... 88
 19. Anchorage Overlook Trail ......................................... 94
 20. Flattop Mountain Trail .............................................. 97
 21. Backside of Flattop Mountain Trail........................... 103
 22. Williwaw Lakes Trail ................................................ 107
 23. Near Point Trail ....................................................... 113
 24. Wolverine Peak Trail ................................................ 119

**South of Anchorage** ............................................................. 125
 25. Turnagain Arm Trail ................................................. 126
 26. Indian Creek to Girdwood ........................................ 132
 27. Falls Creek Trail ...................................................... 138

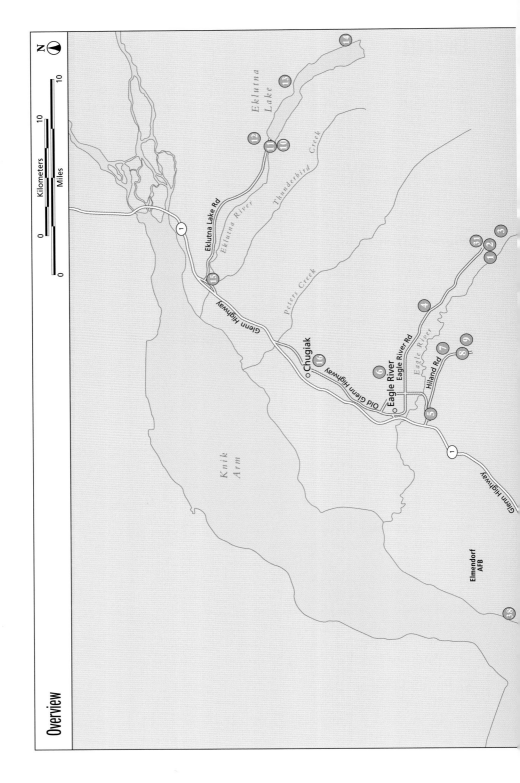

Overview

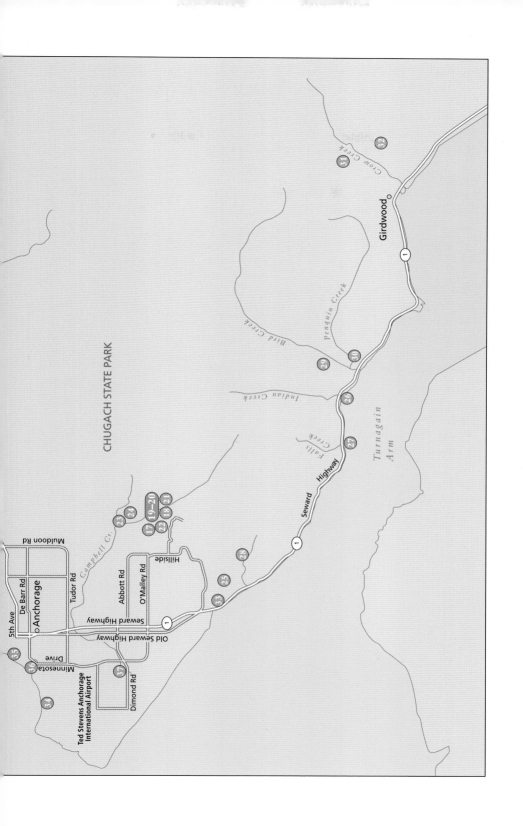

28. McHugh Lake–Rabbit Lake Trail ........................................... 143
29. Bird Ridge Trail ....................................................... 148
30. Bird Creek Trail ...................................................... 152
31. Historic Iditarod (Crow Pass) Trail.................................... 156
32. Winner Creek Trail .................................................... 164
33. Potter Marsh Wildlife Viewing Boardwalk Trail......................... 170

**Anchorage Urban Trails** ................................................ **174**
34. Earthquake Park/Inside the Slide Trail................................ 175
35. Tony Knowles Coastal Trail ........................................... 180
36. Lanie Fleischer Chester Creek Trail .................................. 185
37. Campbell Creek Trail ................................................. 190
38. Ship Creek Trail ..................................................... 195

The Art of Hiking ........................................................ 200
   Trail Etiquette....................................................... 200
   Getting into Shape ................................................... 201
   Preparedness ......................................................... 201
   First Aid............................................................. 203
   Natural Hazards ...................................................... 207
   Navigation............................................................ 208
   Trip Planning......................................................... 209
   Equipment............................................................. 211
   Hiking with Children ................................................. 214
   Hiking with Your Dog ................................................. 215

Hike Index .............................................................. 219
About the Author ........................................................ 220

# Acknowledgments

Being an avid outdoor photographer and adventure seeker means my family has had to make some serious sacrifices. No one has sacrificed more in their life than my wife Madelyn. She has been my life-long companion and travel partner and always supportive of all of my ideas—regardless how outrageous they may seem. My boys Michael and Matthew and their wives Caitlin and Perri have been hugely supportive of my goals while working on this project during the time I was away from home. I could not have completed this book without my family's sacrifices and support. I thank and love you all!

Special thanks to staff at Eagle River Nature Center. They made my life so much easier with their warm and generous hospitality during my stay in Eagle River.

Thank you to Caitlin Romm-Tyson and Amanda Hanson for their photo contributions.

And lastly, thanks to the rangers and trail crews of Chugach State Park, the folks at FalconGuides, and all my old friends in Alaska and all the new ones who helped bring this project to completion.

*Barbara Falls (Hike 5)*

# Introduction

If you are hiking in Alaska for the first time or thousandth time, you will always be left with an enormous admiration for the beauty and pristine qualities of the state. Hiking around Anchorage is primarily accomplished in Chugach State Park, our country's third-largest state park, encompassing nearly 500,000 acres of wilderness. It is the largest park in North America within an urban setting, sitting immediately east of Anchorage, the largest city in Alaska. This book is intended to introduce you to Chugach State Park and other trails in Anchorage and the surrounding area. Many of the major trailheads near town can lead you on your own trail of endless exploration.

For visitors and less-experienced hikers, this book will help you in planning your time and properly preparing for your hikes in the park. GPS coordinates are provided for all the major trailheads, stream crossings, landmarks, and other directional cues for every hike. The trails in this book are divided into four sections: north, east, south, and Anchorage urban trails. They are based on entry points into the park and popular trails within the Anchorage city limits. Directions to each trailhead in this book always use Anchorage as a starting point.

Different regions of Chugach will experience significant differences in weather patterns, which you should always take into account when planning your hike. The trails in Chugach State Park can provide you with a variety of levels of wilderness experiences and can accommodate the skill level of most any hiker, or the busy schedule of a visitor and his or her family. The opportunities for adventure are endless. Strenuous physical challenges into backcountry or forty-five-minute afternoon leisure walks can provide you with glimpses of the true wild Alaska. Stunning alpine lakes, icy glaciers, and a 5,000-foot elevation rise add to the natural wonder of Chugach State Park. Nature and wildlife are bountiful in Chugach, and you won't be disappointed. World-class wildlife viewing or afternoon berry picking is available just minutes from downtown Anchorage. Mountain streams offer opportunities for fishing and even recreational gold panning.

Six mountain ranges can be seen from Anchorage. On a clear day, Mount McKinley and the Alaska Range can be seen to the north, the smaller Tordrillo Mountain range to the west–northwest, the Chugach Mountains to the east, the Talkeetna Mountains to the west, the Kenai Mountains to the south, and the volcanic Chigmit Mountains of the Aleutian Range to the southwest. Cook Inlet sits west of Anchorage and is also visible from several trails within the park.

With nearly a half-million acres of wilderness to explore, the trails in this book merely provide you with a glimpse of the wilderness opportunities Chugach has to offer and the outstanding trail systems within Anchorage itself. This book can get you started on your own road to adventure and will introduce you to some of the most picturesque areas of Alaska—true Alaskan wilderness and hiking trails unrivaled anywhere else in the United States.

## Weather

The Anchorage area has four seasons and a relatively mild winter. This maritime climate allows the park to be utilized year-round. The park itself receives 160 inches of rain each year in the extreme southeast and only 12 inches per year in the northeast. Keep these extremes in mind as you plan your hike. The average temperatures in the Anchorage area range from 65 degrees Fahrenheit in July to 20 degrees Fahrenheit in January. Summer months have a comfortable low temperature of 51 degrees Fahrenheit with very low humidity.

When you come to Alaska, you dress for changing weather. That means wearing layers that you can peel off or put on. The weather can change from sunny and warm to cool and damp within a matter of minutes. It can—and does—change quickly, abruptly, and often.

Summers here are like nowhere else in the world. Unlike many places, you do not need to restrict your hiking to early morning or late afternoon because of high temperatures and high humidity. You will experience cooler temperatures in the mountains, depending on altitude. On the day of the summer solstice, June 21, there are twenty-four hours of functional daylight. Long summer days provide you with plenty of daylight hours for hiking. Winter days are much shorter. On the winter solstice, the shortest day of the year, you will experience a mere five hours and twenty-eight minutes of daylight.

The trails in this book are used year-round by residents and visitors alike. In the higher elevations of Chugach State Park, snow can be on the ground August through May. Fortunately, trail use is not restricted to summer hiking. Many trails are intended for winter outdoor sports and can be explored using snowshoes, cross-country skis, dogsleds, and snow machines. There are more than 130 miles of winter walkways and over 140 miles of groomed ski trails for winter enjoyment by Alaskans and visitors to this amazing area.

## Flora and Fauna

Just about any hike in this book, and certainly any hike in Chugach State Park, will quickly acquaint you with the variety of plant and animal communities existing in the Anchorage area. The interrelationship between the plant and animal communities is actually quite complex and ever changing. The unique ecosystems you'll see throughout Chugach are affected by that particular area's amount of precipitation, slope of the land, elevation, soil, wind, sun exposure, succession, and the people that occupy or use it. As you hike throughout different areas of the park, you will quickly notice the enormous differences in the principal habitats that support the plant and animal communities within them. The primary habitats in the south side of the park are completely different from what you will see on the north or west side. Each ecosystem can actually be broken down into smaller components.

The waters of the Turnagain Arm border the park's south side. This marine ecosystem also includes the intertidal zone, salt marshes, and mudflats—all supporting a variety of wildlife. The marine waters support a population of beluga whales, visible from several points along the Seward Highway. Other wildlife you will see in this area includes spotted sandpipers, gulls, mews, Arctic terns, Canada geese, and several varieties of ducks. The salt marshes and other wetlands in Chugach State Park are home to a variety of wildlife, such as river otters, muskrats, minks, brown bears, red foxes, songbirds, terns, gulls, and waterfowl.

*Bluebells commonly seen on Alaska trails*

Muskegs are a less-prominent habitat in the Anchorage area. A muskeg is basically a poorly drained depression, a former river basin, or old slough—too wet for tree growth. These are good places for bird observation. Numerous varieties of waterfowl, marsh birds, and even short-eared owls are quite common. Muskegs also support a variety of small mammals such as voles, lemmings, muskrats, weasels, and minks and the park's only amphibian, the wood frog. As you observe the wildlife in these areas, also note some of the plant life around you, such as sphagnum moss, lichens, grasses, sedges and rushes, willow, cranberry, bog blueberry, black spruce, and alder.

The riparian habitats are the zones around the lakes, rivers, and streams. The wildlife occupying these areas is many of the same ones you will see in the muskegs. However, the larger mammals such as black and brown bears, moose, river otters, beavers, and wolverines will frequent these zones. Bald eagles are common birds in riparian habitats. The dominant vegetation along the rivers and streams is cottonwood, willow, alder, poplar, and grasses, rushes, and sedges.

There are several plants you will want to be able to identify before taking off onto the trails. One is called cow parsnip. This large leafed plant can cause a skin rash much like poison ivy commonly encountered in other states. Devil's club is a brushy plant with large highly serrated leaves with very pronounced thorns on the stalk, stems and underside of the leaves. This one too should be avoided. It is easily identified. If you like to pick berries, be sure you can identify baneberry. All parts of the baneberry plant are highly toxic and it produces a red and sometimes white berry that is poisonous to children and adults.

Many of Chugach's trails begin in a coniferous forest. Where you are in the park will make a difference in the type of forest you may be standing in. Hemlock spruce forests are found largely in the Turnagain Arm area, along with mountain hemlock at the higher elevations. The dominant trees are a mix of western hemlock and Sitka spruce, towering over 100 feet high. This forest is actually a northern extension of

# THE BEARS OF CHUGACH

Chugach State Park near Anchorage has bears, and you can expect to meet one almost anywhere. This does not mean you will see one; it does mean you should always be prepared on how to react if you do. There are bear encounters in the park every year, and young bears are known to venture into human spaces. However, most bears prefer to avoid people rather than interact with them, and if given the opportunity will do just that.

The park has populations of both black and brown bears, with approximately 300 black bears and 65 brown bears in the Anchorage area and Chugach State Park. The two species cannot be identified merely by the color of their fur. Black bears vary in color from brown to black and have a white patch on the front of the chest. They range in size from 125 to 400 pounds, depending on the gender of the animal. The average length is 5 feet. In comparison, brown bears can be dark brown to blonde. Females weigh 200 to 600 pounds, males weigh 400 to 1,000 pounds, and the bears average 7 to 9 feet in length. Brown bears have a hump on their shoulders and a dish-shaped head. Black bears do not have the hump, and their head has a straight profile.

If you are not bear savvy, become acquainted with bear facts before you venture out. Learn to become "bear aware" as you travel throughout the park and on any of the trails in the Anchorage area. There are several things you can do to ensure a safe and fun hike.

- The first thing to remember is to always keep alert during a hike. Be aware of the trail both in front of you and off to the sides. Bears also use trails and roads just like humans. Look for bear signs along the way such as fresh scat and tracks.
- When you hike, make noise as you proceed along the trail. Wearing bear bells, singing, whistling, and talking will alert any bears up around the next corner. Traveling in groups adds safety by generating more noise and visibility, alerting bears of your presence.
- If you hike with your dog, leashed is safer than unleashed. Many unleashed dogs, retreating from a bear encounter farther up the trail, have brought a running bear back to their owner.
- Try to avoid areas with thick brush or vegetation.
- Know that windy days can make it more difficult for a bear to hear or smell you.
- Avoid areas where there are fresh carcasses of mammals or dead fish. A bear will defend its food aggressively.

Bears are somewhat predictable, but they do not like surprises nor do they like to be crowded. Do not try to approach a bear for a better photograph either on land or in a boat. Always keep a considerable distance between you and the bear, and change your course if possible to avoid the animal. Some bears are more tolerant of human presence than others, but all animals

*Black bears are common in the Anchorage area.*

have an approach distance that makes them feel threatened when you get too close. If you enter that zone, the animal may react aggressively.

If you come upon a bear and the bear does not see you, slowly back up and retreat. If the bear does see you, identify yourself as a human. Do not run. Hold your ground, stand tall, and wave your arms and talk loudly until the bear retreats. A bear that stands up usually is curious and not a threat. If the bear charges, continue waving your arms and speaking in a normal voice. Almost all charges are bluffs, and the bear usually will stop within feet of you and then veer off. Under no circumstances should you run. Running can trigger a bear's chasing instinct, and none of us can outrun a bear.

The best defense against a bear is common sense, being part of a group and being alert when hiking in bear country. Always be reading the habitat around you and be aware of the things bears are interested in, such as salmon, berries, or moose. You can also carry an aerosol bear spray with you as an added measure of defense. However, the spray won't do you any good if it is tucked away or hanging on the back of your pack or you don't know how to use it. Always know which way the wind is blowing.

Firearms are allowed in Chugach State Park. If you choose to carry a firearm, be sure it is one that can stop an adult bear. Unless you are quite skilled in shooting the weapon, it may become a bigger threat to you than the bear. More people are hurt by the guns they carry than by the bears they encounter.

If your hike includes an overnight campout, be sure not to set up camp close to the trail or in an area with a lot of bear activity. Use a tent and camp in an open area where wildlife can see you. Cook at least 100 feet away from the campsite, and learn how to cache your food. And be sure to pack everything out that you carry in.

southeastern Alaska's temperate rain forest. A spruce-hardwood forest contains either white or black spruce. Often, but not exclusively, white spruce is located in the drier areas of the park and on southern slopes. Black spruce is on the north-facing slopes. Some other plants you will see in this type of forest are birch, aspen, balsam poplar, willow, and dwarf dogwood.

The coniferous forest supports a vast variety of wildlife, much of which you'll never see. The eerie fact is that there are a lot of eyes watching you as you go up the trail. Animals such as bears, moose, porcupines, foxes, coyotes, snowshoe hares, martens, squirrels, and lynx are all common. There is also a diverse mix of birds, such as juncos, pine grosbeaks, sparrows, common red polls, chickadees, nuthatches, owls, goshawks, woodpeckers, spruce grouse, and jays. Keep your eyes open and you will spot many of these.

As you make your way up a mountain, you will notice another change in vegetation. The forest thins and the vegetation becomes intensely thicker, with thickets and shrubs. The dominant vegetation is alder, willow, and birch—favorites of the all-powerful moose. Alaska's state bird, the willow ptarmigan, is also found at this level. This area is often called the subalpine, for obvious reasons. The tree line begins to end, just below the alpine tundra.

The alpine tundra is above the tree line and is unique, with an abundance of wildlife, a multitude of miniature plants, and extraordinary views. The open land with low shrubs and wildflowers supports wildlife such as Dall sheep, mountain goats, wolves, coyotes, hoary marmots, wolverine, and brown bears. Forget-me-nots, the state wildflower, grow in the tundra soil. Other flowers such as mountain and bell heather, fireweed, western buttercup, and alpine meadow bistort are also part of the plant community, along with mosses and colorful lichens. Blueberry, crowberry, and cranberry are favorites for many explorers of the tundra terrain each fall.

The variety of ecosystems, habitats, and terrains in Chugach State Park makes hiking this park an extraordinary and rewarding experience. It will create a desire for adventure and exploration and will leave you with a strong admiration for and a unique connection with the awesome beauty and vastness of the park.

## Wilderness Restrictions and Regulations

Alaska's Division of Parks and Outdoor Recreation is dedicated to preserving the wilderness of Chugach State Park and helping you discover the unique features the park has to offer. Chugach State Park Headquarters is located at the Potter Section House State Historic Site, Mile 115, Seward Highway, south of Anchorage. (Call 907-345-5014 or e-mail at csp@dnr.state.ak.us for information.) Although overnight trip plans are not a requirement, they are suggested and can be filed with the rangers at Chugach State Park Headquarters.

There are various rules for different outdoor sports within the park. However, hikers should be aware of the following general regulations while using the park:

- Fireworks are not permitted in the park. They can be dangerous to other visitors, disturb wildlife, and cause fires.

- Berries and edible plants can be gathered for personal consumption but not for sale. Other natural items, such as rocks, trees, and vegetation, should not be disturbed.

- Fires are allowed in portable camp stoves, metal fire rings provided by the park, and on the gravel beds of the Eklutna River, Peters and Bird Creeks, and the main stem of the Eagle River at times of low water. Random campfires can cause scars that last for decades.

- Wood that is dead and lying on the ground can be used for fires in park-provided fire pits.

- Gold panning is allowed year-round, except in streams that support salmon. Only a pan and shovel may be used. No motorized equipment or chemicals are allowed.

- Guns and weapons may be carried for self-protection. No target practice is allowed. During hunting seasons, guns may not be discharged within 0.5 mile of any campground, picnic area, ski area, or roadway in the park, including the Seward Highway.

- Hunting and fishing are permitted during legal seasons. Hunting and fishing licenses are required. Contact the Alaska Department of Fish and Game, 333 Raspberry Road, Anchorage 99518; (907) 267-2344.

- Mudflats are located in the intertidal areas along the Turnagain Arm. Even though they look inviting to explore, they are extremely dangerous. The solid surface of the glacial mud can suddenly change to quicksand. Many people and animals have become trapped in the mud and drowned due to rapidly rising tides. STAY OFF THE MUDFLATS.

- Pets/dogs must be on a leash at all visitor centers and campgrounds; barking is not permitted after 11:00 p.m.

- Vehicles must remain on the roadway, in designated parking areas, or on camping pads. Posted speed limits and parking regulations are enforced.

- Drones are not permitted in Chugach State Park.

Park regulations and other park information can be found at www.dnr.state.ak.us/parks.

### GREEN TIP
Consider the packaging of any products you bring with you.
It's best to properly dispose of packaging at home before you hike.
If you're on the trail, pack it out with you.

## Alaska's Public Lands

The state of Alaska has more than 379 million acres of land. Over 300 million acres of this land is considered public-use land. The state has 33,904 miles of shoreline and is one-fifth the size of the entire lower forty-eight states. With this come enormous opportunities for the traveler and explorer. What brings so many people to the state is the fact that much of this land is untouched by man; it is truly pristine Alaskan wilderness.

Alaska has eight national parks, two national forests, 110 state parks, and 88 percent of the nation's national wildlife refuges. The Tongass and Chugach National Forests are the two largest forests in the United States. Alaska's Wood-Tikchik, nearly 1.6 million acres, is the country's largest state park. At nearly 500,000 acres, Chugach State Park is North America's largest park within an urban setting and the third-largest U.S. state park.

Alaska's public lands provide immense recreational opportunities for everyone. If you are looking for things to do, some of the more popular activities include fishing and hunting, horseback riding, hiking, mountaineering, rock climbing, panning for gold, wildlife viewing, photography, biking, boating, river floating, day cruising, road touring, camping, picnicking, snow skiing, snowshoeing, ice climbing, snow machines and all-terrain vehicles (ATVs), and berry picking.

In addition to Chugach State Park near Anchorage, popular public lands in the state include the Arctic National Wildlife Refuge, Glacier Bay National Park, McNeil River State Game Sanctuary, Portage Glacier and Russian River in Chugach National Forest, Kenai Fords National Park, Denali National Park, and Chilkat Bald Eagle Preserve.

The public lands in Alaska provide not just recreation for Alaskans and visitors but also food to eat, natural resources for extraction industries, and ecotourism opportunities for local economies. In addition to preserving the pristine beauty of the state, these public lands provide vital habitat and protection for wildlife. For more detailed information about Alaska's public lands, contact the Alaska Public Lands Information Center in Anchorage (907-271-2737) or Fairbanks (907-456-0527), or visit www .nps.gov/aplic.

# How to Use This Guide

To aid in quick decision-making, each hike begins with a short description of the hike to whet your appetite. Next come the "hike specs," including where the hike starts; distance and type of hike; approximate hiking time; difficulty rating; elevation gain or loss; trail surface; best hiking season; other trail users; status on dogs; what agency manages the land; town(s) nearest the trailhead; any fees or permits required; useful maps; whom to contact for updated trail information; and special considerations or hazards.

Finding the trailhead gives you directions from Anchorage to where the hike begins. Be aware that Alaska Highway 1 is called the Glenn Highway north of Anchorage and the Seward Highway south of Anchorage. Those are the names that will be used in this book.

The Hike presents this author's impressions of the trail. It isn't possible to cover everything you will see, and who would want that anyway? Taking a hike is not just about exercise or getting outside. It's also about exploring a place and learning about it on your own. The hike description is meant as a guide.

Miles and Directions includes specific mileages and GPS coordinates to identify turns, trail junctions, points of interest, and options such as hike extensions or interesting detours. Hike Information lists sources of additional area information, campgrounds, purveyors of hike tours, outdoor/hiking organizations, outdoor equipment retailers, and local events and attractions.

*Chugach Mountains backdrop downtown Anchorage*

# Trail Finder

| Hike No. | Hike Name | Best Hikes with Children | Best Hikes for Great Anchorage Views | Best Hikes with Peak Climbing | Best Hikes with Rivers/Streams/Marshes | Best Hikes with Waterfalls | Best Hikes for Back-packers | Best Hikes with Multiuse Trails | Best Hikes for Turnagain Arm Views |
|---|---|---|---|---|---|---|---|---|---|
| 1 | Albert Loop Trail | • | | | • | | | | |
| 2 | Rodak Nature Trail | • | | | • | | | | |
| 3 | Dew Mound Trail | | | | • | | | | |
| 4 | River Trail at North Fork Eagle River | | | | • | | | | |
| 5 | Lower Eagle River Trail and Barbara Falls | • | | | • | • | | | |
| 6 | Mount Baldy | • | • | • | | | | | |
| 7 | Rendezvous Peak Trail | | | • | • | | • | | |
| 8 | South Fork Eagle River Valley Trail | | | | • | | • | | |
| 9 | Hanging Valley Trail | | | • | | | • | | |
| 10 | Eklutna Lakeside Trail | | | | • | | | • | |
| 11 | Twin Peaks Trail | | | • | | | | | |
| 12 | Eydlu Bena Loop Trail | • | | | | | | | |
| 13 | Bold Ridge Trail | | | • | | | | | |
| 14 | East Fork Trail to Tulchina Falls | | | | • | • | • | | |
| 15 | Thunderbird Falls Trail | | | | | • | | | |
| 16 | Ptarmigan Valley Trail | • | | | | | | • | |
| 17 | Hillside Trail System (Overview) | • | • | | | | • | | |

| No. | Trail | C1 | C2 | C3 | C4 | C5 | C6 | C7 | C8 |
|---|---|---|---|---|---|---|---|---|---|
| 18 | Powerline Trail | • | • | | | • | | | • |
| 19 | Anchorage Overlook Trail | • | | | | | | • | • |
| 20 | Flattop Mountain Trail | • | | | | | • | • | |
| 21 | Backside of Flattop Mountain Trail | • | | | | | • | • | • |
| 22 | Williwaw Lakes Trail | | | • | | | • | • | |
| 23 | Near Point Trail | | | | | | • | • | |
| 24 | Wolverine Peak Trail | | | | | | • | • | |
| 25 | Turnagain Arm Trail | • | | | | • | | | |
| 26 | Indian Creek to Girdwood | • | • | | | | | | |
| 27 | Falls Creek Trail | • | | | • | | | | |
| 28 | McHugh Lake–Rabbit Lake Trail | • | | • | • | • | | | |
| 29 | Bird Ridge Trail | • | | | | | | | |
| 30 | Bird Creek Trail | • | • | | | | | | |
| 31 | Historic Iditarod (Crow Pass) Trail | | | • | • | • | | | |
| 32 | Winner Creek Trail | | | | | • | | | • |
| 33 | Potter Marsh Wildlife Viewing Trail | | | | | | | • | • |
| 34 | Earthquake Park Inside the Slide | • | | | | | | • | • |
| 35 | Tony Knowles Coastal Trail | • | • | | | | | | • |
| 36 | Lanie Fleischer Chester Creek Trail | • | • | | | | | | • |
| 37 | Campbell Creek Trail | | • | | | | | | • |
| 38 | Ship Creek Trail | | • | | | • | | | • |

# Map Legend

## Transportation

- Freeway/Interstate Highway (80)
- US Highway (101)
- State Highway (1)
- Other Road (1431)
- Unpaved Road
- Railroad

## Trails

- Selected Route
- Trail or Fire Road
- Direction of Travel

## Water Features

- Body of Water
- River or Creek
- Waterfall

## Symbols

- Trailhead
- Bridge
- Boardwalk/Steps

## Symbols (continued)

- Building/Point of Interest
- Campground
- Gate
- Lighthouse
- Mountain/Peak
- Parking
- Pass
- Picnic Area
- Restroom
- Visitor Center/Information
- Towns and Cities
- Tunnel
- Scenic View
- True North (Magnetic North is approximately 15.5° East)

## Land Management

- Local and State Parks
- National Forest and Wilderness Areas
- Natural Area
- Watersheds

# North of Anchorage

Most of the hiking trails north of Anchorage are located in Chugach State Park. The trails on the north side of the park are accessible from various points described in the individual hike descriptions. There is no single road that takes you into the park, and accessing different hikes will often require driving from one area of the park to the next. Sometimes access to the trailhead may even require several miles of hiking before you reach the official "beginning" of the trail.

That said, the trails in this section will lead you into the vast mountain ranges and open tundra of Chugach State Park and provide you with opportunities to view much of Alaska's wildlife. These trails can launch you on vast expeditions across the park through remote wilderness, or they can provide the simple pleasure of a short morning or afternoon walk. Either way, you can trust that these trails will introduce you to some of the most exceptional scenery Alaska has to offer.

*View of Eagle and Symphony Lakes from Rendezvous Peak*

# 1 Albert Loop Trail

This is an excellent hike for the entire family. Amazing scenery, boardwalks, viewing platforms, and an easy, flat trail are the main elements of the hike. The trail slightly descends down along the Eagle River and provides outstanding mountain views, wildflowers, lush vegetation and ample opportunities for spotting wildlife.

**Start:** Trailhead behind the Eagle River Nature Center
**Distance:** 3.2-mile loop
**Approximate hiking time:** 1.5–2 hours
**Difficulty:** Easy due to flat, smooth terrain
**Elevation loss:** 51 feet
**Trail surface:** Gravel and dirt with several boardwalks; can be muddy and wet in some areas
**Seasons:** Best hiking June through early August. Closed during salmon season in mid-August through October.
**Other trail users:** Heavily used during the summer months with school groups, local hikers, and tourists; horses permitted with a special-use permit from the park. Fat tire bike access to river provided during winter.
**Canine compatibility:** Leashed dogs permitted
**Land status:** State park

**Nearest town:** Eagle River
**Fees and permits:** $5 daily parking fee in the nature center's private parking lot; state park parking passes not valid here
**Maps:** Eagle River Nature Center map (available at the center); Imus Geographics Chugach State Park map (www.imusgeographics.com); USGS Anchorage
**Trail contacts:** Eagle River Nature Center, 32750 Eagle River Road, Eagle River 99577; (907) 694-2108; www.ernc.org; open Tuesday through Sunday 10:00 a.m. to 5:00 p.m. June through August. Open Wednesday through Sunday 10 a.m. to 5 p.m. May and September. Open 10:00 a.m. to 5:00 p.m. Friday through Sunday October through April.
**Special considerations:** Portions of this trail are often closed August through November to allow bears undisturbed salmon fishing in the river.

**Finding the trailhead:** Coming from Anchorage, follow the Glenn Highway north toward the town of Eagle River. After about 10 miles veer right onto the Hiland Road/Eagle River Loop exit. Turn right onto Eagle River Loop Road and continue for 2.5 miles. Turn right at the Lighthouse Church onto Eagle River Road and drive 10 miles to the Eagle River Nature Center parking lot. Hike down the trail directly behind the nature center for 0.5 mile. The Albert Loop Trail begins here at the signpost.

## The Hike

This is one of several great trails at Eagle River Nature Center just 10 miles outside of the town of Eagle River. The nature center is a non–profit organization that offers community events, public programs and educational school programs throughout the year. They also offer guided family hikes and daily nature hikes during the summer months. Inside the center is an amazing display of local wildlife and a wealth of information. Start your journey here.

*Common sight on the Albert Loop Trail*

The easy 3-mile loop provides great views of the Eagle River Valley and Polar Bear, Eagle, and Hurdygurdy Mountain. It is a fun hike with wildlife viewing opportunities, wildflowers, boardwalks, bridges, and lush vegetation.

Begin this hike just behind the nature center and proceed down the paved path on the Rodak Nature Trail. This is a popular stretch linking four trails, so plan on lots of company. However, it is closed to bicycles, motor vehicles, and horses (except by special-use permit).

Technically, the trail does not begin until you meet the junction of Dew Mound Trail and the Historic Iditarod (Crow Pass) Trail at slightly less than 0.5 mile from the trailhead. At this point the Albert Loop Trail begins by continuing straight ahead while simultaneously following the Historic Iditarod (Crow Pass) Trail. A left turn is where you begin the Dew Mound Trail. Here the ground becomes wetter, and you cross your first boardwalk to get through the wetland.

Hike another 0.5 mile to an intersection called Four Corners, for good reason. This is a prominent intersection with a resting bench. The Iditarod continues straight ahead, a left turn loops you to the Dew Mound Trail, and a right turn is the continuation of Albert Loop, which is what you want to take.

Continue onto Darren's Bridge and stop and view the large open marshy area on your left. This is a beautiful setting with an abandoned beaver lodge and remnants of the beaver dam that helped form this area. Continue a short distance to reach another signpost. This gives you an opportunity to visit the River Trail Yurt, one of three yurts in the area. . This one, located on the shoreline of the Eagle River, is often used by rafters and kayakers as an overnight resting facility while they travel downstream. It is also a favorite rental location for families and couples. Albert Loop continues to the right.

▶ **The mosquito is often jokingly called Alaska's state bird. The willow ptarmigan actually fills that niche. However, there are twenty-seven species of mosquitoes in the state of Alaska; sixteen are found in Chugach State Park.**

Further up the trail, you will find a well-marked bypass trail veering to the right. This is often used when the river is high or during the muddy season to avoid the lower wet areas near the river. If mud is not a concern for you, take the entire trail that borders along the Eagle River. This portion of the trail allows for off-trail exploring along the stone shore line and presents some awesome views in the valley.

At approximately 2.8 miles you come to several small bridges and a rest stop. From here on, the trail becomes gravel and narrows; the vegetation changes from woodland to tall grasses just prior to meeting the Rodak Nature Trail. You can turn right and head down to the Beaver Viewing Platform or go left, which will return you to the nature center and trailhead.

The Albert Loop Trail is a great nature trail and is used most of the year, other than several months beginning in August when it is closed because of bears fishing the Eagle River. In the winter months it provides excellent snowshoeing, hiking, and cross-country skiing opportunities.

## Miles and Directions

**0.0** Start hiking behind the nature center. N61 14.043 / W149 16.262

**0.9** Continue straight at the Albert Loop trailhead (N61 13.584 / W149 16.107) and begin walking on a boardwalk. N61 13.532 / W149 16.127

**1.0** Turn right at the Four Corners intersection to stay on Albert Loop. N61 13.433 / W149 16.181

**1.2** Reach a marshy area to your left and boardwalk (N61 13.498 / W149 16.371), then cross Daren's Bridge over an old beaver dam. N61 13.499 / W149 16.426

**1.6** Veer right, otherwise straight if going to the river yurt. N61 13.280 / W149 16.914

**1.7** Turn right to stay on the trail or left to view the river. N61 13.876 / W149 17.229

**1.9** Main trail joins the By-pass trail option used during wet seasons. N61° 13.545' W149° 17.084'

**2.7** Come to the first of several bridge crossings and bench. N61 14.055 / W149 16.788

**3.1** The Albert Loop Trail joins the Rodak Nature Trail here. Turn left to return to the nature center. N61 13.967 / W149 16

**3.2** Arrive back at the trailhead. N61 14.043 / W149 16.262

## Hike Information

### *Local information*

Anchorage Visitor Information Center, 546 West Fourth Avenue, Anchorage 99501; (907) 274-3531; www.anchorage.net

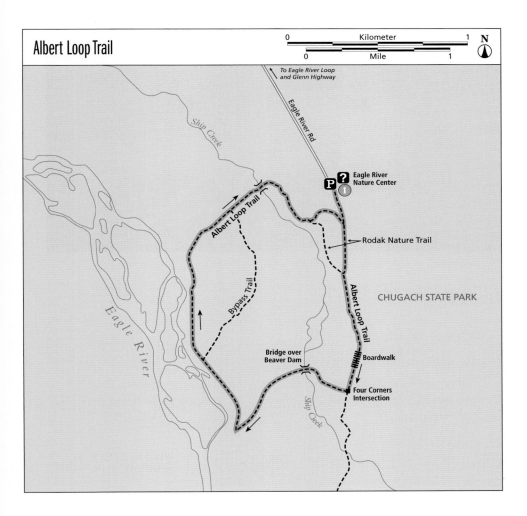

Alaska Department of Natural Resources Public Information Center, Atwood Building, 550 West Seventh Avenue, Suite 1260, Anchorage 99501; (907) 269-8400; www.dnr.state.ak.us/parks

Alaska Public Lands Information Center, 605 West Fourth Avenue, Suite 105, Anchorage 99501; (907) 271-2737; www.nps.gov/aplic

Chugach State Park Headquarters, located at the Potter Section House State Historic Site, Mile 115 Seward Highway (mailing address: HC 52 Box 8999, Indian 99540); (907) 345-5014; e-mail: csp@dnr.state.ak.us; open Monday through Friday 10:00 a.m. to 4:30 p.m.

*Camping*

Eagle River Campground (907-345-5014), Glenn Highway. Exit about 10 miles north of Anchorage onto Eagle River Loop and Hiland Road; nightly camping fee.

*Past beaver activity along Albert Loop Trail*

### Hike tours

Friends of Eagle River (operators of Eagle River Nature Center); (907) 694-2108; e-mail: ERNC@alaska.net

### Local organizations

The Anchorage Adventurers Meetup Group; www.adventurers.meetup.com/109
Mountaineering Club of Alaska, 2633 Spenard Road, Anchorage 99503; (907) 272-1811; www.mcak.org

### Local retailers

Recreational Equipment Inc. (REI), 1200 West Northern Lights Boulevard, Anchorage; (907) 272-4565; www.rei.com
Sportsman's Warehouse, 681 Old Seward Highway, Anchorage; (907) 644-1400; www.sportsmanswarehouse.com
Alaska Mountaineering and Hiking, 2633 Spenard Road, Anchorage; (907) 272-1811; www.alaskamountaineering.com
Cabelas, 155 W 104th, Anchorage; (907) 341-3400; www.cabelas.com/Stores/Anchorage
6th Avenue Outfitters, 520 W 6th Avenue, Anchorage; (907) 276-0233; www.6thavenueoutfitters.com
Bass Pro Shops, 3046 Mountain View Drive, Anchorage; (907) 330-5200; www.basspro.com/Anchorage

### Local events/attractions

Bear Paw Festival, Eagle River; July
Alaska State Fair, Palmer; August and September
An Anchorage calendar of events can be found at www.anchorage.net/events.html.

# 2 Rodak Nature Trail

This popular trail at Eagle River Nature Center is usually packed with hikers, families of all ages and the family dog—all easily accommodated. The trail is wheelchair and stroller accessible, although there is a slight downward hill, which means you have to come up on your return to the center. It begins on a wide path to two viewing platforms—the Beaver Viewing Deck and Salmon Viewing Deck—and Eagle River Valley. There are interpretive signboards, abundant wildflowers, lush vegetation, wildlife viewing opportunities such as bear, moose, songbirds, shorebirds, and waterfowl—all coupled with great scenery throughout the hike. This is definitely a hike to take your camera.

**Start:** Trailhead behind the Eagle River Nature Center

**Distance:** 0.75-mile loop

**Approximate hiking time:** 30 minutes–1 hour

**Difficulty:** Easy

**Elevation loss:** 51 feet

**Trail surface:** Paved path and gravel with seating; wheelchair and stroller accessible

**Seasons:** Best during summer months

**Other trail users:** Heavily used during the summer months with school groups, guided daily nature hikes, local hikers, and tourists

**Canine compatibility:** Leashed dogs permitted

**Land status:** State park

**Nearest town:** Eagle River

**Fees and permits:** $5 daily parking fee in the nature center's private parking lot; state park parking passes not valid here

**Maps:** Eagle River Nature Center map (available at the center); Imus Geographics Chugach State Park map (www.imusgeographics.com); USGS Anchorage

**Trail contacts:** Eagle River Nature Center, 32750 Eagle River Road, Eagle River 99577; (907) 694-2108; www.ernc.org; open Tuesday through Sunday 10:00 a.m. to 5:00 p.m. June through August. Open Wednesday through Sunday 10 a.m. to 5 p.m. May and September. Open 10:00 a.m. to 5:00 p.m. Friday through Sunday October through April.

**Special considerations:** None

**Finding the trailhead:** Coming from Anchorage, follow the Glenn Highway north toward the town of Eagle River. After about 10 miles veer right onto the Hiland Road/Eagle River Loop exit. Turn right onto Eagle River Loop Road and continue for 2.5 miles. Turn right at the Walmart onto Eagle River Road and drive 10 miles to the Eagle River Nature Center parking lot. The trailhead is located behind the nature center.

## The Hike

The Rodak Nature Trail is as popular with local residents as it is with tourists. It provides an easy, quick hike for the entire family on a nice weekend or an evening when you want to take a leisurely walk and just enjoy nature. Prior to walking the trail, take a few moments to go into the nature center. The center and staff can provide a wealth of information about the area—historical, natural history, Alaska's flora and fauna, things to see, and recent sightings along the trail.

*Eagle Peak and Hurdygurdy Mountain from Rodak Trail*

▶ **The wood frog is the only amphibian found in Chugach State Park. This unique little creature's body tissues are capable of completely freezing like a solid chunk of ice, allowing it to survive the harsh subzero winters of Alaska.**

The trailhead is easily found around the back of the center, to the left of the patio and viewing area. A series of interpretive panels along the trail highlight many of the features of Eagle River Valley. In addition, there is always something to see along the trail as you make your way down to the creek. You will trek through deciduous-coniferous woodland where an abundance of spring and summer wildflowers attractively garnish the trail's edge.

The trail passes two separate viewing decks. In late to mid-August and early September, the creek becomes heavily populated with red and silver salmon that are easily viewed from both viewing platforms. Both viewing platforms provide extraordinary views of the mountain ranges and Eagle River Valley. This area is exceptionally beautiful and shouldn't be missed. Bring your camera.

## Miles and Directions

**0.0** Start at the trailhead located directly behind the nature center (N61 14.043 / W149 16.262) and turn right onto the Rodak Nature Trail. N61 26.583 / W149 21.700 (Option: Going straight ahead will allow you to follow the Albert Loop, Historic Iditarod, or Dew Mound Trails.)

**0.1** Veer left at Geology Tour #3 interpretive panel. N61 14.008 / W149 16.377

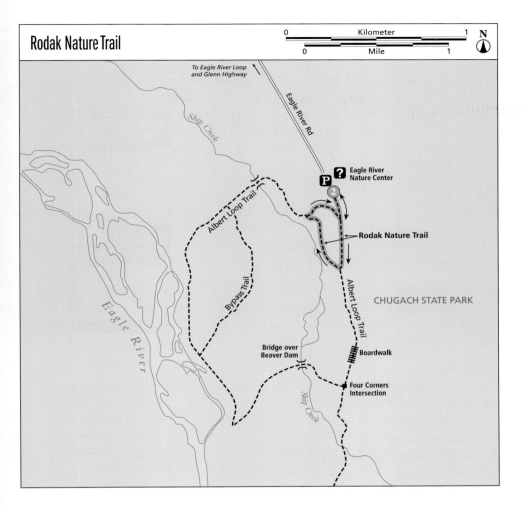

**Rodak Nature Trail**

To Eagle River Loop and Glenn Highway

Eagle River Rd

Ship Creek

Eagle River Nature Center

Albert Loop Trail

Rodak Nature Trail

Bypass Trail

Eagle River

Albert Loop Trail

CHUGACH STATE PARK

Bridge over Beaver Dam

Boardwalk

Four Corners Intersection

Ship Creek

- **0.2** Reach the Beaver Viewing Deck . N61 13.959 / W149 16.405
- **0.3** Reach the Salmon Viewing Deck and a boardwalk. N61 13.852 / W149 16.300
- **0.4** Join the main trail. Turn left to head back to the nature center and trailhead. N61 13.820 / W149 16.221
- **0.75** Arrive back at the trailhead. N61 14.043 / W149 16.262

## Hike Information

*Local information*

Anchorage Visitor Information Center, 546 West Fourth Avenue, Anchorage 99501; (907) 274-3531; www.anchorage.net

Alaska Department of Natural Resources Public Information Center, Atwood Building, 550 West Seventh Avenue, Suite 1260, Anchorage 99501; (907) 269-8400; www.dnr.state.ak.us/parks

Alaska Public Lands Information Center, 605 West Fourth Avenue, Suite 105, Anchorage 99501; (907) 271-2737; www.nps.gov/aplic

Chugach State Park Headquarters, located at the Potter Section House State Historic Site, Mile 115 Seward Highway (mailing address: HC 52 Box 8999, Indian 99540); (907) 345-5014; e-mail: csp@dnr.state.ak.us; open Monday through Friday 10:00 a.m. to 4:30 p.m.

## Camping

Eagle River Campground (907-345-5014), Glenn Highway. Exit about 10 miles north of Anchorage onto Eagle River Loop and Hiland Road; nightly camping fee. Hike tours: Friends of Eagle River (operators of Eagle River Nature Center); (907) 694-2108; e-mail: ERNC@alaska.net

## Local organizations

The Anchorage Adventurers Meetup Group; www.adventurers.meetup.com/109

Mountaineering Club of Alaska, 2633 Spenard Road, Anchorage 99503; (907) 272-1811; www.mcak.org

## Local retailers

Recreational Equipment Inc. (REI), 1200 West Northern Lights Boulevard, Anchorage; (907) 272-4565; www.rei.com

Sportsman's Warehouse, 681 Old Seward Highway, Anchorage; (907) 644-1400; www.sportsmanswarehouse.com

Alaska Mountaineering and Hiking, 2633 Spenard Road, Anchorage; (907) 272-1811; www.alaskamountaineering.com

Cabelas, 155 W 104th, Anchorage; (907) 341-3400; www.cabelas.com/Stores/Anchorage

6th Avenue Outfitters, 520 W 6th Avenue, Anchorage; (907) 276-0233; www.6thavenueoutfitters.com

Bass Pro Shops, 3046 Mountain View Drive, Anchorage; (907) 330-5200; www.basspro.com/Anchorage

## Local events/attractions

Alaskan Scottish Highland Games, Eagle River Lions Park, Anchorage; June
Bear Paw Festival, Eagle River; July
Alaska State Fair, Palmer; August and September
An Anchorage calendar of events can be found at www.anchorage.net/events.html.

# 3 Dew Mound Trail

The Dew Mound Trail runs parallel to the historic Iditarod Trail. Although it is considered a one-way trail to Dew Lake, it is easily traveled as a loop along the historic Iditarod trail back to the nature center. This easy to moderate 6.3-mile loop trail offers four cut-back options along the way to shorten the hike, should you decide to head back sooner. The trail passes through a variety of plant communities showcasing tall grasses, shrubs and thickets, and beautiful spans of spruce, birch and aspen trees. Large boulder fields and rocky ravines add to the adventure of this hike.

**Start:** Trailhead behind the Eagle River Nature Center

**Distance:** 6.3-mile loop

**Approximate hiking time:** 3–4 hours

**Difficulty:** Easy

**Elevation gain:** 365 feet

**Trail surface:** Dirt, wood chips, tree roots, rocks and gravel

**Seasons:** Spring, summer, fall

**Other trail users:** None

**Canine compatibility:** Leashed dogs permitted

**Land status:** State park

**Nearest town:** Eagle River

**Fees and permits:** $5 daily parking in the nature center's private parking lot; state park parking passes not valid here

**Maps:** Eagle River Nature Center map (available at the center); Imus Geographics Chugach State Park map (www.imusgeographics.com); USGS Anchorage

**Trail contacts:** Eagle River Nature Center, 32750 Eagle River Road, Eagle River 99577; (907) 694-2108; www.ernc.org; open Tuesday through Sunday 10:00 a.m. to 5:00 p.m. June through August. Open Wednesday through Sunday 10 a.m. to 5 p.m. May and September. Open 10:00 a.m. to 5:00 p.m. Friday through Sunday October through April.

**Special considerations:** None

**Finding the trailhead:** Coming from Anchorage, follow the Glenn Highway north toward the town of Eagle River. After about 10 miles veer right onto the Hiland Road/Eagle River Loop exit. Turn right onto Eagle River Loop Road and continue for 2.5 miles. Turn right at the Walmart onto Eagle River Road and drive 10 miles to the Eagle River Nature Center parking lot. The trailhead is located behind the nature center.

## The Hike

Begin this hike at the trailhead located behind the Eagle River Nature Center. Head straight down the Albert Loop Trail, following the gravel path. Hike about 0.4 mile and pick up Dew Mound Trail on your left. Proceeding straight will keep you on the Historic Iditarod (Crow Pass) and Albert Loop Trails; turning right will take you to the viewing deck on the Rodak Nature Trail. The trail begins through an open, grassy meadow and eventually takes you into thicker vegetation and then into a mature

*Dew Lake*

forest of birch, aspen and cottonwood trees. Portions of the trail are rough with rocks and roots.

Within another 0.1 mile come to an area with a couple of right-turn options within 15 yards of each other. Either turn will loop back to the main trail and back to the nature center. As you continue straight ahead, notice the orange blazes marking the trail. Several areas along the path are more difficult to follow, and you'll be glad you have the blazes. During the next 0.75 mile you will cross three footbridges and mountain streams, all showcasing the beauty of this area with stands of birch and spruce. Just past the third bridge you have a second opportunity to loop back to the Historic Iditarod (Crow Pass) Trail, which will also lead you back to the nature center. The loop is called the Mountain Meadow Trail. There is one last opportunity to loop back another 0.25 mile up the trail. Turn right to take the Rapids Loop Trail back to the nature center and shorten the hike, or continue straight ahead to stay on the Dew Mound Trail.

The terrain begins to change rapidly with a steeper climb, rocks, and large boulders, which all add to the beauty of this hike. Once you start in the rocky terrain, within 0.5 mile you'll have a small, unbridged stream to cross. You are more likely to get wet feet from the mud than from crossing the stream. After crossing the stream, the trail heads uphill and veers to the right. Be sure to follow the orange blazes in this area. There are several places with some great scenic views from atop of the rocks when you venture slightly off the trail. The trail begins to descend, passes a small pond, and within another 0.5 mile joins the Historic Iditarod (Crow Pass) Trail down at the Eagle River. There is a small designated campsite called Echo Bend right along the river's shoreline. Be sure to use the provided metal fire ring for any campfires.

Just about where the campsite is located, Dew Mound Trail heads back north toward the nature center following the Historic Iditarod (Crow Pass) Trail. It is a 3.2-mile hike back to the trailhead from this point. The trail is very rocky and rough from here on for about 2.0 miles. After about 1.25 miles you will arrive at another point where there is access to the Eagle River. Turn left to descend a steep series of wooden stairs and view the river. An immediate right at the signpost will take you to the Rapids Camp Yurt, which overlooks the river below. Keep in mind that the yurt might be occupied. (Advance reservations are required.) Like with most of the cabins and yurts in the park, firewood, a wood-burning stove, and bunks are provided. As you continue back toward the nature center, remember that the several trails you will be passing on your right are the same optional loop trails you passed when you were heading south on Dew Mound.

Just under 1.0 mile from the Rapids Camp, you'll come to the Paradise Haven public-use cabin signpost. This rustic log cabin, located west of the trail, is quite popular and is rented most of the time. The next intersection is called Four Corners. Turn left if you want to hike the Albert Loop Trail, which will also end up back at the nature center. Otherwise, continue straight ahead. Follow a long, narrow boardwalk over the wetland area and begin a slight uphill walk back to the center.

*View from Dew Mound*

# Miles and Directions

**0.0** Start behind the Eagle River Nature Center and go straight on the Albert Loop Trail. N61 14.045 / W149 16.260

**0.4** Turn left onto Dew Mound Trail. N61 14.046 / W149 16.257 (Options: Straight ahead takes you onto the Historic Iditarod (Crow Pass) Trail. A right turn takes you to a viewing deck on the Rodak Nature Trail.)

**0.5** Keep straight to remain on the Dew Mound Trail. N61 13.441 / W149 15.945 (Option: Turn right to take the Four Corners Cut-off Trail back to the Historic Iditarod (Crow Pass) Trail or back to the nature center.)

**0.8** Arrive at the first footbridge. N61 13.219 / W149 15.817

**1.0** Come to the second footbridge. N61 13.169 / W149 15.857

**1.1** Reach the third footbridge. N61 13.054 / W149 15.790

**1.3** Continue straight on the Dew Mound Trail. N61 12.862 / W149 15.628 (Option: Turn right to take the Mountain Meadow Cut-off Trail back to the Historic Iditarod (Crow Pass) Trail or back to the nature center.)

**1.5** Continue straight on the Dew Mound Trail. N61 12.734 / W149 15.375 (Option: Turn right to take the Rapids Cut-off Trail back to the Historic Iditarod (Crow Pass) Trail or back to the nature center.)

**1.6** Pass large boulders on the trail. N61 12.657 / W149 15.225

**2.25** Cross a small stream and continue straight to Dew Lake. N61 12.371 / W149 14.526

**2.3** Backtrack and veer to the right up a steep hill and follow the orange blazes. N61 12.319 / W149 14.529

**2.4** Veer slightly right onto a side trail to Dew Mound for views of the valley. N61 12.312 / W149 14.602

**3.1** Join the Historic Iditarod (Crow Pass) Trail at the Eagle River. N61 11.802 / W149 14.819

**3.2** Reach the Echo Bend campsite with fire ring along the riverside. N61 11.789 / W149 14.924

**4.3** Come to the Rapids Camp river access (N61 12.570 / W149 15.922), then go straight at the signpost to return to the nature center. N61 12.593 / W149 15.960 (Option: Turn right to visit the Rapids Camp Yurt. N61 12.586 / W149 16.036)

**4.9** The Mountain Meadow Cut-off Trail to the right connects to the first leg of the Dew Mound Trail. Stay straight. N61 12.941 / W149 16.071

**5.3** Reach the signpost for the Paradise Haven public-use cabin. N61 13.286 / W149 16.185

**5.8** Continue straight at the Four Corners intersection. N61 13.427 / W149 16.172

**6.0** Cross wetlands on a long, narrow boardwalk. N61 13.455 / W149 16.176

**6.3** Arrive back at the nature center. N61 14.045 / W149 16.260

## GREEN TIP

Keep your dog on a leash unless you are certain it can follow your voice and sight commands. Even then, keep the leash handy and your dog in sight. Do not let it approach other people and their pets unless invited to do so.

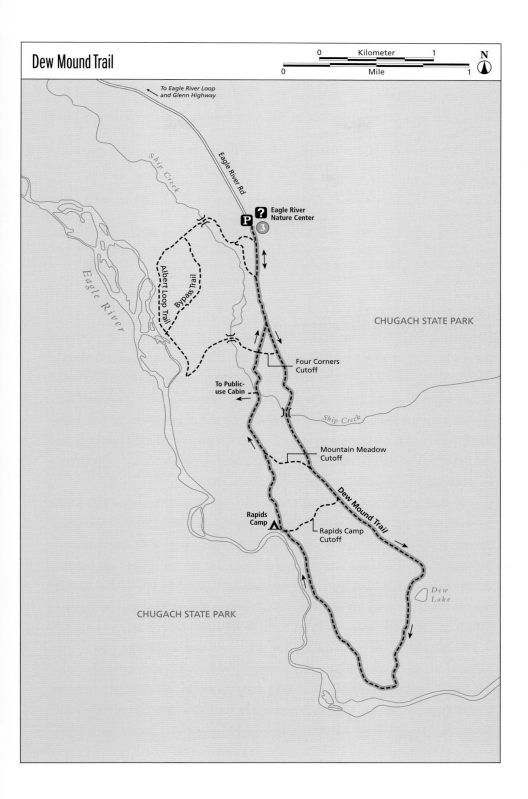

# Dew Mound Trail

0 — Kilometer — 1
0 — Mile — 1

N

To Eagle River Loop
and Glenn Highway

*Ship Creek*

Eagle River Rd

**P** **?** Eagle River
Nature Center
**3**

*Eagle River*

Albert Loop Trail

Bypass Trail

CHUGACH STATE PARK

Four Corners
Cutoff

To Public-
use Cabin

*Ship Creek*

Mountain Meadow
Cutoff

Rapids
Camp

Rapids Camp
Cutoff

Dew Mound Trail

*Dew
Lake*

CHUGACH STATE PARK

# Hike Information

*Local information*

Anchorage Visitor Information Center, 546 West Fourth Avenue, Anchorage 99501; (907) 274-3531; www.anchorage.net

Alaska Department of Natural Resources Public Information Center, Atwood Building, 550 West Seventh Avenue, Suite 1260, Anchorage 99501; (907) 269-8400; www.dnr.state.ak.us/parks

Alaska Public Lands Information Center, 605 West Fourth Avenue, Suite 105, Anchorage 99501; (907) 271-2737; www.nps.gov/aplic

Chugach State Park Headquarters, located at the Potter Section House State Historic Site, Mile 115 Seward Highway (mailing address: HC 52 Box 8999, Indian 99540); (907) 345-5014; e-mail: csp@dnr.state.ak.us; open Monday through Friday 10:00 a.m. to 4:30 p.m.

## IDITAROD YESTERDAY AND TODAY

The Historic Iditarod (Crow Pass) Trail can be started at the Eagle River Nature Center. Its historical significance dates back to the early 1880s, when Alaskan natives created a series of trails in interior Alaska. Segments of these trails later became known as the Iditarod Trail. This was a very complex system of trails stretching from Seward to Nome on the Bering Sea. Dog teams and sleds were the most popular means of travel during the early 1900s and carried freight, gold shipments, and mail. Usually six to twenty scruffy, big-boned dogs (depending on the weight of the load) were harnessed to transport the freight.

The section of the Historic Iditarod, or Crow Pass, Trail between Eagle River Nature Center and Girdwood was originally used for transportation and dog-mushing mailmen, connecting the villages of Knik and Portage. In 1919 the railroad opened and the trails were abandoned. Dogsledding was on the verge of extinction until dog musher Joe Redington Sr. and historian Dorothy Page staged the first dog-mushing race between Knik and Big Lake in 1967. Another race was executed in 1969. The first Iditarod race from Anchorage to Nome was held on March 3, 1973, with thirty-four teams. Twenty-two teams finished thirty-two days later.

The Iditarod became known as the Last Great Race, with competitors from all over the world. In today's races mushers finish in nine to twelve days after crossing two mountain ranges and passing twenty-six checkpoints along the way. In 2004 seventy-seven teams crossed the finish line—the most in Iditarod history. The fastest time is credited to Mitch Seavey, who finished the race in eight days, three hours, forty minutes, and thirteen seconds.

## Camping

Eagle River Campground (907-345-5014), Glenn Highway. Exit about 10 miles north of Anchorage onto Eagle River Loop and Hiland Road; nightly camping fee. Hike tours: Friends of Eagle River (operators of Eagle River Nature Center); (907) 694-2108; e-mail: ERNC@alaska.net

## Local organizations

The Anchorage Adventurers Meetup Group; www.adventurers.meetup.com/109
Mountaineering Club of Alaska, 2633 Spenard Road, Anchorage 99503; (907) 272-1811; www.mcak.org

## Local retailers

Recreational Equipment Inc. (REI), 1200 West Northern Lights Boulevard, Anchorage; (907) 272-4565; www.rei.com
Sportsman's Warehouse, 681 Old Seward Highway, Anchorage; (907) 644-1400; www.sportsmanswarehouse.com
Alaska Mountaineering and Hiking, 2633 Spenard Road, Anchorage; (907) 272-1811; www.alaskamountaineering.com
Cabelas, 155 W 104th, Anchorage; (907) 341-3400; www.cabelas.com/Stores/Anchorage
6th Avenue Outfitters, 520 W 6th Avenue, Anchorage; (907) 276-0233; www.6thavenueoutfitters.com
Bass Pro Shops, 3046 Mountain View Drive, Anchorage; (907) 330-5200; www.basspro.com/Anchorage

## Local events/attractions

Alaskan Scottish Highland Games, Eagle River Lions Park, Anchorage; June
Bear Paw Festival, Eagle River; July
Alaska State Fair, Palmer; August and September
An Anchorage calendar of events can be found at www.anchorage.net/events.html.

# 4 River Trail at North Fork Eagle River

River Trail at North Fork is a quick, easy trail providing a close-up view and access to the Eagle River. The River Trail follows the North Fork Eagle River through a mixed deciduous forest, crosses a bridge, and finally ends on the river's main bank. The area is enhanced with good views of the surrounding mountain ranges and is ideal for birding and wildflowers. This short and simple trail provides a great opportunity for an afternoon outing, a family walk, or a day of fishing.

**Start:** South end of parking lot at mile 7.4 on Eagle River Road
**Distance:** 1.0 mile out and back
**Approximate hiking time:** 30 minutes
**Difficulty:** Easy
**Elevation gain:** Negligible
**Trail surface:** Smooth gravel path
**Seasons:** Year-round
**Other trail users:** None
**Canine compatibility:** Leashed dogs permitted
**Land status:** State park
**Nearest town:** Eagle River

**Fees and permits:** $5 parking fee
**Maps:** Imus Geographics Chugach State Park map (www.imusgeographics.com); USGS Anchorage
**Trail contacts:** Chugach State Park Headquarters located at the Potter Section House State Historic Site, Mile 115 Seward Highway (mailing address: HC 52 Box 8999, Indian AK 99540); (907) 345-5014; e-mail: csp@dnr.state.ak.us; open Monday through Friday 10:00 a.m. to 4:30 p.m.
**Special considerations:** None

**Finding the trailhead:** Coming from Anchorage, follow the Glenn Highway north toward the town of Eagle River. After about 10 miles veer right onto the Hiland Road/Eagle River Loop exit. Turn right onto Eagle River Loop Road and continue for 2.5 miles. Turn right at the Lighthouse Church onto Eagle River Road and drive 7.4 miles. Turn right into the parking lot. The trailhead is located at the south end of the lot.

## The Hike

If you are looking for one extra hike to squeeze in for the day, or a warm-up before you head up the road to the Eagle River Nature Center trails, this could be the one. In addition, this trail provides access to the river for other recreational opportunities such as fishing and rafting. The parking area is quite large, and there are restroom facilities at the south end of the lot.

You will pick up the trail at the south end of the lot. The path is a flat gravel surface, and making good time on it is no problem. After the first several hundred feet, the trail makes an abrupt 90-degree bend to the right. Travel another 300 feet and cross North Fork Creek on a bridge. From here on, it is a straight shot to the Eagle River.

The trail takes you through a mixed spruce forest from beginning to end, with wildflowers evident along the trail's edge. Keep your eyes open for wildlife. Even

*River Trail over N. Fork Eagle River*

though the hike is short, you pass through habitat often occupied by moose, bears, porcupines, and other Alaskan wildlife.

## Miles and Directions

**0.0**  Start at the south end of the parking lot. N61 08.336 / W149 42.695

**0.05** Cross North Fork Creek on a bridge. N61 16.509 / W149 22.740

**0.5**  Reach the Eagle River. Turn around and retrace your steps. N61 16.233 / W149 23.163

**1.0**  Arrive back at the parking lot. N61 08.336 / W149 42.695

## Hike Information

*Local information*

Anchorage Visitor Information Center, 546 West Fourth Avenue, Anchorage 99501; (907) 274-3531; www.anchorage.net

Alaska Department of Natural Resources Public Information Center, Atwood Building, 550 West Seventh Avenue, Suite 1260, Anchorage 99501; (907) 269-8400; www .dnr.state.ak.us/parks

Alaska Public Lands Information Center, 605 West Fourth Avenue, Suite 105, Anchorage 99501; (907) 271-2737; www.nps.gov/aplic

*Camping*

Eagle River Campground (907-345-5014), Glenn Highway. Exit about 10 miles north of Anchorage onto Eagle River Loop and Hiland Road; nightly camping fee.

*Local organizations*

The Anchorage Adventurers Meetup Group; www.adventurers.meetup.com/109

Mountaineering Club of Alaska, 2633 Spenard Road, Anchorage 99503; (907) 272-1811; www.mcak.org

*Local retailers*

Recreational Equipment Inc. (REI), 1200 West Northern Lights Boulevard, Anchorage; (907) 272-4565; www.rei.com

Sportsman's Warehouse, 681 Old Seward Highway, Anchorage; (907) 644-1400; www .sportsmanswarehouse.com

Alaska Mountaineering and Hiking, 2633 Spenard Road, Anchorage; (907) 272-1811; www.alaskamountaineering.com

Cabelas, 155 W 104th, Anchorage; (907) 341-3400; www.cabelas.com/Stores/Anchorage

6th Avenue Outfitters, 520 W 6th Avenue, Anchorage; (907) 276-0233; www.6th avenueoutfitters.com

Bass Pro Shops, 3046 Mountain View Drive, Anchorage; (907) 330-5200; www .basspro.com/Anchorage

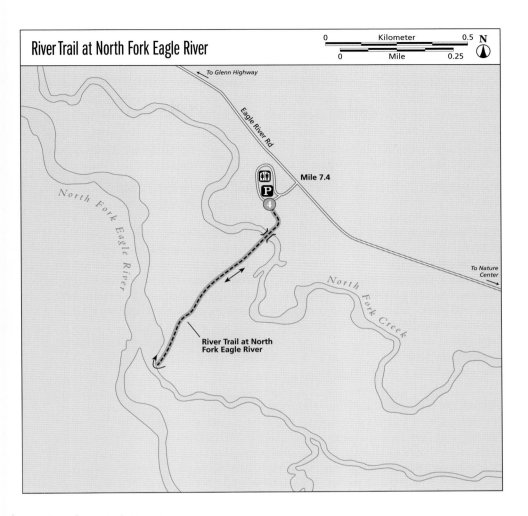

# River Trail at North Fork Eagle River

0     Kilometer     0.5   **N**

0     Mile     0.25

To Glenn Highway

Eagle River Rd

Mile 7.4

North Fork Eagle River

North Fork Creek

To Nature Center

River Trail at North Fork Eagle River

*Local events/attractions*

Alaskan Scottish Highland Games, Eagle River Lions Park, Anchorage; June
Bear Paw Festival, Eagle River; July
Alaska State Fair, Palmer; August and September
An Anchorage calendar of events can be found at www.anchorage.net/events.html.

▶ There are nine species of fish found in Chugach State Park. Because most streams and lakes are glacially fed with silty gray water, fish populations are limited to specific areas within the park. The Eagle River and Bird Creek are the primary salmon waterways. Campbell, Thunderbird, Hunter, Peters, Rabbit, and Penguin Creeks also support fish, as do Eklutna and Rabbit Lakes.

# 5 Lower Eagle River Trail and Barbara Falls

This hike follows a wide, easy path. The trail is mainly level and travels through a mixed spruce and birch forest with views of the Eagle River and surrounding mountains. Wildflowers and other beautiful vegetation make this hike a nice weekend jaunt with the family. The hike offers a great boardwalk through a wetland and waterfowl nesting area and ends at South Fork Eagle River. It can be continued on to Barbara Falls.

**Start:** Briggs Bridge river access on Eagle River Loop
**Distance:** 6.0 miles out and back
**Approximate hiking time:** 2–4 hours
**Difficulty:** Easy
**Elevation gain:** 230 feet
**Trail surface:** Dirt; seasonably muddy
**Seasons:** Best hiking May through September
**Other trail users:** Bikes, horses, and runners
**Canine compatibility:** Leashed dogs permitted
**Land status:** State park
**Nearest town:** Eagle River
**Fees and permits:** $5 daily parking fee

**Maps:** Imus Geographics Chugach State Park map (www.imusgeographics.com); USGS Anchorage
**Trail contacts:** Chugach State Park Headquarters, located at the Potter Section House State Historic Site, Mile 115 Seward Highway (mailing address: HC 52 Box 8999, Indian AK 99540); (907) 345-5014; e-mail: csp@dnr.state.ak.us; open Monday through Friday 10:00 a.m. to 4:30 p.m.
**Special considerations:** There's a bridgeless stream to ford.

**Finding the trailhead:** Coming from Anchorage, follow the Glenn Highway north toward the town of Eagle River. After about 10 miles veer right onto the Hiland Road/Eagle River Loop exit. Turn right onto Eagle River Loop Road and pass through the first stoplight. Travel 0.5 mile downhill to the Chugach State Park Briggs Bridge river access on your right. Turn right on the gravel road. Drive to the end of the gravel road down by the river, where there are picnic tables, restroom facilities, and a large parking area. There is no formal trailhead, but the trail is easy to spot and begins by following the river eastward away from the bridge.

## The Hike

The Lower Eagle River Trail is part of the Eagle River Greenbelt, a collaborative effort of the Alaska State Department of Transportation and Public Facilities, the Alaska Department of Natural Resources Division of Parks and Outdoor Recreation, and the Municipality of Anchorage. The entire trail extends almost 7.0 miles along the south fork of the Eagle River and is probably a more popular trail for local residents for running, biking, horseback riding, day hiking, and various winter activities.

The not so well known yet striking Barbara Falls is definitely a highlight on this trail. However, it is located on private property. If hiking the trail from the trailhead, you will need a permit from Eklutna Inc. to pass through their land. You are on Eklutna Inc. land after crossing the river. You can also access the falls from a different

*Boardwalk through waterfowl nesting area*

location off of Ken Logan Circle which is accessed off of Hiland Road. If you are hiking just to see the falls, be sure not to park by the posted No Parking signs on the cul-de-sac. Rather park further up the street, walk in and cross the bridge and turn right. At the time of this writing this is okay with the private land owner.

The main trail is a haven for local wildlife such as moose and bears that occupy the varied habitat along the river. Because of the low nature of this trail, the river, and low, wet areas, you are likely to find plenty of mosquitoes.

You can begin the trail at the northeast corner of the larger parking area by the river (the Briggs Bridge river access) between the two huge boulders. However, any of the paths coming from the lot will take you to the river trail—just head east away from the bridge. The first path that joins the trail is just the other access point from the first small parking area at the beginning of the gravel road.

After about 0.3 mile you will cross a small mountain stream that carries melting winter snow and rain. The trail is definitely seasonally wet. In late spring and early summer, there will be many low spots in the trail that you will need to travel around to avoid wet feet. At the 0.5-mile point you'll cross a low, wet area on a series of logs laid out over the ground to keep you above the water and mud. There will be one more small runoff stream to cross just beyond the first mile of travel. You will also find several small paths during the first mile that lead you down to the riverbank. If you are the inquisitive type, it's fun to go down and explore the different animal tracks in the mud.

# Lower Eagle River Trail and Barbara Falls

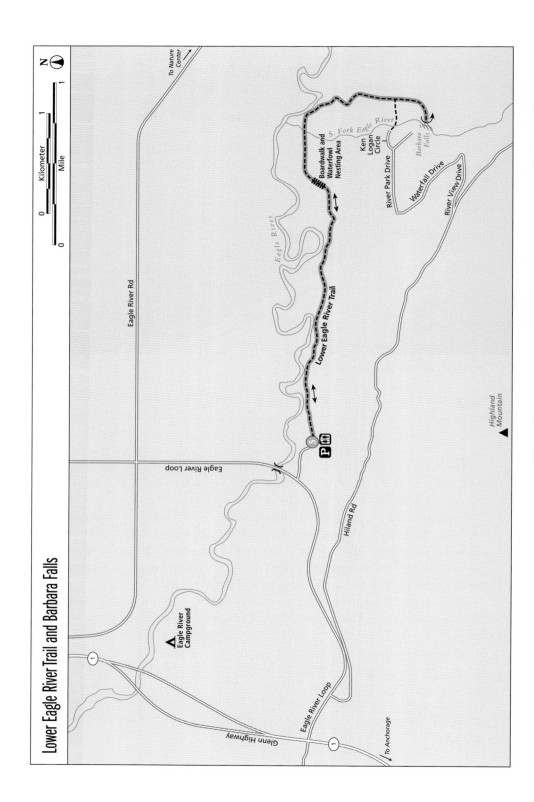

At approximately 1.3 miles another path joins the trail; veer to the left. Take the fork to the right toward the South Fork Eagle River. You will very quickly reach the river and have a choice to make. Most people ford the river at this crossing point. A separate pair of shoes for crossing the river is a good idea. The other option is to look for a log to cross on. You may have to do some bushwhacking to get to a log and back to the trail.

Once you have crossed the river, the trail continues slightly uphill. The property on this side of the river is owned by Eklutna Inc. which requires a permit to enter.

There are also several noticeable side trails. Just keep on the main path. After another 0.5 mile the trail passes under a set of power lines. When you come to a four-way intersection, turn left to continue on the Lower Eagle River Trail. (NOTE: Turning right will take you to a bridge and into private property and a subdivision.) To continue to the falls, take the main trail straight ahead. At approximately 2.8 miles the trail veers sharply left and heads steeply uphill. Turn right onto a small, narrow path. Within 200 feet you will arrive at the top of the falls. There is a heavy steel railing installed for safety.

## Miles and Directions

**0.0** Start between two large boulders at the northeast corner of the Briggs Bridge river access lot. N61 17.796 / W149 31.891

**0.3** Cross a small runoff stream. N61 17.761 / W149 31.391

**0.45** Cross a low, wet area on a series of logs. N61 17.732 / W149 31.178

**1.1** Cross another small stream. N61 17.673 / W149 30.051

**1.3** Veer left at the trail junction. N61 17.619 / W149 29.612

**1.55** Enter private property. N61 17.703 / W149 29.232

**1.8** Leave the private property and turn right at the fork. N61 17.770 / W149 28.781

**1.9** Ford South Fork Eagle River. N61 17.743 / W149 28.721

**2.4** The trail passes under power lines. N61 17.386 / W149 28.350

**2.5** Continue straight ahead at the four-way intersection. N61 17.309 / W149 28.313

**2.8** Turn right off the main trail onto a narrow footpath. N61 17.183 / W149 28.432

**3.0** Reach the falls, then retrace your steps to the trailhead. N61 17.176 / W149 28.523

**6.0** Arrive back at the river access parking lot. N61 17.796 / W149 31.891

## Hike Information

*Local information*

Anchorage Visitor Information Center, 546 West Fourth Avenue, Anchorage 99501; (907) 274-3531; www.anchorage.net

Alaska Department of Natural Resources Public Information Center, Atwood Building, 550 West Seventh Avenue, Suite 1260, Anchorage 99501; (907) 269-8400; www.dnr.state.ak.us/parks

Alaska Public Lands Information Center, 605 West Fourth Avenue, Suite 105, Anchorage 99501; (907) 271-2737; www.nps.gov/aplic

## Camping

Eagle River Campground (907-345-5014), Glenn Highway. Exit about 10 miles north of Anchorage onto Eagle River Loop and Hiland Road; nightly camping fee.

## Local organizations

The Anchorage Adventurers Meetup Group; www.adventurers.meetup.com/109
Mountaineering Club of Alaska, 2633 Spenard Road, Anchorage 99503; (907) 272-1811; www.mcak.org

## Local retailers

Recreational Equipment Inc. (REI), 1200 West Northern Lights Boulevard, Anchorage; (907) 272-4565; www.rei.com
Sportsman's Warehouse, 681 Old Seward Highway, Anchorage; (907) 644-1400; www.sportsmanswarehouse.com
Alaska Mountaineering and Hiking, 2633 Spenard Road, Anchorage; (907) 272-1811; www.alaskamountaineering.com
Cabelas, 155 W 104th, Anchorage; (907) 341-3400; www.cabelas.com/Stores/Anchorage
6th Avenue Outfitters, 520 W 6th Avenue, Anchorage; (907) 276-0233; www.6thavenueoutfitters.com
Bass Pro Shops, 3046 Mountain View Drive, Anchorage; (907) 330-5200; www.basspro.com/Anchorage

## Local events/attractions

Alaskan Scottish Highland Games, Eagle River Lions Park, Anchorage; June
Bear Paw Festival, Eagle River; July
Alaska State Fair, Palmer; August and September
An Anchorage calendar of events can be found at www.anchorage.net/events.html.

# 6 Mount Baldy

Mount Baldy is a popular family trail that starts out on a wide gravel path and eventually turns off, travels through a segment of thick alders, and heads abruptly uphill above the tree line. The trail is easy to follow with multiple trail options once you begin the climb upwards. It provides good views of the town of Eagle River and Eagle River Valley. The trail is steep, has some loose stone, and can be slick when wet. Knowing this however, it is a fun trail for the entire family and the family pet. It can also be hiked as a loop trail by utilizing the trail that goes around Mount Baldy and ascends the peak from the back.

**Start:** At trailhead up the hill from street
**Distance:** 2 miles out and back
**Approximate hiking time:** 2–3 hours
**Difficulty:** Easy to moderate due to steepness
**Elevation gain:** 3,000 feet
**Trail surface:** Gravel, dirt, stone
**Seasons:** May through September
**Other trail users:** Runners
**Canine compatibility:** Leashed dogs permitted
**Land status:** State park
**Nearest town:** Eagle River
**Fees and permits:** None

**Maps:** Imus Geographics Chugach State Park map (www.imusgeographics.com); USGS Anchorage
**Trail contacts:** Chugach State Park Headquarters, located at the Potter Section House State Historic Site, Mile 115 Seward Highway (mailing address: HC 52 Box 8999, Indian AK 99540); (907) 345-5014; e-mail: csp@dnr.state.ak.us; open Monday through Friday 10:00 a.m. to 4:30 p.m.
**Special considerations:** Can be slick when wet

**Finding the trailhead:** From Anchorage, drive approximately 10 miles to the Eagle River Loop / Hiland Road exit. Exit to the right and follow Eagle River Loop Road down the hill and cross Eagle River. You will pass Wal-Mart on your right. Go thru the light and intersection of Eagle River/Eagle River Loop Roads and continue several more blocks. Turn right on Skyview Drive. Skyview will change names a couple of times, however stay on the main road and follow it to the end approximately 2 miles. Parking is limited and is roadside parking only.

## The Hike

Mount Baldy is so named because of its prominently displayed rocky bald top. The trail begins by following a gravel road that starts out abruptly uphill, levels out and switches back toward a series of radio towers. You will want to turn off to your left just twenty or thirty feet prior to a red gate. If you would continue through the gate, the gravel road will take you to the radio towers and eventually back down to the road you drove in on.

After turning left down the narrow dirt path, you will hike through a thick strand of alders, willows and small trees. The path will begin a slight ascent toward Mount Baldy. Just after approximately a ½-mile, you will come to a level area where the

*Top: Mt. Baldy Trail with long range views of Knik Arm*
*Bottom: Mount Baldy ascent*

vegetation begins to thin, and you find yourself moving above the tree line. From here, the trail will become noticeably steeper. Use caution when trail conditions are wet, as the path can become quite slick. The trail surface will become a mix of dirt, loose stone and rock as you get closer to the summit. Once at the top, the views are great and there is plenty of wide-open space and opportunity to continue exploring the surrounding peaks. Use caution as you descend back to the gravel road.

## Miles and Directions

**0.0**  Start the trail at the end of the road and beginning of uphill gravel road. N61 20.280 W149 30.730

**0.2**  Turn left slightly downhill just before a gate. N61 20.242 W149 30.716

**0.6**  You will come to flat area before starting a steep ascent. N61 20.239 W149 30.055

**1.0**  Arrive at the top of Mount Baldy. N61 20.165 W149 29.629

**2.0**  Return to parking area. N61 20.280 W149 30.730

### Local information

Anchorage Visitor Information Center, 546 West Fourth Avenue, Anchorage 99501; (907) 274-3531; www.anchorage.net

Alaska Department of Natural Resources Public Information Center, Atwood Building, 550 West Seventh Avenue, Suite 1260, Anchorage 99501; (907) 269-8400; www.dnr.state.ak.us/parks

Alaska Public Lands Information Center, 605 West Fourth Avenue, Suite 105, Anchorage 99501; (907) 271-2737; www.nps.gov/aplic

### Camping

Eagle River Campground (907-345-5014), Glenn Highway. Exit about 10 miles north of Anchorage onto Eagle River Loop and Hiland Road; nightly camping fee.

### Local organizations

The Anchorage Adventurers Meetup Group; www.adventurers.meetup.com/109

Mountaineering Club of Alaska, 2633 Spenard Road, Anchorage 99503; (907) 272-1811; www.mcak.org

### Local retailers

Recreational Equipment Inc. (REI), 1200 West Northern Lights Boulevard, Anchorage; (907) 272-4565; www.rei.com

Sportsman's Warehouse, 681 Old Seward Highway, Anchorage; (907) 644-1400; www.sportsmanswarehouse.com

Alaska Mountaineering and Hiking, 2633 Spenard Road, Anchorage; (907) 272-1811; www.alaskamountaineering.com

Cabelas, 155 W 104th, Anchorage; (907) 341-3400; www.cabelas.com/Stores/Anchorage

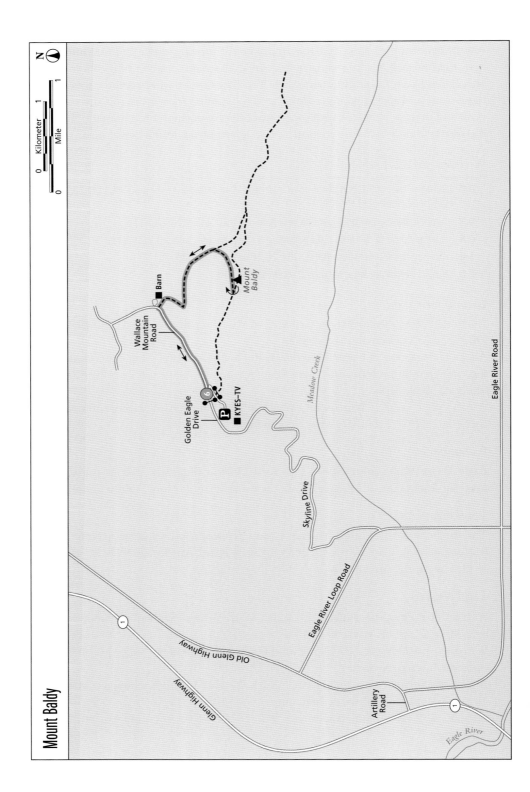

# Mount Baldy

6th Avenue Outfitters, 520 W 6th Avenue, Anchorage; (907) 276-0233; www.6th avenueoutfitters.com

Bass Pro Shops, 3046 Mountain View Drive, Anchorage; (907) 330-5200; www .basspro.com/Anchorage

## Local events/attractions

Alaskan Scottish Highland Games, Eagle River Lions Park, Anchorage; June

Bear Paw Festival, Eagle River; July

Alaska State Fair, Palmer; August and September

An Anchorage calendar of events can be found at www.anchorage.net/events.html.

# 7  Rendezvous Peak Trail

The trail to Rendezvous Peak presents some of the best views of Anchorage. At nearly 4100 feet and appropriately a 1300-foot elevation gain, you can view the Cook Inlet, Knik Arm, the Anchorage Bowl, Mount Susitna, Fire Island, Eagle River Valley and Ship Creek. The trail starts out easy and becomes a bit more difficult as you ascend the peak. Wildlife is evident such as Artic ground squirrels, moose and bears along with wild flowers and seasonal berry picking.

**Start:** Trailhead behind kiosk or trail next to Artic Valley building
**Distance:** 3.2 miles loop trail
**Approximate hiking time:** 3-4 hours
**Difficulty:** Easy starting out, moderate while ascending peak
**Elevation gain:** 1354 feet
**Trail surface:** Dirt and stone
**Seasons:** June through August
**Other trail users:** runners
**Canine compatibility:** Dogs must be leashed

**Land status:** Chugach State Park, Military land
**Nearest town:** Eagle River
**Fees and permits:** $5 parking fee. The trailhead is maintained by the Anchorage Ski Club.
**Maps:** National Geographic, Alaska, Chugach State Park Anchorage, Trails Illustrated Topographical Map
**Trail contacts:** Chugach State Park, Artic Valley Ski Club
**Special considerations:** Military land. Please respect the boundaries.

**Finding the trailhead:** The Arctic Valley trailhead is at the end of Arctic Valley Road. Coming from Anchorage, take the Glenn Highway to the Arctic Valley exit. This road will become gravel after two to three miles. Follow this for approximately eight miles to the parking area run by the Anchorage Ski Club. There is a $5 parking fee payable at the fee station where you will also find the trailhead. Your state park or military parking pass is not valid here.

Note: This trail is also accessible from Eagle River. Take the Glenn Highway from Anchorage to the Eagle River Loop / Hiland Road exit. Turn right off the highway, and then another right onto Hiland Road. Follow about seven miles to the end. Turn right on South Creek Road, then another right on West Creek Drive. The parking area for the trailhead will be on your left. There is no parking fee at this location.

## The Hike

The trail description in this book is hiking from the Arctic Valley side. Several miles prior to the trailhead you will drive on a gravel road. Driving slowly on this very rough road can save some unnecessary wear on your vehicle. You will be driving through and hiking near military land, so respect all signs. You will also notice military installation signs on the land. These are restricted areas, and access is prohibited. Also note the road is gated and is open from 6:00 am to 10:00 pm, so plan your hike accordingly. The old Nike missile site is also visible from the trail, but is also on restricted land.

*Awesome views while ascending Rendezvous Peak*

The official trailhead is located at the kiosk and fee station. The hike can be started here or through the gate to the left of the ski lodge building. The trail by the building is wide, well-traveled and proceeds slightly uphill.

From the official trailhead start, you will see a small signpost with two signs with arrows pointing up the trail behind the kiosk. One reads Rendezvous Peak Trail and the other reads South Fork Overlook. Hike about 200 feet in the direction the sign is pointing and look for a second narrower dirt trail off to your right. There is no sign at this turning point. Turn right and follow the meandering foot trail about ¼ mile to a bridge that is crossing the Tokklat Creek. Rather than crossing the bridge continue straight ahead on the path. If you start your hike coming from the wide trail passing the lodge, you would cross this bridge and continue ahead on this same trail.

Travel this path slightly uphill for about ½ mile. You will come to a ridgeline at the Southfork Overlook area with beautiful views of the valley below. Going left will take you to Mount Gordon Lyons. Turning right will take you up to Rendezvous Peak. You will traverse another ½ mile along the saddle and the trail will go steeply uphill as it wraps around the peak and brings you to the summit. Continue on the trail while still wrapping around the peak to head back down the mountain and loop back to the trailhead and parking lot.

## Miles and Directions

**0.0**   Start at the trailhead and pay station. N61° 14.815′ W149° 32.103′
**0.1**   Pass through gate. N61° 14.814′ W149° 32.088′

# Rendezvous Peak Trail

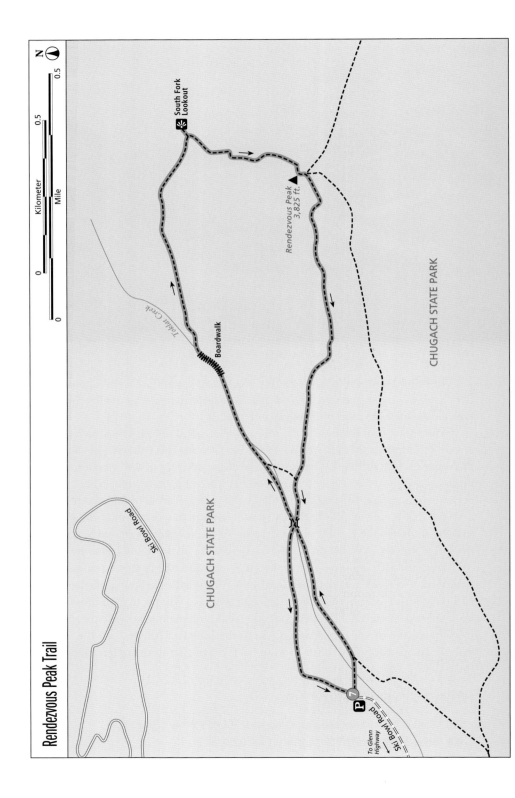

CHUGACH STATE PARK

CHUGACH STATE PARK

Ski Bowl Road

Tickit Creek

Boardwalk

South Fork Lookout

Rendezvous Peak 3,825 ft.

To Glenn Highway

Ski Bowl Road

N

Kilometer

Mile

**0.4** Cross over bridge and Toklat Creek. N61° 14.966' W149° 31.549'

**0.6** Cross small bridge. N61° 15.034' W149° 31.366'

**0.8** Cross over short boardwalk. N61° 14.966' W149° 31.549'

**1.5** View of South Fork Eagle River below. N61° 15.269' W149° 30.197'

**1.9** Arrive at top of peak. N61° 14.970' W149° 30.372'

**2.8** Turn right at fork and cross bridge to continue return loop. N61° 14.952' W149° 31.569

**3.1** Turn left to return to main trail and trailhead. N61° 14.945' W149° 32.045'

**3.2** End back at trailhead. N61° 14.817' W149° 32.098'

## Local information

Anchorage Visitor Information Center, 546 West Fourth Avenue, Anchorage 99501; (907) 274-3531; www.anchorage.net

Alaska Department of Natural Resources Public Information Center, Atwood Building, 550 West Seventh Avenue, Suite 1260, Anchorage 99501; (907) 269-8400; www.dnr.state.ak.us/parks

Alaska Public Lands Information Center, 605 West Fourth Avenue, Suite 105, Anchorage 99501; (907) 271-2737; www.nps.gov/aplic

## Camping

Eagle River Campground (907-345-5014), Glenn Highway. Exit about 10 miles north of Anchorage onto Eagle River Loop and Hiland Road; nightly camping fee.

## Local organizations

The Anchorage Adventurers Meetup Group; www.adventurers.meetup.com/109
Mountaineering Club of Alaska, 2633 Spenard Road, Anchorage 99503; (907) 272-1811; www.mcak.org

## Local retailers

Recreational Equipment Inc. (REI), 1200 West Northern Lights Boulevard, Anchorage; (907) 272-4565; www.rei.com

Sportsman's Warehouse, 681 Old Seward Highway, Anchorage; (907) 644-1400; www.sportsmanswarehouse.com

Alaska Mountaineering and Hiking, 2633 Spenard Road, Anchorage; (907) 272-1811; www.alaskamountaineering.com

Cabelas, 155 W 104th, Anchorage; (907) 341-3400; www.cabelas.com/Stores/Anchorage

6th Avenue Outfitters, 520 W 6th Avenue, Anchorage; (907) 276-0233; www.6thavenueoutfitters.com

Bass Pro Shops, 3046 Mountain View Drive, Anchorage; (907) 330-5200; www.basspro.com/Anchorage

# 8 South Fork Eagle River Valley Trail

This great day hike takes you down to the South Fork Eagle River and eventually leads you to Eagle and Symphony Lakes. At the end of the trail, you can expect great views of the valley, the lakes, Triangle Peak, Hurdygurdy Mountain, and surrounding peaks. This is a popular place for overnight camping and opportunities for further exploration into the open tundra.

**Start:** At the trailhead located 7.5 miles from the intersection of Eagle River Loop and Hiland Roads

**Distance:** 12.2 miles out and back

**Approximate hiking time:** 6–8 hours

**Difficulty:** Easy at the beginning; moderate toward the end, with heavy rockslide/boulder area

**Elevation gain:** 1,080 feet

**Trail surface:** Begins as dirt and gravel, boardwalks; heavy rockslide/boulders toward end

**Seasons:** Best hiking late May through September

**Other trail users:** Horse access to Ship Creek; cross-country and backcountry skiers and snow-shoers in winter

**Canine compatibility:** Leashed dogs permitted

**Land status:** State park

**Nearest town:** Eagle River

**Fees and permits:** No fees or permits required

**Maps:** Imus Geographics Chugach State Park map (www.imusgeographics.com); USGS Anchorage

**Trail contacts:** Chugach State Park Headquarters, located at the Potter Section House State Historic Site, Mile 115 Seward Highway (mailing address: HC 52 Box 8999, Indian 99540); (907) 345-5014; e-mail: csp@dnr.state.ak.us; open Monday through Friday 10:00 a.m. to 4:30 p.m.

**Special considerations:** This can be a very dangerous trail in wintertime; the area is prone to avalanches.

**Finding the trailhead:** Coming from Anchorage, follow the Glenn Highway north toward the town of Eagle River. After about 10 miles veer right onto the Hiland Road/Eagle River Loop exit. Turn right onto Eagle River Loop Road and then make an immediate right at the first stoplight onto Hiland Road. From this point it is 7.5 miles to the trailhead.

Travel approximately 5 miles and cross the South Fork Eagle River. Turn right onto South Creek Road at the state park sign and travel for a short distance to West River Drive. Make a sharp right and park in the small dirt parking lot located on the left side of the road. The lot fills up quickly. Please respect private homeowners surrounding this area, and do not park in yards or in front of driveways when the main lot is full.

## The Hike

The long-range views from down in the valley as you follow the South Fork Eagle River and the approach to the final destination looking at Symphony and Eagle Lakes are definite highlights of this hike. Like all trails in Chugach State Park, this hike has something unique to offer—amazing valley views. The trail begins with an easily followed path, though the last couple miles are a bit more difficult to accomplish.

*Bridge crossing to boulder field*

If you decide not to hike the entire length, there are several places that make good turnaround points along the way. Down in the valley near the first bridge crossing is an excellent place for lunch and an easy place to shorten the hike. Otherwise, plan on six to eight hours for the hike to the lakes and the return trip. For the more adventurous there are some areas around the south side of Eagle Lake to camp and, like most of Chugach State Park, other trails and more tundra to explore.

The trail commences by heading gently uphill across a narrow boardwalk with views of scattered homes along the hillside, which quickly diminish as you continue onward. Vast open views of mountains and the valley are prominent throughout the hike. The trail is well defined from plenty of use, but is rough with rocks and an uneven terrain.

After the first mile or so, the trail starts heading down into the valley. Slightly past the 2.0-mile mark, come to the first bridge crossing. During the course of the next mile, plan on several small mountain stream crossings where you'll make use of stepping-stones and single-plank boardwalks. The area tends to be wet and muddy, and you'll pass several small ponds or wet depressions.

Venture away from the lower valley area and continue slightly upward and into more rock and less vegetation. Then abruptly head back down toward the valley and river again. At approximately 4.5 miles you come to the second bridge. The water is flowing rapidly from the glacier-fed lake, so use caution in crossing the bridge.

This is where the next part of the adventure begins. The area is the result of a past rockslide, and everything for the next 1.0 mile is boulder and rock. Be prepared for

*View of Eagle and Symphony Lakes*

some rough walking and some boulder hopping. You won't see any trail, so look for the cairns, or rock piles, built as markers along the way to keep you going in the right direction. If you lose sight of the markers, don't be alarmed. You can't really get lost at this point, since you'll be hiking right down the center of the valley.

Toward the end of the boulder field, the trail begins a slight ascent through sparse vegetation where an old octagonal hut is evident. Although the hut is not really an adequate place to spend the night, during a storm it might serve as a last resort. Both Symphony and Eagle Lakes, quite apparent at this point, look completely different. Symphony Lake has a blue cast and is fed from melting snow and rain. Eagle Lake is a silty greenish color, caused by glacier runoff.

The trail continues along a ridge as a divide between the two lakes and begins a more rapid ascent at the far south end. The trail virtually disappears in the thin, ankle-high vegetation and becomes exceedingly steep. If you are here during late summer or early fall, wild blueberries are abundant. The flattened area ahead provides outstanding views of the lakes, peaks, and valley. You can continue to explore the park as far as you wish or sit and enjoy the view before the hike back.

## Miles and Directions

**0.0**  Start at the parking lot on West River Drive. N61 13.954 / W149 27.361
**2.1**  Cross South Fork Eagle River on a bridge. N61 12.601 / W149 25.815

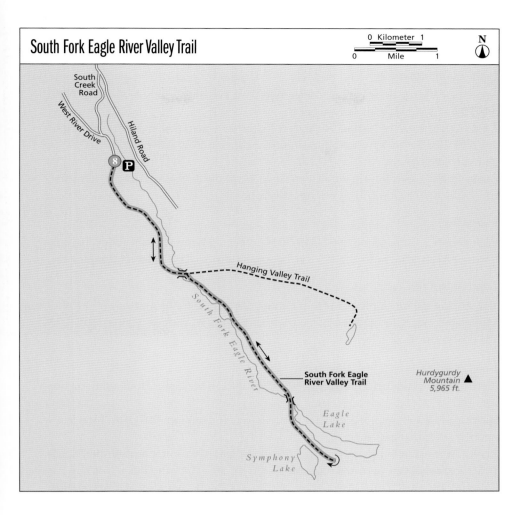

0   Kilometer  1

0          Mile          1

N

**2.2**  Cross a small stream on stepping-stones. N61 12.582 / W149 25.760

**2.3**  Cross another small stream. N61 12.544 / W149 25.493

**2.8**  Pass a small pond and take advantage of a single-plank boardwalk. N61 12.320 / W149 24.867

**4.5**  Enter a rockslide area and pass a small pond. Three cairns mark the trail. N61 178 / W149 23.346

**5.0**  Cross a small, sturdy bridge over a fast-moving stream into an area of boulders. Follow the cairns to stay on the trail. N61 11.091 / W149 23.162

**5.5**  Reach an old homestead site. N61 10.615 / W149 22.834

**6.1**  Reach the hillside viewpoint. Enjoy the views of the lakes, peaks, and valley before retracing your steps. N61 10.265 / W149 22.272

**12.2**  Arrive back at the trailhead. N61 13.954 / W149 27.361

# Hike Information

## Local information

Anchorage Visitor Information Center, 546 West Fourth Avenue, Anchorage 99501; (907) 274-3531; www.anchorage.net

Alaska Department of Natural Resources Public Information Center, Atwood Building, 550 West Seventh Avenue, Suite 1260, Anchorage 99501; (907) 269-8400; www.dnr.state.ak.us/parks

Alaska Public Lands Information Center, 605 West Fourth Avenue, Suite 105, Anchorage 99501; (907) 271-2737; www.nps.gov/aplic

## Camping

Eagle River Campground (907-345-5014), Glenn Highway. Exit about 10 miles north of Anchorage onto Eagle River Loop and Hiland Road; nightly camping fee.

## Local organizations

The Anchorage Adventurers Meetup Group; www.adventurers.meetup.com/109

Mountaineering Club of Alaska, 2633 Spenard Road, Anchorage 99503; (907) 272-1811; www.mcak.org

## Local retailers

Recreational Equipment Inc. (REI), 1200 West Northern Lights Boulevard, Anchorage; (907) 272-4565; www.rei.com

Sportsman's Warehouse, 681 Old Seward Highway, Anchorage; (907) 644-1400; www.sportsmanswarehouse.com

Alaska Mountaineering and Hiking, 2633 Spenard Road, Anchorage; (907) 272-1811; www.alaskamountaineering.com

Cabelas, 155 W 104th, Anchorage; (907) 341-3400; www.cabelas.com/Stores/Anchorage

6th Avenue Outfitters, 520 W 6th Avenue, Anchorage; (907) 276-0233; www.6thavenueoutfitters.com

Bass Pro Shops, 3046 Mountain View Drive, Anchorage; (907) 330-5200; www.basspro.com/Anchorage

## Local events/attractions

Alaskan Scottish Highland Games, Eagle River Lions Park, Anchorage; June

Bear Paw Festival, Eagle River; July

Alaska State Fair, Palmer; August and September

An Anchorage calendar of events can be found at www.anchorage.net/events.html.

# 9 Hanging Valley Trail

This trail is an offshoot of the South Fork Trail that leads to Eagle and Symphony Lakes. It provides some awesome views of the Eagle River Valley and South Fork Eagle River as it works its way up into the hanging valley perched above the Eagle River Valley floor. The final destination for most hikers, near the end of the valley, is the hidden Hanging Valley Tarn, nestled in a secluded cirque. This is an excellent camping area garlanded with wildflowers and alpine mosses, accompanied by the scurrying activity of Arctic ground squirrels. The lake provides a tranquil environment for camping and a stopping ground for several species of waterfowl such as gulls, harlequin ducks, and Barrow's goldeneye. The surrounding rocky boulders also provide habitat for the rock ptarmigan.

**Start:** South Fork trailhead
**Distance:** 10.0 miles out and back from the parking lot
**Approximate hiking time:** 7–10 hours
**Difficulty:** Easy to moderate
**Elevation gain:** 1,030 feet
**Trail surface:** Dirt
**Seasons:** Best hiking June through September
**Other trail users:** None
**Canine compatibility:** Leashed dogs permitted
**Land status:** State park
**Nearest town:** Eagle River
**Fees and permits:** No fees or permits required

**Maps:** Imus Geographics Chugach State Park map (www.imusgeographics.com); USGS Anchorage
**Trail contacts:** Chugach State Park Headquarters, located at the Potter Section House State Historic Site, Mile 115 Seward Highway (mailing address: HC 52 Box 8999, Indian 99540); (907) 345-5014; e-mail: csp@dnr.state.ak.us; open Monday through Friday 10:00 a.m. to 4:30 p.m.
**Special considerations:** This trail can be very dangerous in wintertime; the area is prone to avalanches.

**Finding the trailhead:** Coming from Anchorage, follow the Glenn Highway north toward the town of Eagle River. After about 10 miles veer right onto the Hiland Road /Eagle River Loop exit. Turn right onto Eagle River Loop Road and then make an immediate right at the first stoplight onto Hiland Road. From this point it is 7.5 miles to the parking lot.

Travel approximately 5 miles and cross South Fork Eagle River. Turn right onto South Creek Road at the state park sign and travel for a short distance to West River Drive. Make a sharp right and park in the small dirt parking lot located on the left side of the road.

The hikes that leave from this parking facility are popular, and consequently the small lot fills up quickly. Please respect private homeowners surrounding this area; do not park in yards or in front of driveways when the main lot is full.

## The Hike

Begin the hike at the boardwalk and trailhead at the corner of the lot. The path begins abruptly uphill and heads through a mixed spruce forest. The first 0.3 mile

*Top: Hanging Valley Tarn*
*Bottom: View of Hanging Valley*

climbs until you reach the top of the ridge that will follow the river below for about 1.5 miles. The path then heads down to the river to a bridge crossing, which is a little past the 2.0-mile point. Cross two more small streams and walk up a short boardwalk. Watch for a fork in the trail just after these landmarks.

▶ **You will not encounter any snakes in Chugach State Park. In fact, there are no reptiles in the entire state of Alaska. This is because of the lack of heat in summer, not the cold of winter.**

The Hanging Valley Trail is unmarked, narrow, slightly overgrown, and easy to miss. The top of a large buried boulder is visible at the foot of the path. The main trail heads back toward the river. Take the narrower, less-traveled trail to the left (east) and head up toward the valley and the sound of running water.

Now that you are on the trail, hike steeply uphill through some heavy vegetation and up to the valley above, where the vegetation thins out. From the lookout point near the top of the hill, you can see the Eagle River Valley below and the trail you came in on. Stay on the main trail heading toward the end of the valley. You will notice several game trails along the way, but keep your destination in mind as you hike and you won't have any problem. The entire valley is about 2.0 miles long.

At approximately the 4.5-mile mark, pass a small tarn on the right side as you near the end of the valley. Continue past the tarn and soon come to an abrupt pinnacle in the trail. The path surface changes to loose stone and becomes very narrow and very steep. Climb the short distance to the top of this pinnacle and stop. Turn 90 degrees to your right and proceed up the hill about 100 feet. The trail that leads to the tarn is not immediately visible, but you will see it if you start up the hill and will reach it within that 100-foot walk. (NOTE: If you miss the turn, you will come to a rambling creek coming from your right.)

Head up the hill on your right to reach the hidden tarn above. Once you are at the top, the views of the valley below are truly outstanding. The best sites to set up camp are located at the far end of the lake where another small runoff stream feeds into this tarn, adding to the wilderness ambience. Bears frequent the area and the ground squirrels are inquisitive, so watch your gear.

## Miles and Directions

**0.0** Start at the parking lot on West River Drive. N61 13.954 / W149 27.361

**2.1** Come to the first bridge crossing. N61 12.600 / W149 25.810

**2.2** Cross a small stream and a boardwalk. N61 12.546 / W149 25.491

**2.7** Turn left (east) at the junction with the Hanging Valley Trail. N61 12.518 / W149 25.099

**3.3** Come to a lookout at the high point on the ridge. N61 12.587 / W149 24.824

**4.5** Pass a small tarn on the right. N61 12.251 / W149 22.161

**4.8** Turn 90 degrees right at the top of the pinnacle. N61 12.164 / W149 21.706

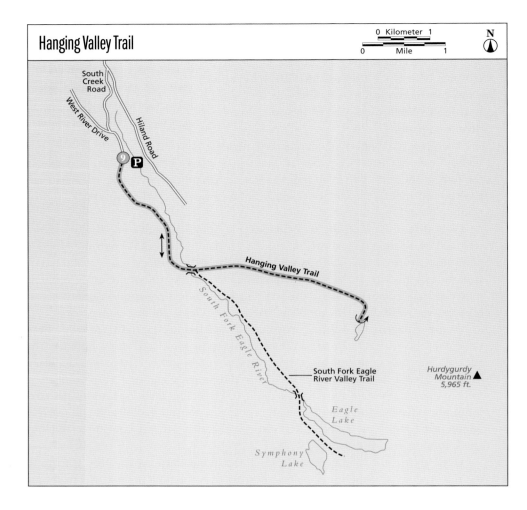

0 Kilometer 1

0 Mile 1

N

South Creek Road

West River Drive

Hiland Road

Hanging Valley Trail

South Fork Eagle River

South Fork Eagle River Valley Trail

Hurdygurdy Mountain ▲ 5,965 ft.

Eagle Lake

Symphony Lake

**5.0** Reach the hidden tarn and campsites. Retrace your steps to the parking lot. N61 12.010 / W149 21.679

**10.0** Arrive back at the parking lot. N61 13.952 / W149 27.359

## Hike Information

*Local information*

Anchorage Visitor Information Center, 546 West Fourth Avenue, Anchorage 99501; (907) 274-3531; www.anchorage.net

Alaska Department of Natural Resources Public Information Center, Atwood Building, 550 West Seventh Avenue, Suite 1260, Anchorage 99501; (907) 269-8400; www .dnr.state.ak.us/parks

Alaska Public Lands Information Center, 605 West Fourth Avenue, Suite 105, Anchorage 99501; (907) 271-2737; www.nps.gov/aplic

## Camping

Eklutna Lake Campground at Eklutna Lake; (907) 345-5014. Follow the Glenn Highway north from Anchorage for 25 miles to the Thunderbird Falls exit. Veer right and continue for 0.5 mile. Turn right onto Eklutna Lake Road and continue for 10 miles; nightly camping fee.
Eagle River Campground (907-345-5014), Glenn Highway. Exit about 10 miles north of Anchorage onto Eagle River Loop and Hiland Road; nightly camping fee.

## Local organizations

The Anchorage Adventurers Meetup Group; www.adventurers.meetup.com/109
Mountaineering Club of Alaska, 2633 Spenard Road, Anchorage 99503; (907) 272-1811; www.mcak.org

## Local retailers

Recreational Equipment Inc. (REI), 1200 West Northern Lights Boulevard, Anchorage; (907) 272-4565; www.rei.com
Sportsman's Warehouse, 681 Old Seward Highway, Anchorage; (907) 644-1400; www.sportsmanswarehouse.com
Alaska Mountaineering and Hiking, 2633 Spenard Road, Anchorage; (907) 272-1811; www.alaskamountaineering.com

## Local events/attractions

Alaskan Scottish Highland Games, Eagle River Lions Park, Anchorage; June
Bear Paw Festival, Eagle River; July
Alaska State Fair, Palmer; August and September
An Anchorage calendar of events can be found at www.anchorage.net/events.html.

### GREEN TIP
Wash dishes or clothes at least 200 feet from a river or lake.
Bring the water to a spot with good drainage, and use only
biodegradable soap in the smallest amount.

# 10 Eklutna Lakeside Trail

This popular trail is utilized year-round by local Alaskans for most every type of outdoor recreational activity. The well-traveled, extremely scenic, and easy-to-follow trail allows for various means of travel. Many people bike this trail or use ATVs (on designated days), allowing them to make the out-and-back trip in one day. If you hike it, you will probably want to make it a two-day trip. The trail follows the Eklutna Lake shoreline for most of the way and then runs along glacial gravel bars. Waterfalls, steep canyon walls, and wildlife such as bears, moose, Dall sheep, mountain goats, and numerous bird species are prominent in the area.

**Start:** Trailhead signpost located just after crossing the small bridge north of the parking lot

**Distance:** 12.7 miles one-way

**Approximate hiking time:** 5–6 hours

**Difficulty:** Easy to moderate

**Elevation gain/loss:** 300 feet

**Trail surface:** Gravel road

**Seasons:** The trails are used year-round, but fall is extraordinary, with foliage colors in their prime. Campground is open May 1 through September 30.

**Other trail users:** Horses, ATVs (Monday through Wednesday only), bikes; snow machines and skiers when snow levels are adequate

**Canine compatibility:** Leashed dogs permitted

**Land status:** State park

**Nearest town:** Eagle River

**Fees and permits:** $5 parking fee

**Maps:** Imus Geographics Chugach State Park map (www.imusgeographics.com); USGS Anchorage

**Trail contacts:** Chugach State Park Headquarters, located at the Potter Section House State Historic Site, Mile 115 Seward Highway (mailing address: HC 52 Box 8999, Indian 99540); (907) 345-5014; e-mail: csp@dnr.state.ak.us; open Monday through Friday 10:00 a.m. to 4:30 p.m.

**Special considerations:** Motorcycles are prohibited on the trail.

**Finding the trailhead:** From Anchorage travel 25 miles north on the Glenn Highway. Take the Thunderbird Falls exit and follow the road to the right. Drive beyond the Thunderbird Falls trailhead and parking lot on your right, and cross the Eklutna River. Just after crossing the river, turn right onto Eklutna Lake Road. This road runs 10 miles uphill to the pay station and Eklutna Lake. There are two large day-use parking lots. Coming from the north side of the parking lots, cross a small bridge and turn right at the main trailhead.

## The Hike

The Eklutna Lakeside Trail follows the shoreline of Eklutna Lake, which provides thirty-five million gallons of drinking water and electricity for the city of Anchorage. The lake is 7 miles long and offers year-round unspoiled beauty and recreation for Alaskans and visitors alike.

*Eklutna Lake*

The trail is basically a gravel road, but it is in good condition. The road is easily hiked and biked and is also popular with ATV riders. But don't let the ATV traffic discourage you from the hike. They won't be in your way. The trail branches often, with high road and low road routes. The high road is intended for the ATVs; the low route is a much narrower trail intended for hikers and will take you on a more intimate hike along the shoreline. These forks along the trail are frequent, very well marked, and easily identified. The first fork appears at Mile 1.0. Veer right onto a narrow trail; the ATVs will take the high wide road straight ahead.

At 2.65 miles you will come to the first stream crossing and bridge. The stream is called Yuditna Creek. Proceed ahead; the trail makes an abrupt right-hand turn back toward the lake. (FYI: Another right turn will take you to one of the state park's public-use cabins—the Yuditna Creek Cabin, with an outstanding view of the lake. Cabins are available by reservation only and are very popular, so you need to plan well in advance if you want to use one. Please respect others' privacy if the cabin is occupied.) Pass the trail to the cabin and continue to follow the lake shoreline. Cross Bold Creek at approximately 4.8 miles. There is an excellent waterfall on the north side of the bridge and a picturesque view as the creek enters the lake on the south side. Just after you cross the bridge, a trailhead marks the access point to Bold Ridge Trail on your left. This is a steep 3.5-mile one-way trip.

After you pass the turnoff to Bold Ridge, the Eklutna Lakeside Trail narrows and follows a steep gravelly ridge along the lake. Come to a third creek, 8-Mile

> **Less than 10 percent of Chugach State Park is covered in ice—roughly 73 square miles and steadily declining. Glaciers have played an important role in the formation and beauty of the park, and many are visible from its trails.**

Creek, at approximately 7.7 miles. This is at the far south end of the lake. The trail starts heading in a westerly direction and then turns south again. Just after crossing the creek, pass a route on your right that will take you to Bold Airstrip. Continue on the main trail that winds to your left. Pay attention to the steep ledges on your left as you continue traveling along the glacial gravel bar. A pair of binoculars will come in handy for spotting Dall sheep on the rocky ledges.

At 8.4 miles come to the first campground, Eklutna Alex Campground, with picnic tables, primitive campsites, and restroom facilities. Just remember that since this is bear country, there is no trash service. What you pack in you need to pack out. When you reach Mile 10.0, the trailhead for East Fork Trail is on your left. This is an approximately 4.0-mile one-way hike to scenic Tulchina Falls.

You will encounter one other campground, Kanchee Campground, along the trail at Mile 11.0. Both Eklutna Alex and Kanchee Campgrounds are good places to camp when making this an overnight trip. The Serenity Falls public-use cabin is another alternative for overnight stays. The cabin is located between Miles 11.0 and 12.0, and access is on the path that travels straight ahead. Turn right to stay on the main trail. Cross a large bridge with a view of two large waterfalls.

Continue on the main trail to reach Serenity Falls at approximately 11.8 miles. The trail becomes very rocky, with large loose stones, and heads uphill. If you are riding, you will probably need to secure your bikes somewhere along the path or else walk them from here to the river shoreline. Reach the end of the trail at 12.7 miles where a large flat boulder overlooks the river. You can continue for another 0.3 mile along the water's edge on a rocky path and ledge to view what used to be the site of the Eklutna Glacier, which has receded.

## Miles and Directions

**0.0** Start at the trailhead signpost in front of the rental concession building. N61 24.622 / W149 08.103

**1.0** Veer right and follow the trail along the lakeshore. N61 24.248 / W149 06.159 (FYI: ATVs go straight ahead.)

**2.65** Cross the bridge over Yuditna Creek and continue to follow the lakeshore. N61 23.513 / W149 03.781 (Option: Turn right to reach the public-use cabin at 2.75 miles. N61 23.430 / W149 03.687)

**5.0** Cross Bold Creek on a bridge and pass the Bold Ridge Trail on your left. N61 22.543 / W149 01.320 (Option: Bold Ridge is a steep 3.5-mile one-way trail.)

**7.7** Cross 8-Mile Creek. N61 20.357 / W148 59.293

**8.0** Pass the route to Bold Airstrip on the right. N61 20.274 / W148 59.818

**8.4** Reach Eklutna Alex Campground. N61 19.931 / W148 59.948

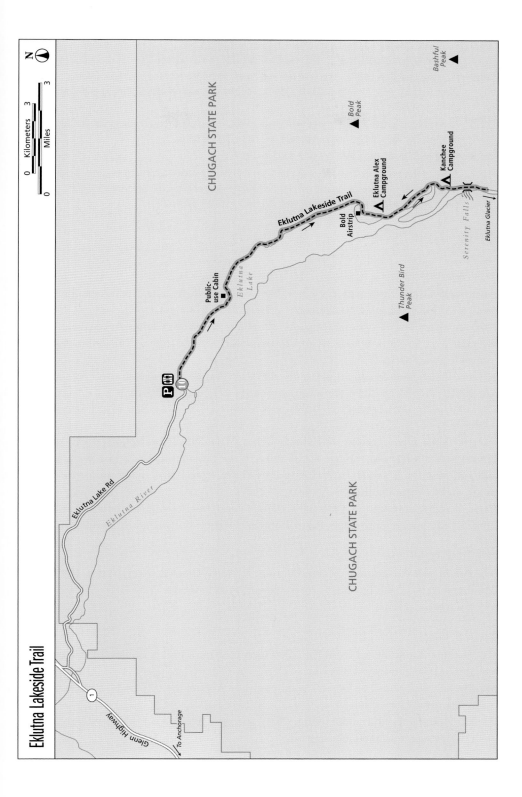

**10.0** Pass the Kanchee Campground. N61 18.437 / W148 58.598 (FYI: Kanchee means porcupine in Athapaskan.)

**10.5** Pass the East Fork trailhead on your left and cross the bridge over the East Fork Eklutna River. N61 18.862 / W148 58.340 (Option: Follow the East Fork Trail 2.9 miles one-way to Tulchina Falls.)

**11.5** Turn right and cross a large bridge with views of two waterfalls. Proceed straight ahead to the Serenity Falls public-use cabin. N61 17.703 / W148 58.512

**11.8** Arrive at Serenity Falls. N61 17.542 / W148 58.776

**12.7** Arrive at the riverbank and end of the trail. N61 17.106 / W148 58.494 (Option: You can walk another 0.3 mile along the river to the Eklutna Glacier overlook. Unfortunately, the glacier has receded from this point. N61 16.943 / W148 58.402)

# Hike Information

## Local information

Anchorage Visitor Information Center, 546 West Fourth Avenue, Anchorage 99501; (907) 274-3531; www.anchorage.net

Alaska Department of Natural Resources Public Information Center, Atwood Building, 550 West Seventh Avenue, Suite 1260, Anchorage 99501; (907) 269-8400; www.dnr.state.ak.us/parks

Alaska Public Lands Information Center, 605 West Fourth Avenue, Suite 105, Anchorage 99501; (907) 271-2737; www.nps.gov/aplic

## Camping

Eklutna Lake Campground at Eklutna Lake; (907) 345-5014. Follow the Glenn Highway north from Anchorage for 25 miles to the Thunderbird Falls exit. Veer right and continue for 0.5 mile. Turn right onto Eklutna Lake Road and continue for 10 miles; nightly camping fee.

Eagle River Campground (907-345-5014), Glenn Highway. Exit about 10 miles north of Anchorage onto Eagle River Loop and Hiland Road; nightly camping fee.

## Local organizations

The Anchorage Adventurers Meetup Group; www.adventurers.meetup.com/109

Mountaineering Club of Alaska, 2633 Spenard Road, Anchorage 99503; (907) 272-1811; www.mcak.org

## Local retailers

Recreational Equipment Inc. (REI), 1200 West Northern Lights Boulevard, Anchorage; (907) 272-4565; www.rei.com

Sportsman's Warehouse, 681 Old Seward Highway, Anchorage; (907) 644-1400; www.sportsmanswarehouse.com

Alaska Mountaineering and Hiking, 2633 Spenard Road, Anchorage; (907) 272-1811; www.alaskamountaineering.com

*Eklutna Lake is a beautiful glacial melt lake surrounded by mountains.*

Cabelas, 155 W 104th, Anchorage; (907) 341-3400; www.cabelas.com/Stores/Anchorage
6th Avenue Outfitters, 520 W 6th Avenue, Anchorage; (907) 276-0233; www.6th avenueoutfitters.com
Bass Pro Shops, 3046 Mountain View Drive, Anchorage; (907) 330-5200; www .basspro.com/Anchorage

*Local events/attractions*
St. Nicholas Russian Orthodox Church and Cemetery, Mile 26 Glenn Highway, Eklutna Road, Eklutna.
An Anchorage calendar of events can be found at www.anchorage.net/events.html.

## GREEN TIP
Pass it down—the best way to instill good green habits in your children is to set a good example.

# 11 Twin Peaks Trail

Twin Peaks Trail is one Chugach's most popular trails—and with good reason. It combines great scenery with adventure, Alaskan wilderness, and opportunity for exploration. The trail gains an elevation of 1,500 feet and affords extraordinary views of Eklutna Lake and Twin Peaks. East Twin Peak climbs to 5,873 feet; West Twin is 5,401 feet. The trail is steep but easy to follow. On some days you will literally be walking in the clouds. There are a couple of benches along the first part of the trail where you can sit and take a break or just pause to marvel at the outstanding views of the valley and Twin Peaks.

**Start:** Approximately 230 feet to the left of the equipment rental building and Eklutna Lakeside trailhead

**Distance:** 7.4 miles out and back

**Approximate hiking time:** 8–10 hours

**Difficulty:** Moderate to difficult, steep trail with some scrambling

**Elevation gain:** 1,500 feet

**Trail surface:** Gravel, loose stone, and dirt

**Seasons:** Spring, summer, and fall

**Other trail users:** None

**Canine compatibility:** Leashed dogs permitted

**Land status:** State park

**Nearest town:** Eagle River

**Fees and permits:** $5 parking fee

**Maps:** Imus Geographics Chugach State Park map (www.imusgeographics.com); USGS Anchorage

**Trail contacts:** Chugach State Park Headquarters, located at the Potter Section House State Historic Site, Mile 115 Seward Highway (mailing address: HC 52 Box 8999, Indian 99540); (907) 345-5014; e-mail: csp@dnr.state.ak.us; open Monday through Friday 10:00 a.m. to 4:30 p.m.

**Special considerations:** Loose stone on the trail

**Finding the trailhead:** From Anchorage travel 25 miles north on the Glenn Highway. Take the Thunderbird Falls exit and follow the road to the right. Drive beyond the Thunderbird Falls trailhead and parking lot on your right and cross the bridge. Just after crossing the river, turn right onto Eklutna Lake Road. This road runs 10 miles uphill to the pay station and Eklutna Lake. There are two large day-use parking lots. From the north side of the lots, cross a small bridge over Twin Peaks Creek and turn left at the main trail marker. The Twin Peaks Trail is approximately 230 feet straight ahead.

## The Hike

The Twin Peaks Trail is an abandoned dirt road. It is wide and well maintained, making it easy to follow. This is an amazingly gorgeous hike in the fall, and like many of the late summer and early fall hikes in the park, the berry picking is great. You're also very likely to spot Dall sheep when you venture above the tree line into the tundra.

Begin the hike at the Twin Peaks trailhead, located just over 200 feet north of the equipment rental building and main trailpost. The trail begins a quick, steep ascent

*View of Eklutna Lake from Twin Peaks Trail*

into the spruce-birch forest and makes several switchbacks as it continues to climb. Just past the 1.5-mile point, the vegetation opens up and provides an outstanding view of Eklutna Lake below and Bold Peak in the distance. There is also a resting bench where you can sit and take in the view. The trail makes an abrupt turn to the north here and continues to climb.

At approximately 2.4 miles the wide trail basically comes to an end. You've reached the top of the tree line, and scrubby vegetation lies ahead. There is a resting bench here with a perfect view of Twin Peaks. Just beyond the bench is a narrow footpath that winds its way through the brush and leads up to open tundra. Instead take the small, narrow path just below the bench that heads abruptly downhill. Follow the downhill trail into the valley, using caution when descending. The trail is dirt, very steep, and particularly slick on wet days.

▷ **The highest peak in Chugach State Park is Bashful Peak (8,005 feet), located near Eklutna Lake.**

The trail crosses a small creek at the bottom and begins to ascend into the open tundra. Blueberry and high-bush cranberry picking is superb through this whole area. The narrow path crosses one more creek and then begins to follow a narrow gorge up the steep, long climb to the ridge above.

The top of the ridge is your destination. From here you will have breathtaking views of the Matanuska Valley, Knik River, Matanuska River, the town of Palmer, and Goat Creek, plus be right next to East Twin Peak. Some hikers venture left or right along this ridge to further explore the rocky terrain. Keep your eye out for Dall sheep in this area and down the valley.

## Miles and Directions

**0.0** Start at the Twin Peaks trailhead. N61 24.608 / W149 08.093

**1.6** Arrive at the first bench with a view. N61 25.167 / W149 08.219

**2.4** Arrive at a second bench, with views of Twin Peaks. N61 25.754 / W149 07.599

**2.8** Cross a small stream. N61 25.852 / W149 07.569

**2.9** Cross another small stream. N61 26.110 / W149 07.362

**3.7** Reach the ridgetop. Explore further or just enjoy the view before retracing your steps. N61 26.539 / W149 06.361

**7.4** Arrive back at the trailhead. N61 24.608 / W149 08.093

## Hike Information

*Local information*

Anchorage Visitor Information Center, 546 West Fourth Avenue, Anchorage 99501; (907) 274-3531; www.anchorage.net

Alaska Department of Natural Resources Public Information Center, Atwood Building, 550 West Seventh Avenue, Suite 1260, Anchorage 99501; (907) 269-8400; www.dnr.state.ak.us/parks

*View of Twin Peaks from trail*

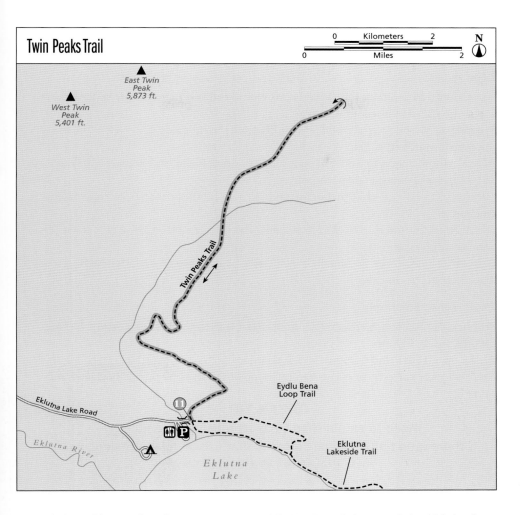

Alaska Public Lands Information Center, 605 West Fourth Avenue, Suite 105, Anchorage 99501; (907) 271-2737; www.nps.gov/aplic

## Camping

Eklutna Lake Campground at Eklutna Lake; (907) 345-5014. Follow the Glenn Highway north from Anchorage for 25 miles to the Thunderbird Falls exit. Veer right and continue for 0.5 mile. Turn right onto Eklutna Lake Road and continue for 10 miles; nightly camping fee.

Eagle River Campground (907-345-5014), Glenn Highway. Exit about 10 miles north of Anchorage onto Eagle River Loop and Hiland Road; nightly camping fee.

## Local organizations

The Anchorage Adventurers Meetup Group; www.advenurers.meetup.com/109

Mountaineering Club of Alaska, 2633 Spenard Road, Anchorage 99503; (907) 272-1811; www.mcak.org

*Local retailers*

Recreational Equipment Inc. (REI), 1200 West Northern Lights Boulevard, Anchorage; (907) 272-4565; www.rei.com

Sportsman's Warehouse, 681 Old Seward Highway, Anchorage; (907) 644-1400; www.sportsmanswarehouse.com

Alaska Mountaineering and Hiking, 2633 Spenard Road, Anchorage; (907) 272-1811; www.alaskamountaineering.com

Cabelas, 155 W 104th, Anchorage; (907) 341-3400; www.cabelas.com/Stores/Anchorage

6th Avenue Outfitters, 520 W 6th Avenue, Anchorage; (907) 276-0233; www.6thavenueoutfitters.com

Bass Pro Shops, 3046 Mountain View Drive, Anchorage; (907) 330-5200; www.basspro.com/Anchorage

*Local events/attractions*

St. Nicholas Russian Orthodox Church and Cemetery, Mile 26 Glenn Highway, Eklutna Road, Eklutna

Alaska State Fair, Palmer; August and September

An Anchorage calendar of events can be found at www.anchorage.net/events.html.

## GREEN TIP
Keep to established trails as much as possible.
If there aren't any, stay on surfaces that will be least affected, like rock, gravel, dry grasses, or snow.

# 12 Eydlu Bena Loop Trail

Eydlu Bena Loop Trail is an easy forested walk. It begins on a wide old roadbed, narrows into a dirt and gravel path, and eventually loops down to join the Eklutna Lakeside Trail. This is a good hike if your time is limited in this section of the park or as an extra activity if you came to the park for biking or just for an afternoon at the lake. The trail is well marked and easy to follow, with relatively low elevation gain, making it an ideal trail for the entire family. This trail can also be hiked in early spring, when other trails in the park are still closed.

**Start:** Approximately 230 feet to the left of the equipment rental building and Eklutna Lakeside trailhead
**Distance:** 2.0-mile loop
**Approximate hiking time:** 1–2 hours
**Difficulty:** Easy
**Elevation gain:** 300 feet
**Trail surface:** Dirt road, gravel
**Seasons:** Year-round
**Other trail users:** Groomed for cross-country skiing in winter
**Canine compatibility:** Leashed dogs permitted
**Land status:** State park

**Nearest town:** Eagle River
**Fees and permits:** $5 daily parking fee
**Maps:** Imus Geographics Chugach State Park map (www.imusgeographics.com); USGS Anchorage
**Trail contacts:** Chugach State Park Headquarters, located at the Potter Section House State Historic Site, Mile 115 Seward Highway (mailing address: HC 52 Box 8999, Indian 99540); (907) 345-5014; e-mail: csp@dnr.state.ak.us; open Monday through Friday 10:00 a.m. to 4:30 p.m.
**Special considerations:** None

**Finding the trailhead:** From Anchorage travel 25 miles north on the Glenn Highway. Take the Thunderbird Falls exit and follow the road to the right. Drive beyond the Thunderbird Falls trailhead and parking lot on your right and cross the bridge. Just after crossing the Eklutna River, turn right onto Eklutna Lake Road. This road runs 10 miles uphill to the pay station and Eklutna Lake. There are two large day-use parking lots. From the north side of the lots, cross a small bridge over Twin Peaks Creek and turn left at the main trail marker. The Eydlu Bena trailhead is just ahead on your right.

## The Hike

After leaving the parking lot, locate the main trailhead and signpost in front of the park's equipment rental building; turn left and walk about 100 feet. The Eydlu Bena Loop Trail begins on your right. The trail starts out on a dirt road, leaving the road at about 0.33 mile from the starting point. At this point veer left and continue heading uphill. This is probably the steepest portion of the trail.

### GREEN TIP
**Hiking and snowshoeing are great carbon-free winter activities.**

*Beautiful view from Eydlu Bena Trail*

The trail travels through a spruce-hardwood forest. Common animals here are black and brown bears, moose, porcupines, and both red and northern flying squirrels. Although you won't always see wildlife, footprints and other signs along the trail are often evident. After approximately 0.9 mile come to a trailpost directing you to the right to the Eklutna Lakeside Trail. This is the trail you want. The path to your left is an unmaintained dead-end trail that continues upward through a tunnel of trees and eventually to a rocky boulder area often used by Dall sheep ewes to lamb in the spring.

▶ Chugach is a tribal name for the Eskimos who once inhabited the upper Cook Inlet region. Early Russian explorers recorded the name as "chugatz."

Turn right at the signpost and loop back down toward the lake. Views of Eklutna Lake will become apparent as you hike downhill. The Eydlu Bena Loop Trail joins the Eklutna Lakeside Trail at approximately 1.25 miles. Turn right at this junction and follow the road along the Eklutna Lake shoreline back to the parking lot.

## Miles and Directions

**0.0** Start at the main trailhead in front of the equipment rental building and go left. The trail begins just past the building on the right. N61 24.611 / W149 07.503

**0.9** Turn right at the trail marker post and head downhill. N61 24.523 / W149 06.568

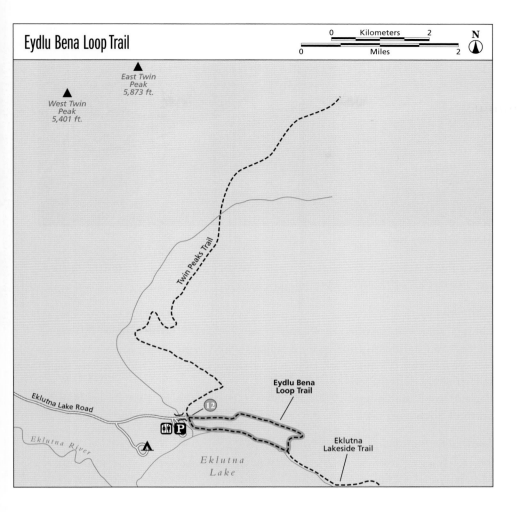

Eydlu Bena Loop Trail

**1.3** Reach the junction with the Eklutna Lakeside Trail. Turn right onto the gravel road and head back toward the parking lot. N61 24.465 / W149 07.055

**2.0** Arrive back at the trailhead. N61 24.611 / W149 07.503

# Hike Information

## Local information

Anchorage Visitor Information Center, 546 West Fourth Avenue, Anchorage 99501; (907) 274-3531; www.anchorage.net

Alaska Department of Natural Resources Public Information Center, Atwood Building, 550 West Seventh Avenue, Suite 1260, Anchorage 99501; (907) 269-8400; www .dnr.state.ak.us/parks

*Moose sign along trail*

Alaska Public Lands Information Center, 605 West Fourth Avenue, Suite 105, Anchorage 99501; (907) 271-2737; www.nps.gov/aplic

## Camping

Eklutna Lake Campground at Eklutna Lake; (907) 345-5014. Follow the Glenn Highway north from Anchorage for 25 miles to the Thunderbird Falls exit. Veer right and continue for 0.5 mile. Turn right onto Eklutna Lake Road and continue for 10 miles; nightly camping fee.

Eagle River Campground (907-345-5014), Glenn Highway. Exit about 10 miles north of Anchorage onto Eagle River Loop and Hiland Road; nightly camping fee.

## Local organizations

The Anchorage Adventurers Meetup Group; www.adventurers.meetup.com/109
Mountaineering Club of Alaska, 2633 Spenard Road, Anchorage 99503; (907) 272-1811; www.mcak.org

## Local retailers

Recreational Equipment Inc. (REI), 1200 West Northern Lights Boulevard, Anchorage; (907) 272-4565; www.rei.com

Sportsman's Warehouse, 681 Old Seward Highway, Anchorage; (907) 644-1400; www.sportsmanswarehouse.com

Alaska Mountaineering and Hiking, 2633 Spenard Road, Anchorage; (907) 272-1811; www.alaskamountaineering.com

## Local events/attractions

St. Nicholas Russian Orthodox Church and Cemetery, Mile 26 Glenn Highway, Eklutna Road, Eklutna

Alaska State Fair, Palmer; August and September

An Anchorage calendar of events can be found at www.anchorage.net/events.html.

# 13 Bold Ridge Trail

The Bold Ridge Trail is steep and difficult, but it takes you to some of the most breathtaking scenery in Chugach State Park. Outstanding views of Eklutna Lake below, Knik Arm, Twin Peaks, Bold Peak, and the Eklutna Glacier make this hike one of the best. The glacial-carved valleys, high ridges, and open tundra, along with the abundance of alpine wildflowers and Arctic ground squirrels, add to the allure and natural beauty of this hike.

**Start:** Bold Ridge trailhead, just past Mile 5.0 on the Eklutna Lakeside Trail
**Distance:** 7.0 miles out and back (17.0 miles out and back from Eklutna Lakeside trailhead parking lot)
**Approximate hiking time:** 4–5 hours (7–10 hours from Eklutna Lakeside trailhead parking lot)
**Difficulty:** Difficult due to steepness
**Elevation gain:** 2,850 feet
**Trail surface:** Dirt, loose stone
**Seasons:** June through September
**Other trail users:** None
**Canine compatibility:** Leashed dogs permitted; under voice control after trailhead

**Land status:** State park
**Nearest town:** Eagle River
**Fees and permits:** $5 daily parking fee
**Maps:** Imus Geographics Chugach State Park map (www.imusgeographics.com); USGS Anchorage
**Trail contacts:** Chugach State Park Headquarters, located at the Potter Section House State Historic Site, Mile 115 Seward Highway (mailing address: HC 52 Box 8999, Indian 99540); (907) 345-5014; e-mail: csp@dnr.state.ak.us; open Monday through Friday 10:00 a.m. to 4:30 p.m.
**Special considerations:** Snow levels can still be deep in the higher elevations in early spring.

**Finding the trailhead:** From Anchorage travel 25 miles north on the Glenn Highway. Take the Thunderbird Falls exit and follow the road to the right. Drive beyond the Thunderbird Falls trailhead and parking lot on your right and cross the bridge. Just after crossing the Eklutna River, turn right on Eklutna Lake Road. This road runs 10 miles down to the pay station and Eklutna Lake. There are two large day-use parking lots. From the north side of the lots, cross a small bridge over Twin Peaks Creek and turn right at the main trailhead. This wide gravel road is the Eklutna Lakeside Trail. Follow it to just beyond the 5.0-mile marker. Bold Ridge Trail is located on the mountainside just after you cross the bridge over Bold Creek.

## The Hike

This hike requires a 5.0-mile trek along the Eklutna Lakeside Trail to reach the trailhead and is often passed by because of the additional effort required. However, the scenery and views far outweigh this inconvenience. The first 5.0 miles, prior to the Bold Ridge trailhead, follow the shoreline of Eklutna Lake. The trail is a wide gravel road, making for easy travel. You will cross several bridged creeks with continual outstanding views of the lake, and magnificent snowcapped mountains in the

*Looking toward the Eklutna Glacier from the Bold Ridge Trail*

background providing amazing scenery along the way. The fall season is particularly beautiful on this stretch of trail.

Many people rent bicycles at the rental hut in the park or bring along their own to bike the first 5.0 miles, chain up the bike in the forested area, and then begin the hike.

As you begin the Bold Ridge Trail, it immediately starts its nearly 3,000-foot ascent. The path is wide and steep and will take you through a dense spruce forest that changes to a predominately hardwood forest as you gain elevation. There are several switchbacks as you work your way up the mountainside. At the 1.0-mile mark the path goes slightly downhill to a large, flat open-meadow area. At this point you'll have the first really unobstructed view of the lake below. During the next 0.5 mile you'll begin to notice significant changes in the vegetation as it transitions from forest to tundra. At 1.75 miles into the hike, enter an open alpine meadow, with more amazing views that continue to get even better as you travel onward.

As you continue climbing in elevation, look for a single large boulder on the left side of the trail. This is the hike's 2.0-mile point and showcases the East and West Twin Peaks, Eklutna Lake, and the Knik Arm below. Just after passing the boulder, the path steeply inclines onto a ridge and heads away from the lake. Follow this ridge for slightly more than 0.5 mile. The wide trail you have been following ends; leave the ridge by veering to the right. Follow what appears to be a narrow sheep path that heads steeply uphill to the next mountain ridge. This is Bold Ridge and is made up of a series of peaks, each one progressively higher.

The path virtually disappears amid the rock and stone. Continuing on the faint trail along the ridge will take you near the base of the snow-covered Bold Peak, at which point you'll be forced to quit.

The tundra is covered with an abundance of mosses, wildflowers, and berries in season and is ideal habitat for ground squirrels. Binoculars will come in handy for scanning the surrounding mountainsides for Dall sheep, moose, bears, and other Alaskan wildlife. The ridge provides incredible views of Eklutna Lake, the Eklutna Glacier, Eklutna Valley, and the Knik Arm of Cook Inlet.

## Miles and Directions

**0.0**  Start at the trailhead 5.0 miles along the Eklutna Lakeside Trail. N61 22.519 / W149 01.310

**1.0**  Head slightly downhill to a flat, open meadow with a clear view of the lake below. N61 22.695 / W148 59.991

**1.75** Reach an alpine meadow. N61 22.632 / W148 59.347

**2.0**  Come to a large boulder on the north side of the trail. N61 22.630 / W148 58.958

**2.6**  Depart from the wide path and head up a steep hill to Bold Ridge. N61 22.411 / W148 58.156

**3.5**  Trail nearly disappears at a rocky mound. Turn around and retrace your steps. N61 21.963 / W148 57.513

**7.0**  Arrive back at the Eklutna Lakeside Trail. N61 22.519/W149 01.310

## Hike Information

*Local information*

Anchorage Visitor Information Center, 546 West Fourth Avenue, Anchorage 99501; (907) 274-3531; www.anchorage.net

Alaska Department of Natural Resources Public Information Center, Atwood Building, 550 West Seventh Avenue, Suite 1260, Anchorage 99501; (907) 269-8400; www .dnr.state.ak.us/parks

Alaska Public Lands Information Center, 605 West Fourth Avenue, Suite 105, Anchorage 99501; (907) 271-2737; www.nps.gov/aplic

*Camping*

Eklutna Lake Campground at Eklutna Lake; (907) 345-5014. Follow the Glenn Highway north from Anchorage for 25 miles to the Thunderbird Falls exit. Veer right and continue for 0.5 mile. Turn right onto Eklutna Lake Road and continue for 10 miles to the campground; nightly camping fee.

Eagle River Campground (907-345-5014), Glenn Highway. Exit about 10 miles north of Anchorage onto Eagle River Loop and Hiland Road; nightly camping fee.

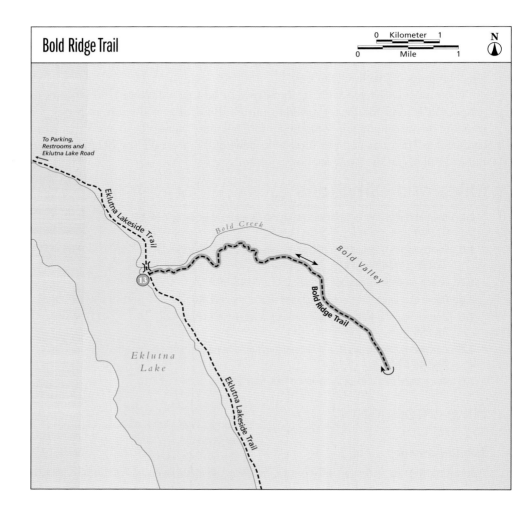

## Local organizations

The Anchorage Adventurers Meetup Group; www.adventurers.meetup.com/109
Mountaineering Club of Alaska, 2633 Spenard Road, Anchorage 99503; (907) 272-1811; www.mcak.org

## Local retailers

Recreational Equipment Inc. (REI), 1200 West Northern Lights Boulevard, Anchorage; (907) 272-4565; www.rei.com
Sportsman's Warehouse, 681 Old Seward Highway, Anchorage; (907) 644-1400; www.sportsmanswarehouse.com
Alaska Mountaineering and Hiking, 2633 Spenard Road, Anchorage; (907) 272-1811; www.alaskamountaineering.com
Cabelas, 155 W 104th, Anchorage; (907) 341-3400; www.cabelas.com/Stores/Anchorage

# EKLUTNA LAKE

Eklutna Lake is formed by a dam located downstream from Eklutna Lake Campground. The Eklutna Glacier carved this valley and left its sign as it retreated to the south beyond Eklutna Lake. In addition to hiking the popular trails near the lake, there are a multitude of other things to do and things happening. Wildlife is abundant. Brown and black bears, Dall sheep, wolves, moose, mountain goats, foxes, lynx, marmots, porcupines, ground squirrels, and many other small mammals live here. Golden eagles, hawks, ptarmigans, grouse, and songbirds are also prevalent. The vegetative ecosystems vary extensively with changes in elevation, from dense spruce forests to meadows of wildflowers to tundra mosses and blueberries.

*Early fall snow above Eklutna Lake*

The area is used extensively year-round for photography, hiking, snow-machining, boating, horseback riding, skiing, dog mushing, fishing, all-terrain vehicles, and camping and picnicking. Eklutna Lake also provides the drinking water to the residents of Anchorage.

6th Avenue Outfitters, 520 W 6th Avenue, Anchorage; (907) 276-0233; www.6th avenueoutfitters.com

Bass Pro Shops, 3046 Mountain View Drive, Anchorage; (907) 330-5200; www .basspro.com/Anchorage

*Local events/attractions*

St. Nicholas Russian Orthodox Church and Cemetery, Mile 26 Glenn Highway, Eklutna Road, Eklutna

Alaska State Fair, Palmer; August and September

An Anchorage calendar of events can be found at www.anchorage.net/events.html.

# 14 East Fork Trail to Tulchina Falls

The East Fork Trail to Tulchina Falls is an excellent waterfall hike. The falls are spectacular from the bottom and can also be climbed—carefully—for a different view. The biggest drawback with this trail is getting to it. It is a relatively short hike to the falls, but it is a 10.5-mile venture to the trailhead. The path parallels the east fork of the Eklutna River, travels through the valley and across a variety of terrain, including mixed forests, rockslides, riverbanks, unbridged stream crossings, and shrubby vegetation. The trail continues on another 4 miles to the back of the valley and open tundra.

**Start:** Mile 10.5 of the Eklutna Lakeside Trail
**Distance:** 5.8 miles out and back to base of falls; 26.8 miles out and back from Eklutna Lakeside trailhead
**Approximate hiking time:** 3–4 hours. Out and back on the Eklutna Lakeside Trail could take anywhere from a half day to 2 days depending on mode of transportation to the trailhead.
**Difficulty:** Moderate
**Elevation gain:** 700 feet
**Trail surface:** Dirt and stone
**Seasons:** Best hiking mid-May through June
**Other trail users:** None
**Canine compatibility:** Leashed dogs permitted; under voice control after trailhead
**Land status:** State park

**Nearest town:** Anchorage
**Fees and permits:** $5 daily parking; reservation required to spend the night in the public-use cabin
**Maps:** Imus Geographics Chugach State Park map (www.imusgeographics.com); USGS Anchorage
**Trail contacts:** Chugach State Park Headquarters, located at the Potter Section House State Historic Site, Mile 115 Seward Highway (mailing address: HC 52 Box 8999, Indian 99540); (907) 345-5014; e-mail: csp@dnr.state.ak.us; open Monday through Friday 10:00 a.m. to 4:30 p.m.
**Special considerations:** It is 10.5 miles to the trailhead; the trail becomes easily overgrown.

**Finding the trailhead:** From Anchorage travel 25 miles north on the Glenn Highway. Take the Thunderbird Falls exit and follow the road to the right. Drive beyond the Thunderbird Falls trailhead and parking lot on your right, and cross the bridge. Just after crossing the Eklutna River, turn right onto Eklutna Lake Road. This road runs 10 miles down to the pay station and Eklutna Lake. There are two large day-use parking lots. From the north side of the parking lots, cross a small bridge over Twin Peaks Creek and turn right at the Eklutna Lakeside trailhead. Hike to Mile 10.5 on the Eklutna Lakeside Trail to access the East Fork trailhead on your left.

## The Hike

This is one of several trails in the Eklutna Lake area. The Tulchina Falls are impressive and the trail is scenic as it ventures through the valley along the base of sheer, steep mountainsides and follows the East Fork Eklutna River. The beginning of the hike follows the rocky confines of Bold Peak to the north. The high, steep rocky ledges are

*Tulchina Falls*

habitat for mountain goats, particularly on the opposite side of the river. Bashful Peak, at 8,005 feet the highest peak in the park, is viewable and directly east of the falls.

Getting to the trailhead is more than half the battle for this hike, since it is located at Mile 10.5 on the Eklutna Lakeside Trail. There are several options available to you. Many people bike to the trailhead. You can bring a bicycle or rent one at the concession stand near the parking lot. You can also drive an ATV to the site. Either of these options allows you to do this hike in one day. Otherwise you can camp at either the Eklutna Alex or Kanchee Campgrounds, located on the Eklutna Lakeside Trail at Miles 8.0 and 10.0, respectively. A third place to stay is the Serenity Falls public-use cabin, located at Mile 12.0. This cabin must be reserved in advance and is a multiple-party public-use hut, meaning that you'll be sharing it with others. However, it is a great cabin with an outstanding view of Serenity Falls and highly recommended.

Follow the Eklutna Lakeside Trail on the wide gravel road for 10.5 miles. When you pass the Eklutna Alex Campground, you know you're close to the turnoff. Once you've arrived at the trailhead, located just before the bridge, the path veers up an embankment and heads into the forest. The narrow, rooted dirt path follows the bank of the river along impressive lichen- and moss-covered boulders. A short 0.25 mile into the hike, the path closely follows the river's edge over a rockslide area. The mountainside vegetation is completely wiped out through this stretch. This continues for another 0.3 mile; the path then heads back into the forest.

Come to a small unbridged stream crossing at approximately 0.9 mile. Just beyond this point you'll encounter another stretch of rockslide. Follow the cairns across the rocky area to the wooded path on the other side. Over the next 0.25 mile you'll cross a couple more small streams. All the stream crossings have old logs in place, making the crossings pretty easy.

At 1.7 miles come to a small lake, often occupied by waterfowl, and then cross a small footbridge. The trail turns south. From here on, the trail remains narrow and is often obstructed by downed trees, making it a little more difficult to follow. Cross one more stream. Immediately on the other side is a small sign pointing you toward the falls. Turn left here and follow the old stone riverbed. As you get closer to the falls, you will have to work your way through a short stand of thick vegetation.

## Miles and Directions

**0.0** Start at the East Fork trailhead, located at Mile 10.5 on the Eklutna Lakeside Trail. N61 18.900 / W148 58.338

**0.9** Cross an unbridged stream. N61 18.568 / W148 56.923

**1.1** Cross a small stream on a log. N61 18.501 / W148 56.760

**1.35** Come to another logged stream crossing. N61 18.333 / W148 56.502

**1.5** Cross a third small stream on a log. N61 18.238 / W148 56.252

**1.7** Reach a small lake and cross a stream on a footbridge. N61 18.210 / W148 56.076

**2.5** Cross another stream on a log. Turn left at the sign and follow the riverbed toward the falls. N61 17.569 / W148 55.707

# East Fork Trail to Tulchina Falls

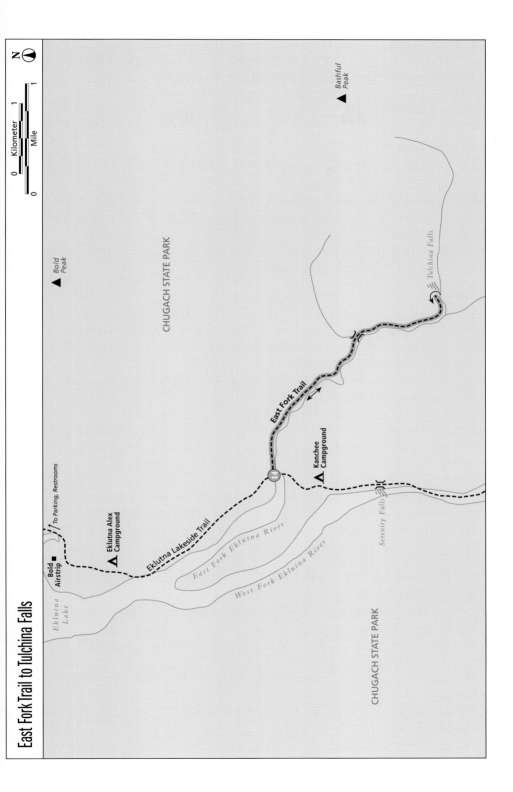

**2.9** Reach the base of the falls. Retrace your steps to the trailhead. N61 17.601 / W148 55.427

**5.8** Arrive back at the East Fork trailhead. N61 18.900 / W148 58.338

# Hike Information

*Local information*

Anchorage Visitor Information Center, 546 West Fourth Avenue, Anchorage 99501; (907) 274-3531; www.anchorage.net

Alaska Department of Natural Resources Public Information Center, Atwood Building, 550 West Seventh Avenue, Suite 1260, Anchorage 99501; (907) 269-8400; www.dnr.state.ak.us/parks

Alaska Public Lands Information Center, 605 West Fourth Avenue, Suite 105, Anchorage 99501; (907) 271-2737; www.nps.gov/aplic

*Camping*

Eklutna Lake Campground at Eklutna Lake; (907) 345-5014. Follow the Glenn Highway north from Anchorage for 25 miles to the Thunderbird Falls exit. Veer right and continue for 0.5 mile. Turn right onto Eklutna Lake Road and continue for 10 miles to the campground; nightly camping fee.

Eklutna Alex and Kanchee Campgrounds; there is no fee for using these remote campgrounds on the Eklutna Lakeside Trail.

Serenity Falls public-use cabin; (907) 269-8400 for fee information

Eagle River Campground (907-345-5014), Glenn Highway. Exit about 10 miles north of Anchorage onto Eagle River Loop and Hiland Road; nightly camping fee.

*Local organizations*

The Anchorage Adventurers Meetup Group; www.adventurers.meetup.com/109

Mountaineering Club of Alaska, 2633 Spenard Road, Anchorage 99503; (907) 272-1811; www.mcak.org

*Local retailers*

Recreational Equipment Inc. (REI), 1200 West Northern Lights Boulevard, Anchorage; (907) 272-4565; www.rei.com

Sportsman's Warehouse, 681 Old Seward Highway, Anchorage; (907) 644-1400; www.sportsmanswarehouse.com

Alaska Mountaineering and Hiking, 2633 Spenard Road, Anchorage; (907) 272-1811; www.alaskamountaineering.com

Cabelas, 155 W 104th, Anchorage; (907) 341-3400; www.cabelas.com/Stores/Anchorage

6th Avenue Outfitters, 520 W 6th Avenue, Anchorage; (907) 276-0233; www.6th avenueoutfitters.com

Bass Pro Shops, 3046 Mountain View Drive, Anchorage; (907) 330-5200; www
.basspro.com/Anchorage

*Local events/attractions*

St. Nicholas Russian Orthodox Church and Cemetery, Mile 26 Glenn Highway,
Eklutna Road, Eklutna
Alaska State Fair, Palmer; August and September
An Anchorage calendar of events can be found at www.anchorage.net/events.html.

## GREEN TIP
Pack out what you pack in—even food scraps,
because they can attract wild animals.

# 15 Thunderbird Falls Trail

This is a short and relatively easy hike through one of Alaska's scenic deciduous forests. Even though the length and duration of the hike are short compared to other hikes in the park, it is one you will not want to miss. A viewing deck on the left side of the trail is located above a steep gorge with views of East and West Twin Peaks and the Eklutna River below. Another 0.5 mile brings you to a second platform with an unobstructed view of historic Thunderbird Falls. An optional side trail takes you down to Thunderbird Creek.

**Start:** Trailhead at the edge of the parking lot
**Distance:** 2.0 miles out and back
**Approximate hiking time:** 1-2 hours
**Difficulty:** Easy
**Elevation gain:** 300 feet
**Trail surface:** Dirt and stone path
**Seasons:** Year-round
**Other trail users:** None
**Canine compatibility:** Leashed dogs permitted
**Land status:** State park
**Nearest town:** Eagle River
**Fees and permits:** $5 daily parking

**Maps:** Imus Geographics Chugach State Park map (www.imusgeographics.com); USGS Anchorage
**Trail contacts:** Chugach State Park Headquarters, located at the Potter Section House State Historic Site, Mile 115 Seward Highway (mailing address: HC 52 Box 8999, Indian 99540); (907) 345-5014; e-mail: csp@dnr.state.ak .us; open Monday through Friday 10:00 a.m. to 4:30 p.m.
**Special considerations:** The trail has extremely steep and dangerous banks. Stay on the trail.

**Finding the trailhead:** From Anchorage follow the Glenn Highway north for 25 miles to the Thunderbird Falls exit. Veer right and continue for 0.25 mile. The well-developed parking lot located on the right-hand side of the road has restroom facilities and picnic tables.

## The Hike

The trail for this hike is wide, relatively straight, and easy to follow. The scenery is particularly enjoyable as you walk through a mixed deciduous–spruce forest. The path traverses the hillside with ups and downs as you proceed along the trail. The right side of the trail is occupied by private property and homes; directly on the left side is a deep gorge revealing the Eklutna River and eventually Thunderbird Creek.

After approximately 0.5 mile come upon a viewing platform looking out toward the West and East Twin Peaks and down on the glacially silty water of the Eklutna River. As you continue on the path, reach a fork in the trail that turns abruptly to your left downhill. The Thunderbird Trail continues straight ahead and joins a boardwalk. The boardwalk ends at the second viewing deck with an unobstructed view of the falls.

The fork to the left takes you steeply downhill into the gorge and to Thunderbird Creek. This portion of the trail can be particularly muddy at the bottom, but it is

*Beautiful Thunderbird Falls*

worth exploring. Proceeding along the creek shoreline, you will arrive at a viewing area near the bottom of the falls. The trail ends here. The view of the falls is not unobstructed from the bottom, but the hike down is still worth it just to observe the beauty of the huge boulders and rock-lined creek. When heading back up, stay on the main trail rather than taking the shortcuts up the hill; this will help in erosion control.

This trail is popular throughout the year. It is a great summer day hike, extremely beautiful in the fall, and equally scenic in the winter months, when amazing ice sculptures often form at the foot of the frozen falls.

## Miles and Directions

**0.0**  Start at the trailhead at the edge of the parking lot. N61 26.946 / W149 22.223

**0.5**  Reach the first viewing platform with a view of the Eklutna River. N61 26.740 / W149 21.958

**0.85** The trail continues straight ahead on a boardwalk. N61 26.583 / W149 21.700 (Option: Take the left-hand trail down to Thunderbird Creek [N61 26.628 / W149 21.623] and the fenced viewing area near the bottom of the falls [N61 26.595 W149 21.531] for an additional 0.5-mile round-trip.)

**1.0**  Reach the end of the trail and the second viewing platform with a view of Thunderbird Falls. N61 26.546 / W149 21.634

**2.0**  Arrive back at the parking lot. N61 26.946 / W149 22.223

## Hike Information

### Local information

Anchorage Visitor Information Center, 546 West Fourth Avenue, Anchorage 99501; (907) 274-3531; www.anchorage.net

Alaska Department of Natural Resources Public Information Center, Atwood Building, 550 West Seventh Avenue, Suite 1260, Anchorage 99501; (907) 269-8400; www.dnr.state.ak.us/parks

Alaska Public Lands Information Center, 605 West Fourth Avenue, Suite 105, Anchorage 99501; (907) 271-2737; www.nps.gov/aplic

### Camping

Eklutna Lake Campground at Eklutna Lake; (907) 345-5014. Follow the Glenn Highway north from Anchorage for 25 miles to the Thunderbird Falls exit. Veer right and continue for 0.5 mile. Turn right onto Eklutna Lake Road and continue for 10 miles to the campground; nightly camping fee.

Eagle River Campground (907-345-5014), Glenn Highway. Exit about 10 miles north of Anchorage onto Eagle River Loop and Hiland Road; nightly camping fee.

### Local organizations

The Anchorage Adventurers Meetup Group; www.adventurers.meetup.com/109

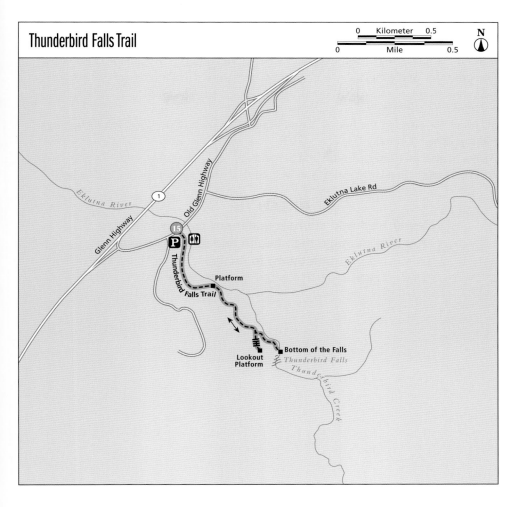

Mountaineering Club of Alaska, 2633 Spenard Road, Anchorage 99503; (907) 272-1811; www.mcak.org

*Local retailers*

Recreational Equipment Inc. (REI), 1200 West Northern Lights Boulevard, Anchorage; (907) 272-4565; www.rei.com

Sportsman's Warehouse, 681 Old Seward Highway, Anchorage; (907) 644-1400; www.sportsmanswarehouse.com

Alaska Mountaineering and Hiking, 2633 Spenard Road, Anchorage; (907) 272-1811; www.alaskamountaineering.com

Cabelas, 155 W 104th, Anchorage; (907) 341-3400; www.cabelas.com/Stores/Anchorage

6th Avenue Outfitters, 520 W 6th Avenue, Anchorage; (907) 276-0233; www.6th avenueoutfitters.com

Bass Pro Shops, 3046 Mountain View Drive, Anchorage; (907) 330-5200; www .basspro.com/Anchorage

*Local events/attractions*

St. Nicholas Russian Orthodox Church and Cemetery, Mile 26 Glenn Highway, Eklutna Road, Eklutna

Alaska State Fair, Palmer; August and September

An Anchorage calendar of events can be found at www.anchorage.net/events.html.

## GREEN TIP

Never feed wild animals under any circumstances.
You may damage their health and expose yourself
(and them) to danger.

# 16 Ptarmigan Valley Trail

The easy-to-follow Ptarmigan Valley Trail guides you through forested slopes and eventually to open alpine tundra in the Ptarmigan Valley. It starts out relatively steep and gradually climbs until you hit the tundra above the tree line. The area provides excellent habitat for moose and numerous bird species including the willow ptarmigan. A variety of trail users are likely to be enjoying this multiuse trail throughout the year; however, mountain bikes are not allowed. There are good views of Knik Arm and the Alaskan Range along the way, with extraordinary views from the tundra.

**Start:** Trailhead at the south side of the upper parking lot
**Distance:** 8.2 miles out and back
**Approximate hiking time:** 4–6 hours
**Difficulty:** Easy to moderate
**Elevation gain:** 1,800 feet
**Trail surface:** Dirt and gravel
**Seasons:** Year-round
**Other trail users:** Horses; snow machines and skiers in winter
**Canine compatibility:** Leashed dogs permitted; voice control after trailhead
**Land status:** State park
**Nearest town:** Anchorage

**Fees and permits:** No fees or permits required
**Maps:** Imus Geographics Chugach State Park map (www.imusgeographics.com); USGS Anchorage
**Trail contacts:** Chugach State Park Headquarters, located at the Potter Section House State Historic Site, Mile 115 Seward Highway (mailing address: HC 52 Box 8999, Indian 99540); (907) 345-5014; e-mail: csp@dnr.state.ak.us; open Monday through Friday 10:00 a.m. to 4:30 p.m.
**Special considerations:** Areas of the trail are avalanche prone.

**Finding the trailhead:** From Anchorage head north on the Glenn Highway 16 miles to the North Birchwood exit. Drive east on Birchwood Loop Road 0.25 mile. Turn right (south) onto Old Glenn Highway. There is a gravel parking lot 0.5 mile up the road on your left side with state park signs. Park in the lot and walk up the gravel road from the lower parking area to another closed-off parking lot. The trailhead is located on the south side of the lot.

## The Hike

The hike begins at the trailhead located in the upper parking area. Take note of the information board next to the trailhead and the multiuse trail information displayed. Be aware of trail users besides hikers. The trail begins as a gentle ascent on a wide path into the spruce forest. It increases in steepness and winds back and forth as you climb upward. The entire trail is well maintained and marked with small orange-metal flags on the trees all the way to the open alpine tundra.

At approximately 0.5 mile the path takes you to the top of a hill and then makes a sudden and steep descent into a valley. It's not a difficult hike down, but you will certainly feel it in your legs coming up on the return trip. You'll hike several hundred

*Taking in the view from Ptarmigan Valley Trail*

feet across the bottom and immediately head back up, where the trail begins to level out for another short distance. This portion of the hike is through a beautiful forested area that's excellent habitat for Alaskan critters. Cross a small stream at slightly more than 0.75 mile. At the 1.0-mile marker the trail becomes very steep. Several switchbacks afford some great views behind you of the Knik Arm, Slipping Lady, and the beautiful Alaskan Range as a backdrop.

After 1.6 miles the wide main trail makes an "S" and continues to head in a southerly direction. At this point a small sign that reads SUMMER TRAIL directs you to the left (east). The trail abruptly leaves the forest and heads into shrubby vegetation, following along the mountain ledge. The Summer Trail is a narrow, more scenic path that eventually leads back into the spruce forest and rejoins the wider main trail, forming a loop.

At around 2.0 miles the trail begins to level off again and runs parallel to Little Peters Creek to the east. The level section doesn't last, and the trail soon continues a slow ascent toward the open tundra. Cross Little Peters Creek on a small footbridge at about 3.5 miles. For the next 0.5 mile keep an eye out for Alaska's state bird, the willow ptarmigan, easily spotted in early spring before the vegetation leafs out. The vegetation will continue to thin as you continue to gain altitude.

At just beyond 4.0 miles, you climb above the tree line and the brushy vegetation ends. The trail continues as a narrow footpath across the alpine meadow and crosses a small creek. The narrow path heads up the ridge into the tundra as you enter Ptarmigan Valley. The view is outstanding, and the area is an ideal place to camp.

You can continue for another 4.0 miles or so to explore other peaks within the park. However, there is no marked trail. Be sure to have your compass/GPS and map with you and know how to use them if you decide to continue.

## Miles and Directions

**0.0**  Start at the upper parking area. N61 23.364 / W149 28.069

**0.15** Arrive at the trailhead. N61 23.364 / W149 28.069

**0.85** Cross a small stream. N61 22.899 / W149 28.092

**1.0**  The trail becomes steep and begins to switchback. N61 22.834 / W149 28.363

**1.6**  Veer left at the sign for Summer Trail. N61 22.561 / W149 27.837

**2.1**  Descend into spruce forest and walk parallel to Little Peters Creek. N61 22.545 / W149 27.114

**3.4**  Cross Little Peters Creek on a small footbridge. N61 21.517 / W149 26.788

**4.1**  The established trail ends and the narrow footpath begins. Retrace your steps. N61 20.955 / W149 27.102

**8.2**  Arrive back at the parking lot. N61 23.364 / W149 28.069

*View of Knik Arm and Mt. Susitna*

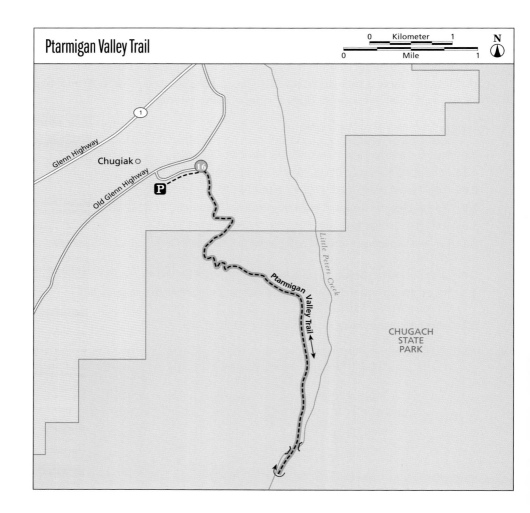

# Hike Information

*Local information*

Anchorage Visitor Information Center, 546 West Fourth Avenue, Anchorage 99501; (907) 274-3531; www.anchorage.net

Alaska Department of Natural Resources Public Information Center, Atwood Building, 550 West Seventh Avenue, Suite 1260, Anchorage 99501; (907) 269-8400; www.dnr.state.ak.us/parks

Alaska Public Lands Information Center, 605 West Fourth Avenue, Suite 105, Anchorage 99501; (907) 271-2737; www.nps.gov/aplic

## Camping

Eklutna Lake Campground at Eklutna Lake; (907) 345-9014. Follow the Glenn Highway north from Anchorage for 25 miles to the Thunderbird Falls exit. Veer right and continue for 0.5 mile. Turn right onto Eklutna Lake Road and continue for 10 miles to the campground; nightly camping fee.

Eagle River Campground (907-345-5014), Glenn Highway. Exit about 10 miles north of Anchorage onto Eagle River Loop and Hiland Road; nightly camping fee.

## Local organizations

The Anchorage Adventurers Meetup Group; www.adventurers.meetup.com/109
Mountaineering Club of Alaska, 2633 Spenard Road, Anchorage 99503; (907) 272-1811; www.mcak.org

## Local retailers

Recreational Equipment Inc. (REI), 1200 West Northern Lights Boulevard, Anchorage; (907) 272-4565; www.rei.com

Sportsman's Warehouse, 681 Old Seward Highway, Anchorage; (907) 644-1400; www.sportsmanswarehouse.com

Alaska Mountaineering and Hiking, 2633 Spenard Road, Anchorage; (907) 272-1811; www.alaskamountaineering.com

Cabelas, 155 W 104th, Anchorage; (907) 341-3400; www.cabelas.com/Stores/Anchorage

6th Avenue Outfitters, 520 W 6th Avenue, Anchorage; (907) 276-0233; www.6th avenueoutfitters.com

Bass Pro Shops, 3046 Mountain View Drive, Anchorage; (907) 330-5200; www.basspro.com/Anchorage

## Local events / attractions

St. Nicholas Russian Orthodox Church and Cemetery, Mile 26 Glenn Highway, Eklutna Road, Eklutna

Alaska State Fair, Palmer; August and September

An Anchorage calendar of events can be found at www.anchorage.net/events.html.

# East of Anchorage

The trails east of Anchorage are located in the foothills of the Chugach Mountains, an area that could be considered the city's backyard—although it's a wild backyard for sure. There are four major access points, just minutes from downtown, that allow hikers to enter the Hillside Trail System and enjoy a vast array of trails. These trails can lead you north or south along the front range of the Chugach Mountains, or into the open tundra and heart of Chugach State Park.

Strong winds are common in this area, particularly at the higher elevations. When hiking any of these trails, always be prepared for changing weather conditions along with great variances in temperatures as you gain elevation. The Hillside Trail System, even though it is right at the doorstep of the city, is prime habitat for bears and moose. On all Anchorage area trails, be prepared for and know how to react to wildlife encounters.

*View of valley from Powerline Trail (Hike 18)*

# 17 Hillside Trail System (Overview)

Access to the western trails in Chugach State Park is gained from the hillside of east Anchorage. Four major trailheads access the assortment of trails called the Hillside Trail System, ranging from easy, wide old roadbeds to more difficult routes requiring mountaineering skills. Trail highlights include excellent alpine scenery and lakes, wildflowers, wildlife, fall berry picking, and outstanding views of Anchorage, the Alaska Range, and Cook Inlet. This area of the park has something for everyone.

**Start:** Prospect Heights, O'Malley, Upper Huffman, or Glen Alps trailheads
**Distance:** 0.25 mile to 22.0 miles one-way
**Approximate hiking time:** 30 minutes–overnight
**Difficulty:** Easy to difficult
**Elevation gain:** 700 to 4,075 feet
**Trail surface:** Loose stone, dirt, mud
**Seasons:** Best hiking summer and fall
**Other trail users:** Mountain bikes, runners, cross-country skiers in winter
**Canine compatibility:** Leashed dogs permitted
**Land status:** State park
**Nearest town:** Anchorage
**Fees and permits:** $5 parking fee at Glen Alps and Prospect Heights trailheads

**Maps:** Imus Geographics Chugach State Park map (www.imusgeographics.com); Alaska Department of Natural Resources: Chugach State Park Hillside Trail System Map; USGS Anchorage
**Trail contacts:** Chugach State Park Headquarters, located at the Potter Section House State Historic Site, Mile 115 Seward Highway (mailing address: HC 52 Box 8999, Indian 99540); (907) 345-5014; e-mail: csp@dnr.state.ak .us; open Monday through Friday 10:00 a.m. to 4:30 p.m.
**Special considerations:** Risk of avalanches, falls, and hypothermia on trails; use caution.

**Finding the trailhead:** For the Prospect Heights trailhead, drive south from downtown Anchorage on Seward Highway to the O'Malley Road exit. Drive east toward the mountains for 3.5 miles; the street runs into Hillside Drive. After the road curves to the left, make an immediate right-hand turn onto Upper O'Malley Road. Follow this road for 0.5 mile to the first intersection and turn left onto Prospect Drive. Follow Prospect Drive for another 1 mile to the Prospect Heights trailhead. There are plenty of parking spaces and restroom facilities. Trailhead GPS: N61 08.341 / W149 42.633

For the O'Malley trailhead, drive south from downtown Anchorage on Seward Highway to the O'Malley Road exit. Drive east toward the mountains for 3.5 miles; the street runs into Hillside Drive. After the road curves to the left, make an immediate right-hand turn onto Upper O'Malley Road. Follow this road for 0.5 mile to the first intersection and turn right onto Longhorn Street. After another 0.5 mile the road veers left and becomes Cobra Street. Take the first right-hand turn onto Shebanof Avenue and travel 0.25 mile until the road ends at a T. There is a small parking area off to the side of the road in front of the trailhead. Trailhead GPS: N61 07.163 / W149 42.875

For the Upper Huffman trailhead, drive south from downtown Anchorage on Seward Highway to the O'Malley Road exit. Drive east toward the mountains for 3.5 miles; the street runs into Hillside Drive as it curves left. Turn right, heading south, and travel approximately 1 mile. Turn left at the Upper Huffman Road sign. Follow this road a short distance to an intersection and turn left onto Sultana Drive. The state park sign and large paved parking lot are just up the road on your right. Trailhead GPS: N61 06.725 / W149 42.645

For the Glen Alps trailhead, drive south from downtown Anchorage on Seward Highway to the O'Malley Road exit. Drive east toward the mountains for 3.5 miles. Turn right onto Hillside Drive, heading south, and travel approximately 1 mile. Turn left at the Upper Huffman Road sign. Follow this road a short distance to an intersection and turn right onto Toilsome Hill Road. Travel for about 2 miles as the road winds around, climbs, and eventually changes from pavement to dirt. The parking lot is on your left. Trailhead GPS: N61 06.187 / W149 40.986

## The Hikes

The trails on the hillside are used year-round by local residents as well as visitors. They are heavily used in summer and fall and equally popular in winter with snow machines and skiers. The trails form a network that enables them to be accessed from various points on the hillside. The common trails and routes in the system are listed below under the trailhead where they are most commonly accessed. The hikes with detailed descriptions in this book are marked with an asterisk.

The Powerline Trail is the major artery used to connect to many of the other trails in the network. It can be accessed from all four trailheads and continues down to the Indian Valley trailhead near the Seward Highway.

The following trails are accessible from the four trailheads:

Prospect Heights: ★Near Point, Williwaw Lakes, Powerline, Middle Fork Loop, and ★Wolverine Peak

O'Malley: Powerline

Upper Huffman: Picnic Loop, Silver Fern Spur, Powerline, Upper Huffman Snowmobile Trail

Glen Alps: ★Powerline, Middle Fork Loop, ★Williwaw Lakes, Gasline, Hidden Lakes, Ship Pass Route, O'Malley Gulley Route, O'Malley Peak, ★Flattop Mountain, Anchorage Overlook.

## Hike Information

### Local information

Anchorage Visitor Information Center, 546 West Fourth Avenue, Anchorage 99501; (907) 274-3531; www.anchorage.net

Alaska Department of Natural Resources Public Information Center, Atwood Building, 550 West Seventh Avenue, Suite 1260, Anchorage 99501; (907) 269-8400; www.dnr.state.ak.us/parks

*Hillside Trail System east of Anchorage*

Alaska Public Lands Information Center, 605 West Fourth Avenue, Suite 105, Anchorage 99501; (907) 271-2737; www.nps.gov/aplic

## Camping

Bird Creek Campground; (907) 345-5014; located southeast of Anchorage at Mile Marker 101 on Seward Highway; nightly camping fee

## Local organizations

The Anchorage Adventurers Meetup Group; www.adventurers.meetup.com/109 Mountaineering Club of Alaska, 2633 Spenard Road, Anchorage 99503; (907) 272-1811; www.mcak.org

## Local retailers

Recreational Equipment Inc. (REI), 1200 West Northern Lights Boulevard, Anchorage; (907) 272-4565; www.rei.com

Sportsman's Warehouse, 681 Old Seward Highway, Anchorage; (907) 644-1400; www.sportsmanswarehouse.com

Alaska Mountaineering and Hiking, 2633 Spenard Road, Anchorage; (907) 272-1811; www.alaskamountaineering.com

Cabelas, 155 W 104th, Anchorage; (907) 341-3400; www.cabelas.com/Stores/Anchorage

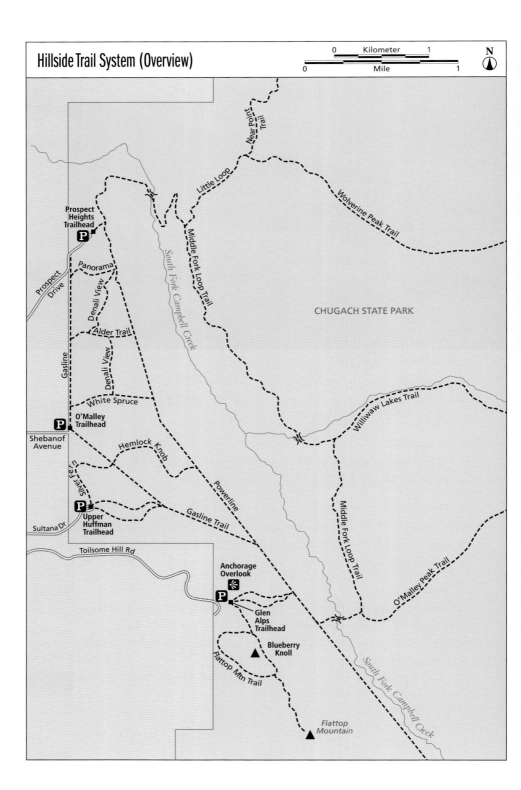

# Hillside Trail System (Overview)

0 Kilometer 1
0 Mile 1

N

Near Point Trail

Little Loop

Wolverine Peak Trail

Prospect Heights Trailhead

P

Prospect Drive

Panorama

Denali View

Middle Fork Loop Trail

South Fork Campbell Creek

CHUGACH STATE PARK

Alder Trail

Gasline

Denali View

White Spruce

Williwaw Lakes Trail

P O'Malley Trailhead

Shebanof Avenue

Hemlock Knob

Silver Fern

Powerline

Middle Fork Loop Trail

P Upper Huffman Trailhead

Gasline Trail

Sultana Dr

Toilsome Hill Rd

O'Malley Peak Trail

Anchorage Overlook

P

Glen Alps Trailhead

Blueberry Knoll

South Fork Campbell Creek

Flattop Mtn Trail

Flattop Mountain

6th Avenue Outfitters, 520 W 6th Avenue, Anchorage; (907) 276-0233; www.6th avenueoutfitters.com

Bass Pro Shops, 3046 Mountain View Drive, Anchorage; (907) 330-5200; www .basspro.com/Anchorage

*Local events/attractions*

Kincaid Park, 9401 West Raspberry Road, southwest Anchorage—1,400 acres of rolling forested hills, beautiful scenery, and wildlife

Mayor's Marathon and Half Marathon, Anchorage; June

Great Alaska Salmon Bake and Fly-by, Anchorage; July

Anchorage Market and Festival, between C and E Streets off West Third Avenue, Anchorage; Saturday and Sunday, mid-May to early September; www.anchoragemar-kets.com/index.html

An Anchorage calendar of events can be found at www.anchorage.net/events.html. Information on events and festivals in the Hillside Trails area is available at www.muni .org/contents1/events.cfm.

## ANCHORAGE TRAILS

The city of Anchorage sits at the base of the Chugach Mountains. Consequently this book uses Anchorage as a starting point for access to all the trailheads in Chugach State Park. You will more than likely spend some time in Anchorage and may want to check out some of the city's award-winning trails. Anchorage has more than 665 miles of paved and unpaved trails. Residents and visitors alike take advantage of the hiking, bicycling, and multiuse trails year-round. The city has more than 10,000 acres of municipal parkland, 200 parks, and over 250 miles of paved trails and greenbelts that connect neighborhoods with open space and wildlife habitat.

Anchorage's long winters allow residents to enjoy 130 miles of plowed and maintained winter paths. There are more than 100 miles of groomed ski trails, 24 miles of lighted ski trails, and 36 miles of dog-mushing trails. On the southwest side of Anchorage sits Kincaid Park, one of two Nordic ski areas certified for international 5K, 10K, 15K, and 30K competition.

# 18 Powerline Trail

At first glance the Powerline Trail doesn't appear to be much more than a long dirt road connecting to Indian Valley. The first 6.0 miles of this trail are uniquely different from the last 5.0 miles in regard to terrain, vegetation, and even wildlife. Steep mountain walls, mountain peaks, beautiful valleys and streams, mature Sitka spruce forest, and areas rich in wildlife provide plenty of enjoyment along the way. The trail is generally wide and uphill until it reaches the pass and then becomes very steep as it heads down to Indian. This year–round multiuse trail provides access to other trails in the Hillside Trail System.

**Start:** From the Glen Alps trailhead parking lot, head down the hill next to the wood stairs. This trail can also be started from the Indian trailhead located at Mile 102 of the Seward Highway.
**Distance:** 11.3 miles one-way to Indian; 12.0 miles out and back to top of pass from Glen Alps trailhead; 10.3 miles out and back to top of pass from Indian trailhead
**Approximate hiking time:** 8–10 hours out and back from Glen Alps; 6–8 hours out and back from Indian
**Difficulty:** Easy to moderate due to steepness
**Elevation gain/loss:** 1,300 feet from Glen Alps; 1,960 feet from Indian
**Trail surface:** Wide road; dirt, gravel, and loose stone
**Seasons:** Best hiking June through mid-September
**Other trail users:** Bikes, horses, cross-country skiers
**Canine compatibility:** Leashed dogs permitted; under voice control after trailhead
**Land status:** State park
**Nearest town:** Anchorage
**Fees and permits:** $5 daily parking at Glen Alps trailhead
**Maps:** Imus Geographics Chugach State Park map (www.imusgeographics.com); Alaska Department of Natural Resources: Chugach State Park Hillside Trail System map; USGS Anchorage
**Trail contacts:** Chugach State Park Headquarters, located at the Potter Section House State Historic Site, Mile 115 Seward Highway (mailing address: HC 52 Box 8999, Indian 99540); (907) 345-5014; e-mail: csp@dnr.state.ak .us; open Monday through Friday 10:00 a.m. to 4:30 p.m.
**Special considerations:** Some areas along this trail are extremely avalanche prone in winter.

**Finding the trailhead:** This trail is easily picked up from the Glen Alps trailhead. Drive south from downtown Anchorage on Seward Highway to the O'Malley Road exit. Drive east toward the mountains for 3.5 miles and turn right onto Hillside Drive. Continue for 1 mile and turn left onto Upper Huffman Road. Travel for 0.75 mile and then turn right onto Toilsome Hill Drive. You will see the Chugach State Park sign at this intersection. The road becomes gravel and continues for another 2 miles. The parking lot is located on your left. The large lot is equipped with a viewing deck—the Anchorage Lookout Trail—and restroom facilities. Follow either one of the paths at the north side of the parking 0.25 mile downhill to the Powerline Trail. (Option: This trail can also be accessed at the south end at Indian trailhead, located at Mile 102 on the Seward Highway south of Anchorage. Turn toward the mountains on Ocean View Road and drive 1.4 miles to the gravel parking lot and trailhead.)

# The Hike

## From Glen Alps Trailhead

Most people begin the Powerline Trail from the Glen Alps trailhead, although it can also be accessed from the Prospect Heights trailhead. From the Glen Alps trailhead, at the north end of the parking lot next to the wood stairs, follow either one of the two trails downhill. You will quickly arrive at a gravel road and the sign indicating that you are at the Powerline Trail. Immediately in front of you spanning east–west is a massive view of South Fork Campbell Creek Valley. Turn right (east). The trail heads downhill for a short distance and then begins a gradual climb for the next several miles. The path follows South Fork Campbell Creek on your left. Keep an eye out for moose along the way, both in the valley and on the trail. The trail follows the parallel power lines through the valley and over the pass. For a good day hike, travel the first 6.0 miles to the top of the pass as a 12.0-mile out-and-back hike. The last 5.0 miles look completely different and are better approached from the Indian trailhead on a separate day.

There are several turnoffs to access different trails within the Hillside Trail System along the way. Almost immediately the path to Middle Fork Loop Trail and Williwaw Lakes descends into the valley on your left. After continuing straight ahead

*View of Powerline Pass*

for approximately 2.0 miles, the Hidden Lake Trailhead veers off into the valley and crosses the bridge over South Fork Campbell Creek. This trail also provides access to Ship Creek Trail.

The Powerline Trail can be very muddy and wet, with a substantial amount of mountain runoff crossing the trail. You will also encounter stream crossings at approximately 4.5 and 9.0 miles. The streams are not bridged, and you can plan on wet feet unless you bring an old pair of shoes or sandals with you.

After crossing the first stream, you soon see two small tarns on your right, the larger being Green Lake. After passing the first tarn, look for a fork to your left heading uphill and take it rather than following the wide road straight ahead that travels past the second tarn. This turnoff will take you up to the pass. If you miss it, you will quickly realize that you need to turn back to get up the steep hillside. This entire area is very avalanche prone and begins to fill with snow by the end of September, so plan your hike accordingly. Once you are at the top of the pass, the views in both directions are amazing. Dall sheep are frequently seen at this elevation.

From here the trail heads abruptly downhill into Indian Valley. There will be a lot of rock and loose stone along the trail, making travel slightly more difficult whether you're coming up the trail or going down. Since most people will hike this trail in two parts, the hike description for the south half starts at the Indian trailhead rather than from the top of the pass.

*From Indian Trailhead*

For a 10.3-mile out-and-back hike from the Indian trailhead parking lot, follow the wet dirt path into the spruce forest along Indian Creek. The trail T's after approximately 0.25 mile. Turn left and cross the bridge just ahead. From here it is 4.9 miles to the pass. The path becomes muddy and wet as it begins to climb, particularly the first couple of miles. At 1.8 miles you will cross a rapidly moving stream that will most likely leave you with wet feet.

The terrain is heavily wooded and provides prime habitat for spruce grouse, bears, moose, and porcupines—the latter being good reason to keep your dog on a leash, at least through this part of the hike. As the trail continues to climb, the views of Turnagain Arm to the south and Indian Valley become increasingly amplified with the increased altitude around 3.0 miles. The path becomes very steep and narrow with loose stone as it travels through thick vegetation and numerous switchbacks, leaving the tree line below. As you approach the final destination, the trail surface changes to rock and stone and climbs steadily to the pass, where it overlooks the South Fork Campbell Creek Valley below.

## Miles and Directions

**North Section**

    **0.0**  Start at the Glen Alps trailhead parking lot. N61 06.184 / W149 40.990

    **0.25** Turn right (east) at the sign onto Powerline Trail. N61 06.239 / W149 40.246

# Powerline Trail

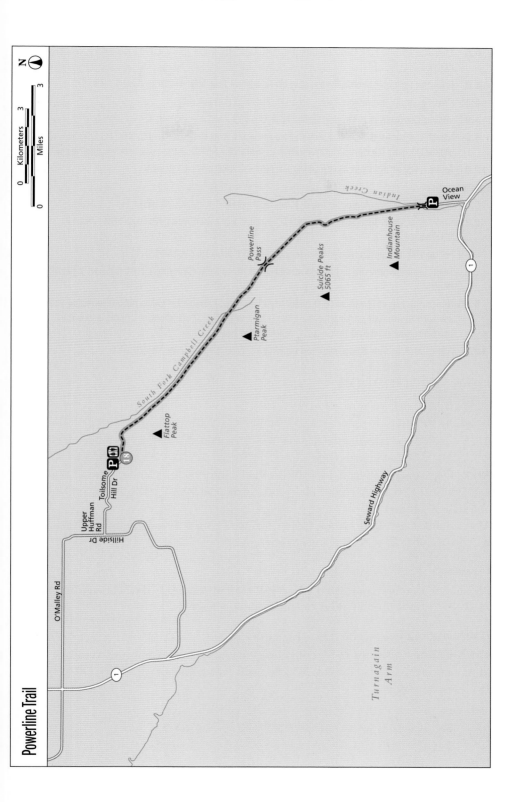

**0.5** Pass the Middle Fork Loop trailhead on your left; continue straight. N61 06.145 / W149 40.107

**2.0** Pass the Hidden Lake trailhead; stay on Powerline Trail. N61 04.965 / W149 38.222

**4.5** Cross a small, unbridged creek. N61 03.798 / W149 34.837

**4.8** Veer left at the fork and head uphill. N61 03.593 / W149 33.740

**6.0** Reach the top of the pass. Enjoy the views before retracing your steps. N61 03.593 / W149 33.740 (Option: Continue down to Indian for an 11.2-mile one-way shuttle hike.)

**12.0** Arrive back at the Glen Alps parking lot. N61 06.184 / W149 40.990

**South Section**

**0.0** Start at the Indian trailhead parking lot. N60 59.974 / W149 29.974

**0.25** Turn left at the T and cross a bridge (10.9 miles from Glen Alps). N61 00.169 / W149 29.955

**0.59** Follow the fork uphill along the power lines. N61 00.438 / W149 30.126

**1.8** Ford a rapidly moving, unbridged stream (9.0 miles from Glen Alps). N61 01.314 / W149 30.657

**5.15** Reach the top of the pass (6.0 miles from Glen Alps). Enjoy the views before retracing your steps to the Indian parking lot. N61 03.593 / W149 33.740 (Option: Continue down to the Glen Alps trailhead for an 11.2-mile shuttle hike.)

**10.3** Arrive back at the Indian trailhead parking lot. N60 59.974 / W149 29.974

# Hike Information

## Local information

Anchorage Visitor Information Center, 546 West Fourth Avenue, Anchorage 99501; (907) 274-3531; www.anchorage.net

Alaska Department of Natural Resources Public Information Center, Atwood Building, 550 West Seventh Avenue, Suite 1260, Anchorage 99501; (907) 269-8400; www.dnr.state.ak.us/parks

Alaska Public Lands Information Center, 605 West Fourth Avenue, Suite 105, Anchorage 99501; (907) 271-2737; www.nps.gov/aplic

## Camping

Bird Creek Campground; (907) 345-5014; located southeast of Anchorage at Mile Marker 101 on Seward Highway; nightly camping fee

## Local organizations

The Anchorage Adventurers Meetup Group; www.adventurers.meetup.com/109
Mountaineering Club of Alaska, 2633 Spenard Road, Anchorage 99503; (907) 272-1811; www.mcak.org

## Local retailers

Recreational Equipment Inc. (REI), 1200 West Northern Lights Boulevard, Anchorage; (907) 272-4565; www.rei.com

Sportsman's Warehouse, 681 Old Seward Highway, Anchorage; (907) 644-1400; www.sportsmanswarehouse.com

Alaska Mountaineering and Hiking, 2633 Spenard Road, Anchorage; (907) 272-1811; www.alaskamountaineering.com

Cabelas, 155 W 104th, Anchorage; (907) 341-3400; www.cabelas.com/Stores/Anchorage

6th Avenue Outfitters, 520 W 6th Avenue, Anchorage; (907) 276-0233; www.6thavenueoutfitters.com

Bass Pro Shops, 3046 Mountain View Drive, Anchorage; (907) 330-5200; www.basspro.com/Anchorage

## Local events/attractions

Kincaid Park, 9401 West Raspberry Road, southwest Anchorage—1,400 acres of rolling forested hills, beautiful scenery, and wildlife

Mayor's Marathon and Half Marathon, Anchorage; June

Great Alaska Salmon Bake and Fly-by, Anchorage; July

Anchorage Market and Festival, between C and E Streets off West Third Avenue, Anchorage; Saturday and Sunday, mid-May to early September; www.anchoragemarkets.com/index.html

An Anchorage calendar of events can be found at www.anchorage.net/events.html. Information on events and festivals in the Hillside Trails area is available at www.muni.org/contents1/events.cfm.

# 19 Anchorage Overlook Trail

The Anchorage Overlook Trail is a short and easy hike delivering great views while only having a distance of slightly more than ¼ mile. On a clear day, this convenient stop can allow for some great photography opportunities. This loop trail is wheelchair accessible and winds its way up the side of a hill to a large viewing platform. There are excellent scenic views of Anchorage, the Alaska Range, Cook Inlet, and Flattop Mountain. Signs of moose are often evident in the immediate area. The loop portion of the trail descends down a gravel path bringing you back by the restroom facilities and parking lot.

**Start:** Glen Alps Trailhead, begin next to restroom facilities
**Distance:** 0.3-mile loop
**Approximate hiking time:** ½ hour
**Difficulty:** Easy
**Elevation gain:** Approximately 53 feet
**Trail surface:** Paved surface, gravel
**Seasons:** Year around
**Other trail users:** Hikers only, heavily used
**Canine compatibility:** Leashed dogs permitted

**Fees and permits:** $5 daily parking fee
**Maps:** Imus Geographics, Chugach State Park Hillside Trail System: Alaska Department of Natural Resources
**Trail contacts:** Chugach State Park Headquarters. Located at the Potter Section House State Historic Site, Mon–Fri 10:00 AM–4:30 PM. csp@dnr.state.ak.us (907) 345-501
**Special considerations:** None

**Finding the trailhead:** This overlook is located at the Glen Alps Trailhead. Follow the Seward Highway south from downtown Anchorage and turn left on the O'Malley Road exit toward the mountains. Travel for 3 ½ miles and turn right onto Hillside Drive. Continue for 1 mile and turn left onto Upper Huffman Road for ¾ mile. Then, turn right onto Toilsome Drive. You will see the Chugach State Park Sign at this intersection. The road becomes gravel and will continue on for another 2 more miles. The parking lot is located on your left. The parking area is sizeable and equipped with a viewing deck and restroom facilities. The lookout trail begins at the west side of the parking lot near the restroom facilities.

## Miles and Directions

**0.0** Start at the paved trail on the west side of the parking lot next to the restrooms. N61 06.210 W149 41.000
**0.1** Come to bench. N61 06.248 W149 41.113
**0.2** Arrive at handicap accessible viewing platform. N61 06.297 W149 41.075
**0.3** End back at parking lot. N61 06.210 W149 41.000

## The Hike

The Anchorage Overlook Trail is part of the Hillside Trail System. There are at least seven popular trails that make up this system. At the Glens Alps Trailhead, there are three other trails besides the Anchorage Overlook to choose from. If there is time in your schedule, Powerline Trail, Williwaw Lakes Trail, and Alaska's most hiked trail—Flattop Mountain are all possibilities to create a half-day or even full-day hike.

Because of the proximity of the hillside with the mountains and the Cook Inlet, this can be a windy place, and wind chill will make the air feel considerably cooler. In Alaska, always dress for change and wear layers.

The Anchorage Overlook Trail begins as a paved trail and reverts to a gravel path on its return trip back to the parking lot. The paved trail will be found on the west side of the lot near the restroom facilities. It's short and sweet. If you are in the area often, visiting this stop at different times during the day will surprise you with changes in the scenic view. This is an ideal place to sit and watch the sunset. It is also a great place to enjoy the tranquility and quietness of nature in the early morning hours. Moose and a variety of birds are also very prevalent in the surrounding landscape. Bringing along a pair of binoculars will be worth your time. Once you are at the platform, take your time and enjoy the scenic views of Anchorage, Alaska Range, and the Cook Inlet.

I would recommend that while you are at the Glen Alps trailhead, walk around and explore the area. There are numerous other trails that you can enjoy for as little or as much time as you choose to allow, and plenty of Alaskan scenery and memory making moments you can take home with you.

*View of Anchorage*

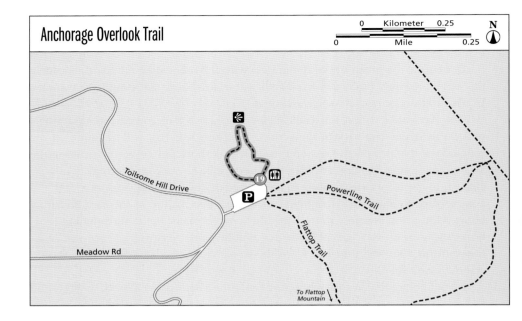

## Anchorage Overlook Trail

# Hike Information

### Local information

Anchorage Visitor Information Center, 546 West Fourth Avenue, Anchorage 99501; (907) 274-3531; www.anchorage.net

Alaska Department of Natural Resources Public Information Center, Atwood Building, 550 West Seventh Avenue, Suite 1260, Anchorage 99501; (907) 269-8400; www.dnr.state.ak.us/parks

Alaska Public Lands Information Center, 605 West Fourth Avenue, Suite 105, Anchorage 99501; (907) 271-2737; www.nps.gov/aplic

### Camping

Bird Creek Campground; (907) 345-5014; located southeast of Anchorage at Mile Marker 101 on Seward Highway; nightly camping fee

### Local organizations

The Anchorage Adventurers Meetup Group; www.adventurers.meetup.com/109

Mountaineering Club of Alaska, 2633 Spenard Road, Anchorage 99503; (907) 272-1811; www.mcak.org

### Local retailers

Recreational Equipment Inc. (REI), 1200 West Northern Lights Boulevard, Anchorage; (907) 272-4565; www.rei.com

# 20 Flattop Mountain Trail

Flattop Mountain is the most climbed peak in all Alaska, so plan on having plenty of company on this trail. But don't let the crowds discourage you if you have never ventured up Flattop. There are extraordinary views of the Alaska Range, Turnagain Arm, Cook Inlet, and Anchorage and a high point of 3,550 feet. The well-maintained trail is fun to hike and a tradition for many.

**Start:** The Glen Alps trailhead, located at the east end of the parking lot. Begin the trail by climbing the wooden stairs.
**Distance:** 3.1 miles out and back
**Approximate hiking time:** 3–5 hours
**Difficulty:** Moderate to difficult; steep trail with scrambling toward the end
**Elevation gain:** 1,300 feet
**Trail surface:** Gravel and rock
**Seasons:** Hiked year-round; best summer and fall
**Other trail users:** Lots of other people
**Canine compatibility:** Leashed dogs permitted but not recommended
**Land status:** State park
**Nearest town:** Anchorage
**Fees and permits:** $5 parking fee

**Maps:** Imus Geographics Chugach State Park map (www.imusgeographics.com); Alaska Department of Natural Resources: Chugach State Park Hillside Trail System map; USGS Anchorage
**Trail contacts:** Chugach State Park Headquarters, located at the Potter Section House State Historic Site, Mile 115 Seward Highway (mailing address: HC 52 Box 8999, Indian 99540); (907) 345-5014; e-mail: csp@dnr.state.ak .us; open Monday through Friday 10:00 a.m. to 4:30 p.m.
**Special considerations:** Some areas of the trail are rough and steep, with loose rock. There have been many fatalities and injuries due to falls, avalanches, hypothermia, and lack of caution.

**Finding the trailhead:** Follow the Seward Highway south from downtown Anchorage to the O'Malley Road exit. Turn left onto O'Malley Road and head toward the mountains. Travel for 3.5 miles; turn right onto Hillside Drive and continue for 1 mile. Turn left onto Upper Huffman Road and drive 0.75 mile. Turn right onto Toilsome Drive. You will see the Chugach State Park sign at this intersection. The road becomes gravel and continues for 2 more miles. The Glen Alps trailhead parking lot is located on your left. The sizable parking area is equipped with a viewing deck and restroom facilities. The trail begins at the east end of the parking lot at the wooden stairs.

## The Hike

Begin the hike by climbing the wooden stairs. The stairway quickly ends, and you begin to follow a winding gravel trail through a brushy hemlock and spruce area. After approximately 500 feet you'll come to a flat, open plateau with a good view of the city of Anchorage. Wildflowers are conspicuous in spring, summer, and fall throughout this area. Just beyond this clearing another 550 to 600 feet is the base of Blueberry Hill, with an information board and resting bench. You have an option at

*Front route to Flattop Mountain*

this obvious intersection to turn right and continue on the trail or follow a loop back to the parking lot.

Stay on the trail and arrive at an area where the trail is bordered by a chain-link fence. This is an effort to help control erosion and keep the high traffic on the main path. Just beyond the end of the fence is an intersection. The trail turns right at this point. Going straight ahead will loop back to the parking lot. You can see where the old foot trail—no longer maintained or in use—converges at this point. Make a right-hand turn to reach a series of wooden steps that climb the side of the mountain. At the top of the steps is a wooden bench, which serves as a good resting spot. This is also a phenomenal place for photo opportunities.

From this point on, the scrambling begins. After 1.25 miles you will come to a sign that states young children and pets are not recommended beyond this point. The trail becomes increasingly more difficult. The rocks are flagged in yellow to help you stay on the trail. There is generally no shortage of other hikers on this trail, and you shouldn't have any problem navigating your way up the mountain. Be prepared, however, to use both hands for balance and climbing. Many hikers use gloves on this hike and collapse their hiking sticks as they climb the rocks.

As you continue to climb, watch for falling rocks that have been dislodged by other hikers above you. Also be careful of rocks you dislodge that might hit hikers below you. Be sure to shout out a warning if this happens. When you reach the summit plateau of Flattop, don't be surprised if it is quite windy. You should be able to

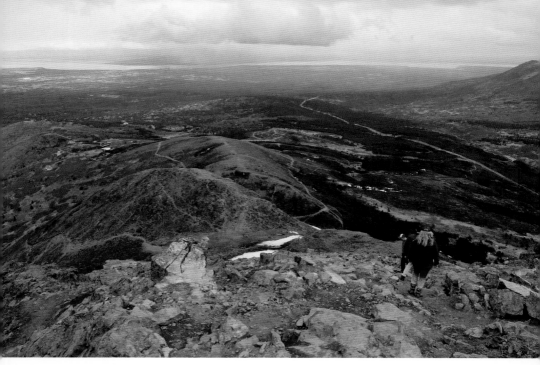

*Stoney retreat from Flattop Mountain*

observe wildflowers, lichens, and Arctic ground squirrels, along with great views of the Anchorage Bowl, Cook Inlet, Denali, and the Alaska Range.

## Miles and Directions

**0.0** Start at the wooden stairway at the east end of the parking lot. N61 06.181 / W149 40.993. After 500 feet you will reach a clear flat area with a great view of Anchorage. N61 06.128 / W149 40.882

**0.2** Arrive at the base of Blueberry Hill, where there is an information board and bench. N61 06.021 / W149 40.766

**0.7** A chain-link fence borders the path. N61 05.774 / W149 40.715

**0.8** Turn right at the trail junction and head toward the second saddle. N61 05.759 / W149 40.600

**0.9** Wooden steps begin. N61 05.648 / W149 40.695

**1.0** Reach a resting bench with a scenic view. N61 05.611 / W149 40.662

**1.25** Come to a trailpost. The trail becomes increasingly rough and rocky. N61 05.561 / W149 40.306

**1.55** Reach the top of Flattop and end of the trail. Enjoy the views and after a well-deserved rest, retrace your path to the trailhead. N61 05.428 / W149 40.110 (Option: Instead of totally retracing your steps, take the loop trail [N61 05.759 W149 40.600] back from the summit. The loop rejoins the main trail at Blueberry Hill in just under 0.5 mile. [N61 06.019 / W149 40.764])

**3.1** Arrive back at the wooden stairs and parking lot. N61 06.181 / W149 40.993

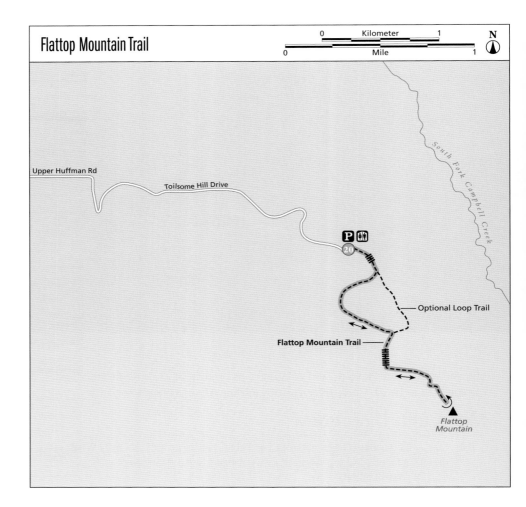

# Hike Information

## Local information

Anchorage Visitor Information Center, 546 West Fourth Avenue, Anchorage 99501; (907) 274-3531; www.anchorage.net

Alaska Department of Natural Resources Public Information Center, Atwood Building, 550 West Seventh Avenue, Suite 1260, Anchorage 99501; (907) 269-8400; www.dnr.state.ak.us/parks

Alaska Public Lands Information Center, 605 West Fourth Avenue, Suite 105, Anchorage 99501; (907) 271-2737; www.nps.gov/aplic

## Camping

Bird Creek Campground; (907) 345-5014; located southeast of Anchorage at Mile Marker 101 on Seward Highway; nightly camping fee

## Local organizations

The Anchorage Adventurers Meetup Group; www.adventurers.meetup.com/109
Mountaineering Club of Alaska, 2633 Spenard Road, Anchorage 99503; (907) 272-1811; www.mcak.org

## Local retailers

Recreational Equipment Inc. (REI), 1200 West Northern Lights Boulevard, Anchorage; (907) 272-4565; www.rei.com

# DOGS, TRAILS, AND PEOPLE

It seems everyone in Alaska owns a dog or two, or three—or maybe forty. Regardless of where you hike, you will run into dogs on the trail. Whether you and your pooch are looking for an afternoon hike or a weekend campout, please follow good dog-trail etiquette. Here are a few suggestions:

- Keep your dog on a leash, especially if there are other people on the trail. Off-leash dogs run the risk of bear and porcupine encounters, and moose attacks. Not all dogs are dog-friendly, and off-leash dogs can present problems for the dog owner whose dog is under control on the lead.
- Be courteous toward other dog owners, and be sure you always have complete control of your dog, both on and off the leash.
- Do not allow your dog to chase wildlife. This is dangerous for you, your dog and people in the area.
- Be sure your dog is current with its vaccinations.
- Carry poop bags to carry out your dog's waste. Dog feces are different from wildlife feces and are more likely to pollute rivers, streams, and lakes through runoff.
- Be prepared to take care of your dog. When you hike with your dog, be sure to bring treats, first-aid supplies, and fresh water. Dogs are also prone to dehydration, over-heating, and giardia from infected water sources. Don't worry about the extra weight. Dogs love to carry their own pack—it gives them a job to do.

The city of Anchorage has areas for off-leash dogs at the following parks: Conners Bog, Far North Centennial Park, Russian Jack, South University Sports Park, and University Lake. For more information on dog-friendly parks, visit www.muni.org/healthmsd/dogparks.cfm.

Sportsman's Warehouse, 681 Old Seward Highway, Anchorage; (907) 644-1400; www
.sportsmanswarehouse.com

Alaska Mountaineering and Hiking, 2633 Spenard Road, Anchorage; (907) 272-
1811; www.alaskamountaineering.com

Cabelas, 155 W 104th, Anchorage; (907) 341-3400; www.cabelas.com/Stores/
Anchorage

6th Avenue Outfitters, 520 W 6th Avenue, Anchorage; (907) 276-0233; www.6th
avenueoutfitters.com

Bass Pro Shops, 3046 Mountain View Drive, Anchorage; (907) 330-5200; www
.basspro.com/Anchorage

*Local events/attractions*

Kincaid Park, 9401 West Raspberry Road, southwest Anchorage—1,400 acres of
rolling forested hills, beautiful scenery, and wildlife

Mayor's Marathon and Half Marathon, Anchorage; June

Great Alaska Salmon Bake and Fly-by, Anchorage; July

Anchorage Market and Festival, between C and E Streets off West Third Avenue,
Anchorage; Saturday and Sunday, mid-May to early September; www.anchoragemar-
kets.com/index.html

An Anchorage calendar of events can be found at www.anchorage.net/events.html.
Information on events and festivals in the Hillside Trails area is available at www.muni
.org/contents1/events.cfm.

## GREEN TIP
**Donate used gear to a nonprofit kids' organization.**

# 21 Backside of Flattop Mountain Trail

The Backside of Flattop Mountain is the newer of the two access points constructed by Alaska State Parks for reaching the popular Flattop Mountain destination. This option trail consists of a series of switchbacks that traverse to the summit making it a much easier hike than hiking the traditional front side of the mountain. Parking is limited to a very small parking lot and road side parking. Great views of Anchorage, wildflowers and amazing scenery are part of this hike to the famous Flattop Mountain peak.

**Start:** Canyon Road Trailhead. Begin along the shoulder of the road at the trail post.
**Distance:** 1.8 miles out and back
**Approximate hiking time:** 2-3 hours
**Difficulty:** Moderate
**Elevation gain:** 1607 feet
**Trail surface:** Dirt, gravel
**Seasons:** April through September
**Other trail users:** Runners, lots of other people
**Canine compatibility:** Leashed pets permitted
**Land status:** State park
**Nearest town:** Basher
**Fees and permits:** $5 daily parking fee

**Maps:** Imus Geographics Chugach State Park map (www.imusgeographics.com); Alaska Department of Natural Resources: Chugach State Park Hillside Trail System map; USGS Anchorage
**Trail contacts:** Chugach State Park Headquarters, located at the Potter Section House State Historic Site, Mile 115 Seward Highway (mailing address: HC 52 Box 8999, Indian 99540); (907) 345-5014; e-mail: csp@dnr.state.ak.us; open Monday through Friday 10:00 a.m. to 4:30 p.m.
**Special considerations:** Slick when wet

**Finding the trailhead:** The trailhead is approximately a 30-minute drive from downtown Anchorage. Coming from downtown Anchorage, head east on 6th Avenue and turn left onto AK-1/Gambell Street. Continue south 8.7 miles to De Armoun Road exit. Continue east on De Armoun Road for 6.3 miles. Keep right onto Canyon Road for about 1 mile. Continue onto Upper Canyon Road for 0.6 mile. This will become Highland Road/Canyon Road for about 0.2 mile. Destination will be on your right.

## The Hike

Hiking the Backside of Flattop Mountain is a new alternative to hiking to the summit of the most widely hiked mountain in the state of Alaska.

Begin the hike at the marked trailhead along the roadside just 100 feet away from the small parking lot. The trail begins immediately with a slight uphill climb and will continue all the way to the top.

After a brief walk of approximately ¼ mile you will come to the first trail marker post. Continue onward as you slowly gain in elevation. The second tailpost marker is at mile 0.3 and a third one is at mile 0.6. You will be hiking through alders the first part of the trail and the vegetation will change to wildflowers and meadows. The trail will continue as a series of switchbacks as it slowly gains in elevation. Keep your eyes

*Summit of Flattop Mountain*

open for Dall sheep on the surrounding mountain ranges as you climb and enjoy the beautiful views of Anchorage and Turnagain Arm.

Once you hike out of the meadows and into the tundra, Arctic ground squirrels will become more evident. The hike will straighten out and take you to the backside of Flattop Mountain. Hike across the rocky flat and head toward the flag, your final destination.

## Miles and Directions

**0.0** Start at trailhead along-side of road. N61° 04.914' W149° 40.884'

**0.2** Arrive at trail marker post. N61° 04.941' W149° 40.713'

**0.3** Arrive at second trail marker post, N61° 04.927' W149° 40.620'

**0.6** Arrive at third trail marker post. N61° 04.908' W149° 40.292'

**1.8** End at flag on top of Flattop Mountain. N61° 05.432' W149° 40.116

## Hike Information

### Local information

Anchorage Visitor Information Center, 546 West Fourth Avenue, Anchorage 99501; (907) 274-3531; www.anchorage.net

Alaska Department of Natural Resources Public Information Center, Atwood Building, 550 West Seventh Avenue, Suite 1260, Anchorage 99501; (907) 269-8400; www.dnr.state.ak.us/parks

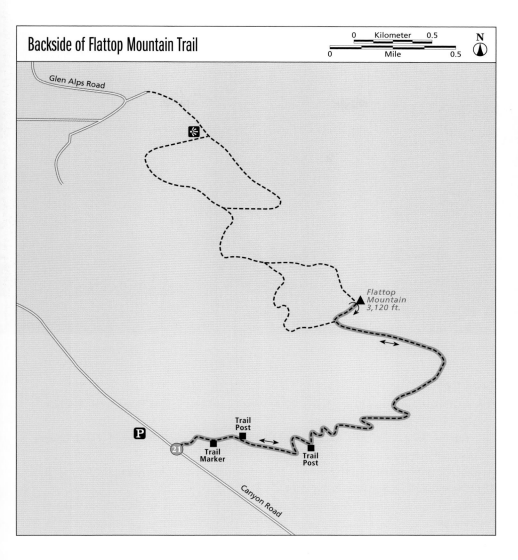

**Backside of Flattop Mountain Trail**

Glen Alps Road

Flattop
Mountain
3,120 ft.

Trail
Post

Trail
Marker

Trail
Post

Canyon Road

Alaska Public Lands Information Center, 605 West Fourth Avenue, Suite 105, Anchorage 99501; (907) 271-2737; www.nps.gov/aplic

*Camping*

Bird Creek Campground; (907) 345-5014; located southeast of Anchorage at Mile Marker 101 on Seward Highway; nightly camping fee

*Local organizations*

The Anchorage Adventurers Meetup Group; www.adventurers.meetup.com/109 Mountaineering Club of Alaska, 2633 Spenard Road, Anchorage 99503; (907) 272-1811; www.mcak.org

*One of many switchbacks*

## Local retailers

Recreational Equipment Inc. (REI), 1200 West Northern Lights Boulevard, Anchorage; (907) 272-4565; www.rei.com

Sportsman's Warehouse, 681 Old Seward Highway, Anchorage; (907) 644-1400; www.sportsmanswarehouse.com

Alaska Mountaineering and Hiking, 2633 Spenard Road, Anchorage; (907) 272-1811; www.alaskamountaineering.com

Cabelas, 155 W 104th, Anchorage; (907) 341-3400; www.cabelas.com/Stores/Anchorage

6th Avenue Outfitters, 520 W 6th Avenue, Anchorage; (907) 276-0233; www.6th avenueoutfitters.com

Bass Pro Shops, 3046 Mountain View Drive, Anchorage; (907) 330-5200; www.basspro.com/Anchorage

# 22 Williwaw Lakes Trail

Williwaw Lakes Trail is a popular day hike to alpine tundra lakes. Wildlife such as moose, bears, Arctic ground squirrels, a variety of songbirds and willow ptarmigan is present in this area. The trail includes a bridged stream crossing; great views of Anchorage, Mount Williwaw, Flattop Mountain, and Wolverine Peak; and the Williwaw Lakes at trail's end. An optional loop trail from the lakes follows Campbell Creek back to the trailhead.

**Start:** From Glen Alps trailhead, head down the hill next to the wooden stairs.
**Distance:** 11.4 miles out and back
**Approximate hiking time:** 8–10 hours
**Difficulty:** Easy to moderate
**Elevation gain/loss:** 1,600 feet
**Trail surface:** Dirt, gravel, and stone
**Seasons:** Best hiking June through September
**Other trail users:** Bikes first 3 miles; hikers only beyond Powerline Trail
**Canine compatibility:** Leashed dogs permitted
**Land status:** State park
**Nearest town:** Anchorage
**Fees and permits:** $5 daily parking fee

**Maps:** Imus Geographics Chugach State Park map (www.imusgeographics.com); Alaska Department of Natural Resources: Chugach State Park Hillside Trail System Map; USGS Anchorage
**Trail contacts:** Chugach State Park Headquarters, located at the Potter Section House State Historic Site, Mile 115 Seward Highway (mailing address: HC 52 Box 8999, Indian 99540); (907) 345-5014; e-mail: csp@dnr.state.ak.us; open Monday through Friday 10:00 a.m. to 4:30 p.m.
**Special considerations:** Some areas of the trail are avalanche prone in winter.

**Finding the trailhead:** Follow the Seward Highway south from downtown Anchorage to the O'Malley Road exit. Turn left onto O'Malley Road and head toward the mountains. Travel for 3.5 miles; turn right onto Hillside Drive and continue for 1 mile. Turn left onto Upper Huffman Road and drive 0.75 mile. Turn right onto Toilsome Hill Drive. You will see the Chugach State Park sign at this intersection. The road becomes gravel and continues for 2 more miles. The Glen Alps trailhead parking lot is located on your left. The sizable parking area is equipped with a viewing deck and restroom facilities. The trail begins at the north side of the parking lot, heading downhill.

## The Hike

The hike begins at the signage board, located near the wooden steps leading to Flattop Mountain. There are two paths leading downhill. Both will take you to the same place. After 0.4 mile come to an intersection with the wide Powerline Trail. This trail is an old dirt road that is also popular with mountain bikers. Turn right onto Powerline Trail. (A left turn will take you to the Prospect Heights trailhead, the other access point for this hike.) This area is good moose habitat, and they are often encountered on the trail itself. Be sure to give them room when going around them.

*Top: Middle Fork Trail enroute to Williwaw*
*Bottom: View of Williwaw Lakes from Wolverine Peak*

Continue on Powerline Trail for several hundred yards until you reach a trail junction with a signpost. Turn left onto Middle Fork Loop Trail and head abruptly downhill. After approximately 0.25 mile cross South Fork Campbell Creek on a footbridge followed by a long boardwalk. Continue for another 0.25 mile to a T in the trail. There is a post, but no signage. You have a choice of traveling left or right. The route to the left is the continuation of the Middle Fork Loop Trail, which will go through some wet muddy areas and then cross a bridged stream after 1.8 miles. At about 2.2 miles you will come to a signpost. Follow the path to the right. Directly after this junction, follow the fork to the left. From here on, the entire route is fairly easy to follow, with little elevation change as the trail goes through the valley, following Campbell Creek, and then directly to the lakes.

## Option

The right-turn option at the fork and signpost is rugged and steep and follows a narrow, loose-stone path up O'Malley Peak and then across a wide-open area, eventually ending with a steep descent to the alpine lakes. Following this option, the path heads immediately uphill and increases in steepness and difficulty along the way.

At the top of the ridge is an area called the Ballpark. The large, expansive area is full of small hills resembling craters and provides ideal habitat for a large community of Arctic ground squirrels. The size of the area is quite misleading because of the ups and downs of the topography.

The stony path follows along the south side of the plateau. At the far end you need to hike down past Black Lake and to the Williwaw Lakes. Hiking down to the lakes can be very challenging. The only way is to descend an extremely steep, unmarked cirque. Try to stay to the side of the loose scree as you head downward. Just keep hiking toward the lakes. Once you reach the bottom, the Williwaw Lakes Trail, which can be an optional loop trail back, becomes evident as it follows the creek bed westward. This trail joins the Middle Fork Loop Trail, which will take you back to the Glen Alps trailhead where you began. You can also head north on the Middle Fork Loop Trail to the Prospect Heights trailhead.

# Miles and Directions

**0.0**   Start at the north end of the parking lot and head downhill on either of two paths. N61 06.187 / W149 40.986

**0.25** Turn right onto Powerline Trail. N61 06.238 / W149 40.240

**0.5**   At the signpost turn left onto Middle Fork Loop Trail. N61 06.145 / W149 40.107

**0.9**   Cross South Fork Campbell Creek on a footbridge followed by a long boardwalk. N61 06.106 / W149 39.711

**1.1**   Turn left at the signpost. N61 06.135 / W149 39.473

**1.8**   Cross a bridge over a stream. N61 06.710 / W149 39.734

**2.2**   Turn right at the signpost. Directly after this turn, follow the fork to the left.

# Williwaw Lakes Trail

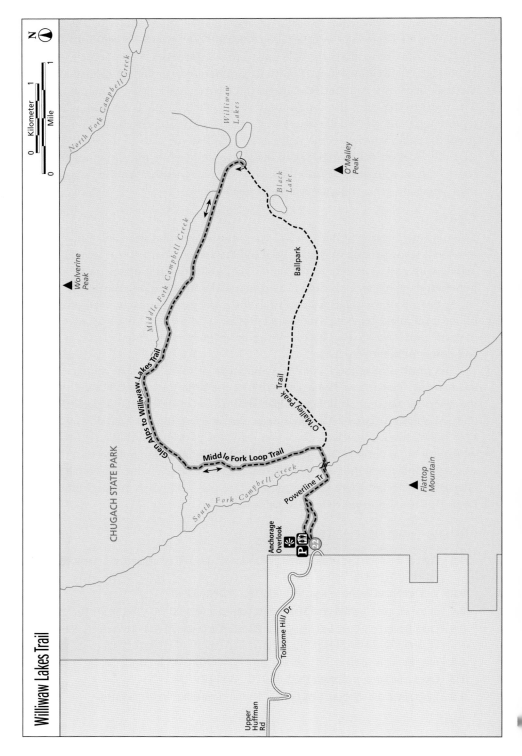

**5.7**  Arrive at Williwaw Lakes, your turnaround point. N61 06.688 / W149 34.605 (Option: Turn right at mile 1.1 at the signpost. Follow the path uphill for a rough and rocky 5.5-mile trek to the lakes via O'Malley Peak and the Ballpark.)

**11.4**  Return to the Glen Alps trailhead parking lot. N61 06.187 / W149 40.986

# Hike Information

## Local information

Anchorage Visitor Information Center, 546 West Fourth Avenue, Anchorage 99501; (907) 274-3531; www.anchorage.net

Alaska Department of Natural Resources Public Information Center, Atwood Building, 550 West Seventh Avenue, Suite 1260, Anchorage 99501; (907) 269-8400; www.dnr.state.ak.us/parks

Alaska Public Lands Information Center, 605 West Fourth Avenue, Suite 105, Anchorage 99501; (907) 271-2737; www.nps.gov/aplic

## Camping

Bird Creek Campground; (907) 345-5014; located southeast of Anchorage at Mile Marker 101 on Seward Highway; nightly camping fee

## Local organizations

The Anchorage Adventurers Meetup Group; www.adventurers.meetup.com/109

Mountaineering Club of Alaska, 2633 Spenard Road, Anchorage 99503; (907) 272-1811; www.mcak.org

## Local retailers

Recreational Equipment Inc. (REI), 1200 West Northern Lights Boulevard, Anchorage; (907) 272-4565; www.rei.com

Sportsman's Warehouse, 681 Old Seward Highway, Anchorage; (907) 644-1400; www.sportsmanswarehouse.com

Alaska Mountaineering and Hiking, 2633 Spenard Road, Anchorage; (907) 272-1811; www.alaskamountaineering.com

Cabelas, 155 W 104th, Anchorage; (907) 341-3400; www.cabelas.com/Stores/Anchorage

6th Avenue Outfitters, 520 W 6th Avenue, Anchorage; (907) 276-0233; www.6thavenueoutfitters.com

Bass Pro Shops, 3046 Mountain View Drive, Anchorage; (907) 330-5200; www.basspro.com/Anchorage

## Local events/attractions

Kincaid Park, 9401 West Raspberry Road, southwest Anchorage—1,400 acres of rolling forested hills, beautiful scenery, and wildlife

Mayor's Marathon and Half Marathon, Anchorage; June

Great Alaska Salmon Bake and Fly-by, Anchorage; July

Anchorage Market and Festival, between C and E Streets off West Third Avenue, Anchorage; Saturday and Sunday, mid–May to early September; www.anchoragemarkets.com/index.html

An Anchorage calendar of events can be found at www.anchorage.net/events.html. Information on events and festivals in the Hillside Trails area is available at www.muni.org/contents1/events.cfm.

# CLEAN WATER AND SAFE DRINKING

Nothing seems more inviting than drinking from a cold, clear mountain stream. However, there are risk factors that probably outweigh the pleasures of quenching your thirst with cold mountain water. Mountain streams are products of runoff and glacial silt, picking up any pollutants along the way. The glacial silt easily clogs water-purification filters and is almost unpalatable. Even more important, pollution can cause illness. An intestinal protozoan called *Giardia lamblia* is shed through the feces of mammals as a cyst and enters the stream water. The cyst can exist for long periods in soil and water, but when ingested the parasite leaves the cyst and attaches itself to the small intestine of its new host. Parasites begin manifesting in two to ten days, causing symptoms of diarrhea, abdominal cramps, pain, fever, weakness, and lack of appetite. The natural immune system of some individuals can rid itself of the parasite, but others may require medical treatment.

If you must drink water from mountain streams, boil it to kill the cysts. Most pathogens will be destroyed when water temperatures reach the boiling point, but boiling water for five minutes will ensure safe drinking water. The effectiveness of iodine, chlorine, and halizone tablets can be questionable depending upon how stable the product is and how long you wait before drinking the water. You can also pump your water through a ceramic filter with excellent results.

Avoid collecting water from areas where there is obvious human and animal activity, such as beavers. Select an area that is clear and still. Microorganisms are more likely to be suspended in moving water and will settle near the bottom in quiet water. Still, depending on the length and duration of your hike, the best practice for ensuring clean, safe water is to carry an adequate supply with you.

# 23 Near Point Trail

This trail is a good full-day hike to the top of a scenic ridge with truly outstanding views of the city of Anchorage. The trail is challenging, yet clearly defined and well-traveled, offering opportunities for wildlife viewing and photography, a mix of vegetative ecosystems, some great views of the Alaska Range and Cook Inlet, and an old homesite at the top of the peak.

**Start:** Prospect Heights trailhead
**Distance:** 8.0 miles out and back
**Approximate hiking time:** 6–8 hours
**Difficulty:** Easy to moderate due to elevation gain
**Elevation gain:** 1,900 feet
**Trail surface:** Loose stone, mud
**Seasons:** Best hiking summer and fall
**Other trail users:** Mountain bikes first 3.0 miles
**Canine compatibility:** Leashed dogs permitted
**Land status:** State park
**Nearest town:** Anchorage
**Fees and permits:** $5 parking fee at Prospect Heights Trailhead

**Maps:** Imus Geographics Chugach State Park map (www.imusgeographics.com); Alaska Department of Natural Resources: Chugach State Park Hillside Trail System map; USGS Anchorage
**Trail contacts:** Chugach State Park Headquarters, located at the Potter Section House State Historic Site, Mile 115 Seward Highway (mailing address: HC 52 Box 8999, Indian 99540); (907) 345-5014; e-mail: csp@dnr.state.ak.us; open Monday through Friday 10:00 a.m. to 4:30 p.m.
**Special considerations:** None

**Finding the trailhead:** The trail is commonly accessed from the Prospect Heights trailhead. From downtown Anchorage drive south on Seward Highway to the O'Malley Road exit. Turn left (east) onto O'Malley Road and drive toward the mountains for 3.5 miles. The street becomes Hillside Drive. After the road curves to the left, make an immediate right-hand turn onto Upper O'Malley Drive. Follow this road for 0.5 mile to the first intersection and turn left onto Prospect Drive. Follow Prospect Drive for another 1 mile to the Prospect Heights trailhead. There are plenty of parking spaces and restroom facilities. This trail can also be accessed from Basher Road.

## The Hike

The trailhead is very obvious at the northeast end of the parking lot. You will also see a large signage board. It's a good idea to stop and read any notices posted by the park rangers, such as bear and bear cub sightings along the trail or other precautionary notices to be aware of while hiking. Begin by following the wide trail several hundred feet to an intersection. Go left, following the power lines, with your first view of Anchorage off in the distance.

At approximately 1.0 mile cross South Fork Campbell Creek on a well-constructed footbridge. The trail switchbacks several times before reaching another intersection.

*View from Near Point*
AMANDA HANSON

To your right is the Middle Fork Loop Trail, which eventually connects to the Glen Alps trailhead. You want to veer left to stay on Near Point Trail.

Cross another stream on a small footbridge. About 1.0 mile past the bridge, a sign directs you to either Wolverine Peak or Near Point. Wolverine Peak is another 3.2 miles on your right. Stay straight ahead for Near Point. (Note: You will often see these types of choices along the way. There are numerous other loop trail opportunities in the Hillside Trail System, and a good map would be very beneficial.)

You've been traveling mostly east up to this point and will now start heading more northerly. The trail narrows and becomes quite steep. At approximately 3.0 miles the ground is extremely muddy and wet, and the trail may become more difficult to follow. This only lasts for several hundred feet. Just keep heading in the same direction and the path will become obvious again.

The landscape changes from forests and trees to shrubby vegetation and eventually tundra. Once you are past the muddy area, you'll be hiking on loose stone and a narrow path. As you wind your way up the mountain, the views of Anchorage below continue to be breathtaking. The ecosystem up here provides good habitat for Arctic ground squirrels and is also a popular area in the fall for wild blueberry picking.

▶ The worst hazards you are likely to encounter on Chugach State Park trails are changes in weather, wildlife encounters, lack of water, and lack of hike preparation. Always be prepared for changes in weather conditions throughout the park. It will vary from one place to the next. Be aware of wildlife and how to react should you encounter an animal, study your route before you head out, and always carry adequate water and be prepared for emergency situations.

Reach your destination at 4.0 miles and 3,050 feet elevation. A cairn has been constructed at the top of the peak, and you can observe the location of an old home-site. It can be very windy up here, so plan accordingly. Once you're up here, exploring the terrain, the vegetation, and taking in the views add to the further gratification of this hike. This is a great place for lunch before you head back down.

## Miles and Directions

**0.0** Begin at the signboard at the northeast end of the parking lot. N61 08.332 / W149 42.692

**1.0** Cross South Fork Campbell Creek on a bridge. N61 08.584 / W149 41.932

**1.5** Reach a trailpost indicating other Hillside Trail options. Veer left to stay on Near Point Trail. N61 08.586 / W149 41.641

**1.7** Continue straight ahead at the trailpost. N61 08.578 / W149 41.327

**2.0** Reach the junction with the Wolverine Peak Loop Trail on your left and right. Continue straight ahead. N61 08.810 / W149 40.813

**2.4** The trail switches back south-southeast, affording a great view of Anchorage. N61 09.142 / W149 40.763

**2.6** Continue on the main trail, heading north. N61 09.147 / W149 40.531 (Option: Take the small, narrow trail on the right at the double spruce trees for an alternate loop route to the top of the plateau.)

**3.0** The trail becomes extremely wet, with low vegetation. N61 09.311 / W149 40.091

**3.6** Cross an area of tundra and loose stone. N61 09.271 / W149 39.155

**4.0** Reach the top of the plateau. Retrace your steps back down to the trailhead. N61 09.273 / W149 39.149

**8.0** Arrive back at the trailhead. N61 08.332 / W149 42.692

## Hike Information

*Local information*

Anchorage Visitor Information Center, 546 West Fourth Avenue, Anchorage 99501; (907) 274-3531; www.anchorage.net

Alaska Department of Natural Resources Public Information Center, Atwood Building, 550 West Seventh Avenue, Suite 1260, Anchorage 99501; (907) 269-8400; www.dnr.state.ak.us/parks

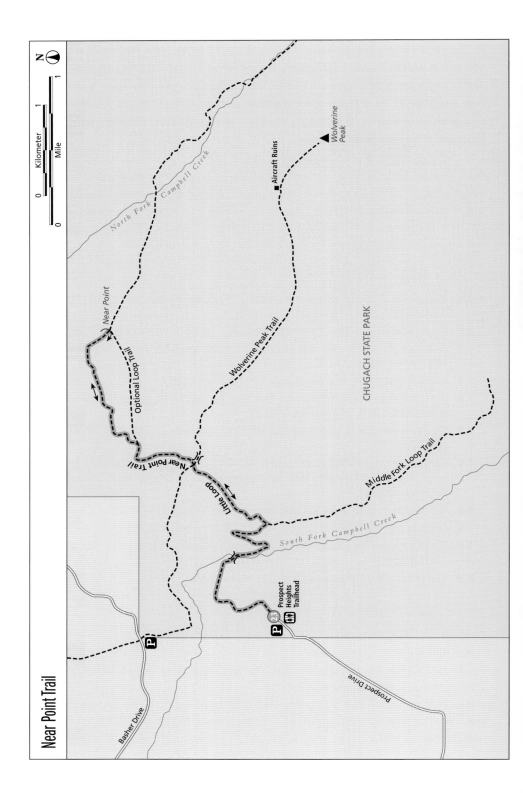

Near Point Trail

*The trail to Near Point Peak*

Alaska Public Lands Information Center, 605 West Fourth Avenue, Suite 105, Anchorage 99501; (907) 271-2737; www.nps.gov/aplic

## Camping

Bird Creek Campground; (907) 345-5014; located southeast of Anchorage at Mile Marker 101 on Seward Highway; nightly camping fee

## Local organizations

The Anchorage Adventurers Meetup Group; www.adventurers.meetup.com/109
Mountaineering Club of Alaska, 2633 Spenard Road, Anchorage 99503; (907) 272-1811; www.mcak.org

## Local retailers

Recreational Equipment Inc. (REI), 1200 West Northern Lights Boulevard, Anchorage; (907) 272-4565; www.rei.com
Sportsman's Warehouse, 681 Old Seward Highway, Anchorage; (907) 644-1400; www.sportsmanswarehouse.com
Alaska Mountaineering and Hiking, 2633 Spenard Road, Anchorage; (907) 272-1811; www.alaskamountaineering.com
Cabelas, 155 W 104th, Anchorage; (907) 341-3400; www.cabelas.com/Stores/Anchorage

6th Avenue Outfitters, 520 W 6th Avenue, Anchorage; (907) 276-0233; www.6th avenueoutfitters.com

Bass Pro Shops, 3046 Mountain View Drive, Anchorage; (907) 330-5200; www .basspro.com/Anchorage

## Local events/attractions

Kincaid Park, 9401 West Raspberry Road, southwest Anchorage—1,400 acres of rolling forested hills, beautiful scenery, and wildlife

Mayor's Marathon and Half Marathon, Anchorage; June

Great Alaska Salmon Bake and Fly-by, Anchorage; July

Anchorage Market and Festival, between C and E Streets off West Third Avenue, Anchorage; Saturday and Sunday, mid-May to early September; www.anchoragemar-kets.com/index.html

An Anchorage calendar of events can be found at www.anchorage.net/events.html. Information on events and festivals in the Hillside Trails area is available at www.muni .org/contents1/events.cfm.

# 24 Wolverine Peak Trail

Wolverine Peak is another excellent day hike. Located just twenty minutes from Anchorage, this is a popular hike with locals. The easy-to-follow trail provides great views of the Alaska Range and Cook Inlet and passes the remains of a small aircraft wreckage near the top. Sightings of Dall sheep, moose, and Arctic ground squirrels are possible, and you can pick berries along the trail in late summer and early fall.

**Start:** Prospect Heights trailhead
**Distance:** 10.4 miles out and back
**Approximate hiking time:** 10–12 hours
**Difficulty:** Moderate due to steep incline
**Elevation gain:** 3,380 feet
**Trail surface:** Loose stone, dirt
**Seasons:** Year-round, but best hiking summer and fall
**Other trail users:** Bikes and horses on first 2.0 miles of hike
**Canine compatibility:** Leashed dogs permitted
**Land status:** State park
**Nearest town:** Anchorage
**Fees and permits:** $5 parking fee

**Maps:** Imus Geographics Chugach State Park map (www.imusgeographics.com); Alaska Department of Natural Resources: Chugach State Park Hillside Trail System Map; USGS Anchorage
**Trail contacts:** Chugach State Park Headquarters, located at the Potter Section House State Historic Site, Mile 115 Seward Highway (mailing address: HC 52 Box 8999, Indian 99540); (907) 345-5014; e-mail: csp@dnr.state.ak .us; open Monday through Friday 10:00 a.m. to 4:30 p.m.
**Special considerations:** None

**Finding the trailhead:** The trail is commonly accessed from the Prospect Heights trailhead. From downtown Anchorage drive south on Seward Highway to the O'Malley Road exit. Turn left (east) onto O'Malley Road and drive toward the mountains for 3.5 miles. The street becomes Hillside Drive. After the road curves to the left, make an immediate right-hand turn onto Upper O'Malley Drive. Follow this road for 0.5 mile to the first intersection and turn left onto Prospect Drive. Follow Prospect Drive for another 1 mile to the Prospect Heights trailhead. There are plenty of parking spaces and restroom facilities. This trail can also be accessed from Basher Road.

## The Hike

Wolverine Peak gives you a perspective of true Alaska wilderness, plus the trailhead is located within twenty minutes of Anchorage, making it one of my favorite hikes. Pick up the trail at the Prospect Heights trailhead. At the beginning of the trail is a signboard with hiking precautions and current ranger notices. Take note of the posted notices for your hiking safety. Because the change in elevation is 3,380 feet on this hike, it can be 52 degrees and partly sunny at the trailhead with cold drizzle, fog, and snow flurries at the peak. Keep this in mind when planning your trip.

The trail begins following the same route you would take to Near Point. Begin by following the trail several hundred feet to an obvious intersection. Go left, following

*Top: Looking back at Anchorage from Wolverine Peak Trail*
*Bottom: Beginning the steep climb to Wolverine Peak*

the power lines a short distance. At approximately the 1.0-mile point, cross South Fork Campbell Creek on a well-constructed bridge. This is a very pretty setting. The trail switchbacks several times on its way to the next intersection. Middle Fork Loop Trail heads right; you want to continue to the left. At 0.2 mile beyond this point, you will pass by a sign that reads LITTLE LOOP TRAIL TO MIDDLE FORK. Continue onward and cross a footbridge over a small stream and arrive at a sign showing the turnoff for Wolverine Peak on your right. (Near Point Trail continues straight ahead.) This is approximately the 2.1-mile point. From this point on, no bicycles or horses are allowed on the trail. The trail narrows significantly and becomes rocky and steep. Cross another small bridge and proceed 0.4 mile to a large boulder, where a beautiful scenic overlook makes a good stopping point for taking pictures.

After another 0.7 mile of climbing, arrive at a flat saddle area. Note the rocky cairn marking your turn slightly to the left. This turn is particularly important on the return trip—you will not want to miss it. Follow the trail along the saddle for about 0.5 mile. The saddle ends and you begin a steep ascent. This next section is the steepest portion of the entire hike. The trail becomes very narrow and stony, almost disappearing.

At 3.9 miles you can see the ruins of a small aircraft on the right side of the trail. The trail makes a slight turn just past the aircraft. The rock formations, lichens, and mosses at this elevation are most amazing. You should also begin to see ground squirrels. At 4,455 feet, the top of the peak affords incredible views of valleys, mountain ranges, and Alaskan wilderness.

# HIKING FOR WEATHER CHANGES

Alaska is known for its quickly changing weather. Changes in altitude can also create rapid changes in the environmental conditions. The north side of Chugach State Park can be experiencing a completely different weather pattern from the south. The western Hillside Trail System is prone to high winds.

When hiking in Chugach, you need to be aware that weather conditions can deviate drastically. A person can be at risk of sunburn, frostbite, and hypothermia all in one hike. When hiking in the park, it's imperative to dress for all weather contingencies. Know where you are going to hike, altitude changes, and current and projected weather conditions. Wear layers and carry a windbreaker or raincoat as well as sunscreen and sunglasses. Be prepared for a variety of temperatures, wind conditions, and precipitation. A little foresight; proper planning; and keeping hydrated, well fueled, and dry will help you avoid most weather-related misfortunes.

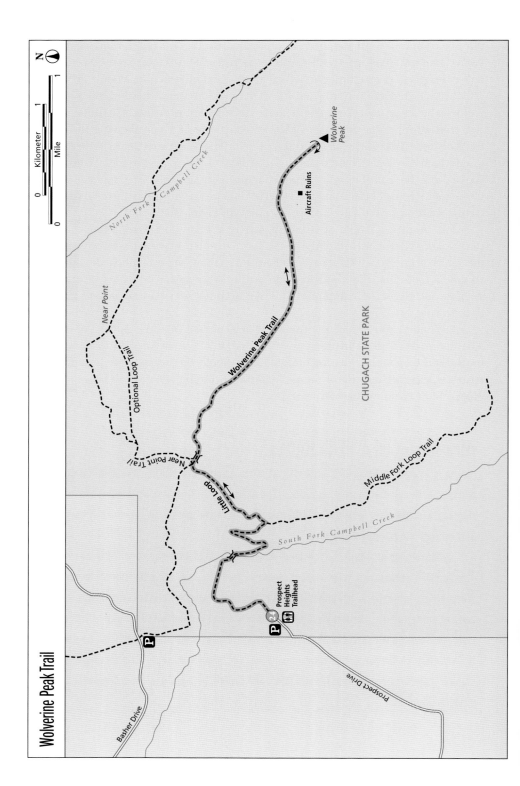

Wolverine Peak Trail

# Miles and Directions

**0.0** Start at Prospect Heights trailhead. N61 08.339 / W149 42.588

**1.0** Cross a bridge over South Fork Campbell Creek. N61 08.584 / W149 41.931

**1.5** Turn left to stay on the Near Point Trail. N61 08.586 / W149 41.644

**1.7** Continue straight at the trailpost. N61 08.579 / W149 41.330

**2.0** Cross a small stream on a footbridge (N61 08.755 / W149 40.905) and then follow Wolverine Trail to the right. N61 08.810 / W149 40.816. Cross a small bridge. N61 08.778 / W149 40.599

**2.5** Reach a scenic overlook at a large boulder. N61 08.666 / W149 39.910

**3.2** Come to a cairn on a saddle. (FYI: Make note of the turn—you don't want to miss it on the way back.) N61 08.296 / W149 39.060

**3.9** Pass the aircraft ruins on the right. N61 08.321 / W149 37.550

**5.2** Reach the top of Wolverine Peak. Enjoy the views before heading back down the trail. N61 08.092 / W149 36.850

**10.4** Arrive back at the trailhead. N61 08.339 / W149 42.588

# Hike Information

## Local information

Anchorage Visitor Information Center, 546 West Fourth Avenue, Anchorage 99501; (907) 274–3531; www.anchorage.net

Alaska Department of Natural Resources Public Information Center, Atwood Building, 550 West Seventh Avenue, Suite 1260, Anchorage 99501; (907) 269–8400; www.dnr.state.ak.us/parks

Alaska Public Lands Information Center, 605 West Fourth Avenue, Suite 105, Anchorage 99501; (907) 271–2737; www.nps.gov/aplic

## Camping

Bird Creek Campground; (907) 345–5014; located southeast of Anchorage at Mile Marker 101 on Seward Highway; nightly camping fee

## Local organizations

The Anchorage Adventurers Meetup Group; www.adventurers.meetup.com/109

Mountaineering Club of Alaska, 2633 Spenard Road, Anchorage 99503; (907) 272–1811; www.mcak.org

## Local retailers

Recreational Equipment Inc. (REI), 1200 West Northern Lights Boulevard, Anchorage; (907) 272–4565; www.rei.com

Sportsman's Warehouse, 681 Old Seward Highway, Anchorage; (907) 644–1400; www.sportsmanswarehouse.com

Alaska Mountaineering and Hiking, 2633 Spenard Road, Anchorage; (907) 272-1811; www.alaskamountaineering.com

Cabelas, 155 W 104th, Anchorage; (907) 341-3400; www.cabelas.com/Stores/Anchorage

6th Avenue Outfitters, 520 W 6th Avenue, Anchorage; (907) 276-0233; www.6thavenueoutfitters.com

Bass Pro Shops, 3046 Mountain View Drive, Anchorage; (907) 330-5200; www.basspro.com/Anchorage

*Local events/attractions*

Kincaid Park, 9401 West Raspberry Road, southwest Anchorage—1,400 acres of rolling forested hills, beautiful scenery, and wildlife

Mayor's Marathon and Half Marathon, Anchorage; June

Great Alaska Salmon Bake and Fly-by, Anchorage; July

Anchorage Market and Festival, between C and E Streets off West Third Avenue, Anchorage; Saturday and Sunday, mid-May to early September; www.anchoragemarkets.com/index.html

An Anchorage calendar of events can be found at www.anchorage.net/events.html. Information on events and festivals in the Hillside Trails area is available at www.muni.org/contents1/events.cfm.

# South of Anchorage

The travel time from the north side of Chugach State Park to the south side can take as long as ninety minutes by car, and the differences between the two areas can be striking. Southeast Alaska's temperate rain forest extends into some of the southernmost trails of Chugach State Park south of Anchorage, and the towering Sitka spruce and mossy vegetation are truly unique to this portion of the park.

The southern trails described here are accessed from the Seward Highway or from side roads that branch off the highway. The Seward Highway follows Turnagain Arm southward from the city, and many of the trails in this section provide exceptional views of the inlet, mountains, and mudflats in the area. Many of these trails are also ideal for spotting spruce grouse, moose, bears, and Dall sheep.

*Overlooking Bird Creek and Turnagain Arm (Hike 30)*

# 25 Turnagain Arm Trail

The Turnagain Arm Trail is a historic trail dating back to 1910, when it was originally used to carry supplies during the construction of the railroad. The trail runs parallel to and above the Seward Highway, the railroad, and the waters of Turnagain Arm. Throughout the trail you'll be able to observe the striking elements of the hike, including stands of birch, aspen, poplar, and spruce trees, highlighted by coastal vegetation, wildflowers, and numerous stream crossings. Wildlife is also abundant, ranging from spruce grouse and bears to moose and Dall sheep.

**Start:** Potter Creek trailhead
**Distance:** 9.3 miles one-way
**Approximate hiking time:** 6–8 hours
**Difficulty:** Easy to moderate
**Elevation gain/loss:** 700 feet
**Trail surface:** Dirt and gravel
**Seasons:** Summer and fall
**Other trail users:** None
**Canine compatibility:** Leashed dogs at trailhead; under voice control after trailhead
**Land status:** State park
**Nearest town:** Anchorage

**Fees and permits:** $5 parking fee
**Maps:** Imus Geographics Chugach State Park map (www.imusgeographics.com); USGS Anchorage
**Trail contacts:** Chugach State Park Headquarters, located at the Potter Section House State Historic Site, Mile 115 Seward Highway (mailing address: HC 52 Box 8999, Indian 99540); (907) 345-5014; e-mail: csp@dnr.state.ak.us; open Monday through Friday 10:00 a.m. to 4:30 p.m.
**Special considerations:** None

**Finding the trailhead:** Heading south on the Seward Highway from Anchorage, look for Mile Marker 115. You will pass Potter Marsh on your left and the state park office on your right. The trailhead is on the left (east) side of the road. Parking is available at this trailhead along with restroom facilities, a resting bench, and a viewing scope. The trail starts on the paved path at the overlook platform.

## The Hike

This hike can easily be split up into three different segments and can be started from four different locations: Potter Creek, McHugh, Rainbow, and Windy Corner. There are parking lots at three of the four places, and at Windy Corner there is room to park along the highway. The hike is numbered from north to south, beginning at the Potter Creek trailhead and ending at Windy Corner. The entire trail is well marked with signposts and mileage markers.

Begin at the overlook platform and interpretive sign display on the south side of the parking lot. Here you will find a good view of the mudflats, the railroad, and the Seward Highway below. The first 0.3 mile of this hike is part of a nature trail and has several interpretive displays along the way. The trail starts out as a paved path and then veers east into the forest and becomes a well-maintained 4-foot-wide gravel path.

*McHugh Creek*

You quickly come to the old Potter Road, part of a shorter loop trail, which goes straight ahead. Turn right to continue on Potter Creek Trail. After approximately 0.5 mile come to a T. Turn right to continue on to McHugh Creek Trail, which is the first third of the Turnagain Arm Trail. (Going left will loop you back to the old Potter Road and back to the parking lot.) The trail becomes a rooted dirt path, levels off, and gets progressively rougher.

Cross a small bridge over a mountain stream at about 0.7 mile. Just beyond this stream, about another 0.1 mile, come to the first resting bench and overlook. After about 1.5 miles of travel, cross another small bridge and stream. The trail has a tendency to be wet, and you'll encounter many small boardwalks along the way.

After about 2.2 miles of travel, reach the junction with the 7.0-mile McHugh Lake Trail on your left. Continue straight ahead on the Turnagain Arm Trail. Slightly farther up the trail, another signpost directs you straight ahead to the next trailhead at Rainbow. (Turning right will take you to the upper-level parking lot of the McHugh Creek State Wayside at Seward Highway Mile Marker 112.)

The next trail section between McHugh and Rainbow becomes narrower with loose stone, rock ledges, and a variety of hiking terrain. About 400 feet from the turn down to the parking lot, a second signpost directs you to make another right-hand

▶ Southeast Alaska's temperate rain forest extends into some of the southernmost trails of Chugach State Park south of Anchorage, and the towering Sitka spruce and mossy vegetation are truly unique to this portion of the park.

turn. After turning, cross two more streams and bridges over the course of the next 1.5 miles. This area also shows evidence of a past wildfire charring the cottonwood landscape. You'll have another bridgeless crossing within another mile. You should be able to hear the water flowing down the series of small falls as you approach. At 6.0 miles the vegetation changes from birch and aspen trees to spruce. Look for spruce grouse on the trail and in the tree branches ahead. They often go unnoticed until you are practically upon them, when they suddenly take flight, startling you as you hike along the path.

The trail begins a slow descent with several switchbacks as it follows the mountain stream on your left. Just before 7.0 miles the trail crosses the stream on a bridge. Beyond the bridge the trail crosses a private drive and heads downhill toward Rainbow Creek. Rainbow is an impressive creek—fast and scenic. If you are into stream photography, this is a good one to photograph as you further explore the shoreline and small falls. Cross the bridge over Rainbow Creek and follow the trail down to the Rainbow parking lot (Seward Highway Mile Marker 108), with an option to stop or continue on to Windy Corner, another 1.9 miles. You'll be able to pick up the trail to Windy Corner at the northeast corner of the lot.

On the last 1.6 miles of the trail, you can expect loose stone and a narrow path with sheer, steep ledges in places. This last segment of the trail, as you get closer to Windy, is through sheep habitat, and you may well get a glimpse of Dall sheep. For about 1.0 mile you'll continue ascending into rocky terrain. Plan on several small stream crossings without bridges—and the possibility of wet feet. Just after Mile 9.0, keep your eye out for Dall sheep on the rocks above. This is a popular place for sheep to congregate, where they entertain the people on the Seward Highway below. The trail quickly descends to the highway and ends at Seward Highway Mile Marker 106.

## Miles and Directions

**0.0**  Start at the overlook platform on paved path on the south side of the parking lot. N61 02.882 / W149 47.540

**0.1**  Veer right off old Potter Road. N61 02.877 / W149 47.462

**0.5**  Turn right at the trailpost to McHugh Creek Trail. N61 02.699 / W149 47.079

**0.7**  Cross a small stream on a bridge. N61 02.515 / W149 46.852

**0.8**  Reach a scenic view with a bench. N61 02.425 / W149 46.901

**1.5**  Cross a small stream on a bridge. N61 02.085 / W149 46.135

**2.2**  The McHugh Lake trailhead is on your left. Continue straight ahead. N61 01.317 / W149 44.267

# Turnagain Arm Trail

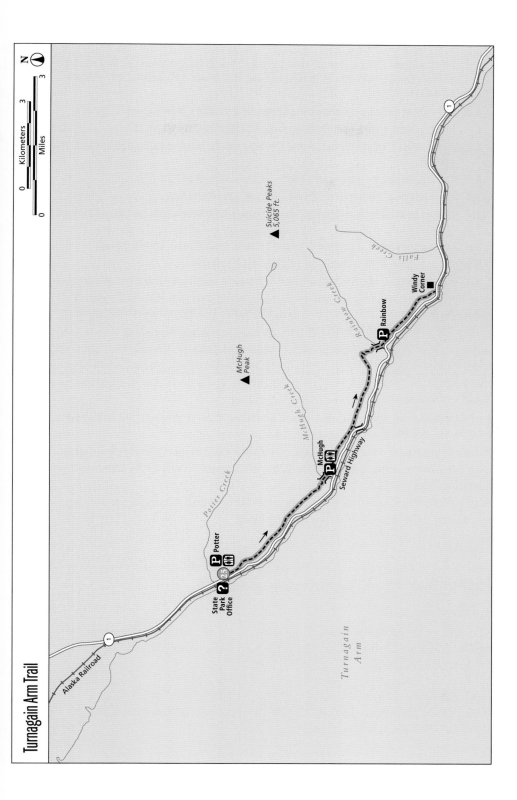

**3.5** At the trailpost continue straight ahead on Turnagain Arm Trail. 112 N61 01.103 / W149 43.988 (Option: Turn right and travel 545 feet to the upper-level parking lot of the McHugh Creek State Wayside, Seward Highway Mile Marker 112. N61 01.187 / W149 43.943)

**3.6** Turn right at the trailpost and cross a bridge. N61 01.114 / W149 43.882

**5.1** Reach a small stream and bridge crossing. N61 00.602 / W149 41.737

**5.9** Reach another small stream crossing, this time with no bridge. N61 00.455 / W149 40.439

**6.9** The trail crosses the stream on a bridge. N61 00.235 / W149 38.747

**7.5** Cross Rainbow Creek on a bridge. N61 00.126 / W149 38.504

**7.7** Reach the Rainbow parking lot at Seward Highway Mile Marker 108. N61 00.013 / W149 38.432

**8.9** Cross several small, unbridged mountain streams. N60 59.419 / W149 36.863

**9.0** Cross another small stream. N60 59.250 / W149 36.554

**9.1** Reach a scenic view. Turn right off the trail to a large boulder. N60 59.199 / W149 36.538

**9.3** Arrive at Windy Corner, Seward Highway Mile Marker 106. Pick up your shuttle or retrace your steps. N60 59.092 / W149 36.270

# Hike Information

*Local information*

Anchorage Visitor Information Center, 546 West Fourth Avenue, Anchorage 99501; (907) 274-3531; www.anchorage.net

Alaska Department of Natural Resources Public Information Center, Atwood Building, 550 West Seventh Avenue, Suite 1260, Anchorage 99501; (907) 269-8400; www.dnr.state.ak.us/parks

Alaska Public Lands Information Center, 605 West Fourth Avenue, Suite 105, Anchorage 99501; (907) 271-2737; www.nps.gov/aplic

*Camping*

Bird Creek Campground; (907) 345-5014; located southeast of Anchorage at Mile Marker 101 on Seward Highway; nightly camping fee

*Local organizations*

The Anchorage Adventurers Meetup Group; www.adventurers.meetup.com/109 Mountaineering Club of Alaska, 2633 Spenard Road, Anchorage 99503; (907) 272-1811; www.mcak.org

*Local retailers*

Recreational Equipment Inc. (REI), 1200 West Northern Lights Boulevard, Anchorage; (907) 272-4565; www.rei.com

*Potter Trailhead*

Sportsman's Warehouse, 681 Old Seward Highway, Anchorage; (907) 644-1400; www.sportsmanswarehouse.com

Alaska Mountaineering and Hiking, 2633 Spenard Road, Anchorage; (907) 272-1811; www.alaskamountaineering.com

Cabelas, 155 W 104th, Anchorage; (907) 341-3400; www.cabelas.com/Stores/Anchorage

6th Avenue Outfitters, 520 W 6th Avenue, Anchorage; (907) 276-0233; www.6thavenueoutfitters.com

Bass Pro Shops, 3046 Mountain View Drive, Anchorage; (907) 330-5200; www.basspro.com/Anchorage

## *Local events / attractions*

Girdwood Forest Fair, Girdwood; July

Alyeska Blueberry and Mountain Arts Festival, Alyeska Ski Resort; August

An Anchorage calendar of events can be found at www.anchorage.net/events.html.

▶ **Turnagain Arm and Cook Inlet have the second-highest tides in North America, second only to eastern Canada's Bay of Fundy. When the tides retreat, extensive areas of mudflats are exposed that possess quicksand-like qualities. The mud is composed of glacial silt and is extremely dangerous and possibly fatal to those who venture out in curiosity.**

# 26 Indian Creek to Girdwood

This scenic trail is totally paved and follows the Turnagain Arm, the Seward Highway, and parts of the Alaskan Railroad. It has several bridge crossings, an underpass, scenic overlooks with viewing scopes, picnic areas and toilet facilities, and opportunities to view numerous varieties of Alaskan wildlife such as beavers, moose, Dall sheep, beluga whales, and various birds. This is also a popular bike trail that can be easily completed in a day. The trail can be picked up at Bird Point on the Seward Highway to shorten the distance or, if you prefer to hike just the south part of the trail, picked up at Gird-wood Station Mall.

**Start:** Indian Creek, at Seward Highway Mile Marker 103
**Distance:** 13.4 miles one-way
**Approximate hiking time:** 6–8 hours
**Difficulty:** Easy
**Elevation gain:** Negligible
**Trail surface:** Paved
**Seasons:** Summer and fall
**Other trail users:** Bikes, joggers
**Canine compatibility:** Leashed dogs permitted
**Land status:** State park
**Nearest town:** Girdwood
**Fees and permits:** $5 parking fee

**Maps:** Imus Geographics Chugach State Park map (www.imusgeographics.com); USGS Anchorage and Seward
**Trail contacts:** Chugach State Park Headquarters, located at the Potter Section House State Historic Site, Mile 115 Seward Highway (mailing address: HC 52 Box 8999, Indian 99540); (907) 345-5014; e-mail: csp@dnr.state.ak .us; open Monday through Friday 10:00 a.m. to 4:30 p.m.
**Special considerations:** Portions of the trail are closed in winter due to avalanche danger.

**Finding the trailhead:** Heading south on the Seward Highway from Anchorage, look for Mile Marker 103 and park on the west side of the road. There is a ball diamond next to the paved parking lot. The paved trail begins at the south side of the lot and immediately veers into the woods, running parallel to the highway.

## The Hike

Begin on the paved trail that leaves the parking lot. It will immediately veer into the forest along the side of the highway. Cross Bird Creek on a bridge at approximately 1.4 miles. This is a popular salmon creek for both anglers and brown bears. This is also a good spot to stop and enjoy the view, which can change dramatically depending on the tide. There is river access and a viewing platform across the bridge. The state park parking lot for Bird Creek is located on the south side of the highway.

Within another 0.3 mile come to Bird Creek Campground. The trail veers slightly south and follows the south side of the campground, giving you a good scope of the facilities as you pass by. On your immediate right is the water from Turnagain Arm. You should see red squirrels and a good variety of birds along this stretch. After

*Girdwood Trail*

approximately 2.5 miles the trail comes to a T. You want to go to your right, cross the bridge, and continue onward. (The trail to your left goes under the road and to a parking lot.)

After a little less than 4.2 miles from the trailhead, the trail makes a sharp left turn and passes through a large culvert under the Seward Highway. You'll be able to see many alluring small waterfalls coming down from the mountains on your left. The trail is now on the north side of the road, passing a large wetland on your left. This muskeg is an ideal habitat for viewing waterfowl and beavers, evidenced by some of the beaver dams in the water.

At approximately 7.0 miles you will arrive at the popular stopping area called Bird Point on the opposite side of the highway. Use the culvert with paved trail to access this area—do not try to cross the highway through the traffic. Bird Point has a large parking area, a picnic area, and restroom facilities. There is also a scenic overlook for viewing the waters of Turnagain Arm, possibly spotting passing beluga whales, and Bradley Peak straight out from the point. As you continue on the trail after Bird Point, expect a steady incline for a short distance.

After about 1.2 miles come to a small picnic shelter and grill. There are pit toilets at this spot. If this isn't a good time for lunch, there will be another opportunity 0.75 mile up the trail. You won't find a shelter here, but there is a grill area and two viewing scopes available. If you started at Indian Creek, you have now traveled about 9.0 miles. The next picnic area is located a little more than 2.0 miles from this point. This picnic area has a small shelter, grills, pit toilets, and two viewing scopes. The nice thing about this trail is that it provides facilities and opportunities for learning about the area with interpretive signs and scopes for observation.

At highway Mile Marker 90.5, 12.7 miles from Indian, arrive at a beautiful setting called Tidewater Slough. There is an interpretive display and viewing platform at this stop. This estuarine marsh filled with grasslike sedges is a popular fall and spring migratory bird stopover. The surrounding Sitka spruce forest and waters of Turnagain Arm also provide habitat for many animals and other birds such as bald eagles, red-tailed hawks, and belted kingfishers. Just up the path a sign indicates that you are leaving the state park boundaries, but keep going.

At highway Mile Marker 90.2 pass the Girdwood Train Depot—a stopping point on the way to Seward for the Alaskan Railroad. The trail heads uphill, turns right, and passes over a wooden bridge that crosses the train tracks. Follow the trail downhill approximately 0.5 mile to the east side of the Girdwood Station Mall. This is a good place to recarb or fill up after working up an appetite. The food selections are excellent for quick foods such as pizza, subs, sandwiches, ice cream, bakery goods, and espresso to keep you going.

## BORE TIDES

Chugach State Park provides extraordinary views of a unique body of water called Cook Inlet. The inlet comprises Turnagain Arm to the southeast and Knik Arm to the north. Both experience bore tides, but the tidal bores in Turnagain Arm are much more prominent and impressive. Turnagain Arm is long and narrow and experiences a very distinct tidal range of over 35 feet.

Because of the shallowness and long length of Turnagain Arm, water is still flowing out after the tide has reversed and is headed back in. The tides are most dramatic when the incoming wall of water takes over the outgoing stream. They can attain heights of more than 6 feet, travel as fast as 10 to 15 miles per hour, and be heard rumbling in as they make their approach. The bore tides vary in size and intensity according to the shallowness and narrowness of the channels they follow. They occur just after low tides and are largest after extreme low tides, such as minus 2 to minus 5. A local tidal chart can help you time your observations.

The Seward Highway has several good points for observing a bore tide, including Beluga Point, Mile Marker 110.5; Indian, Mile Marker 103; and Bird Point, Mile Marker 95. Keep in mind that you can expect to see a bore tide anywhere from one hour to four hours after low tide.

# Indian Creek to Girdwood

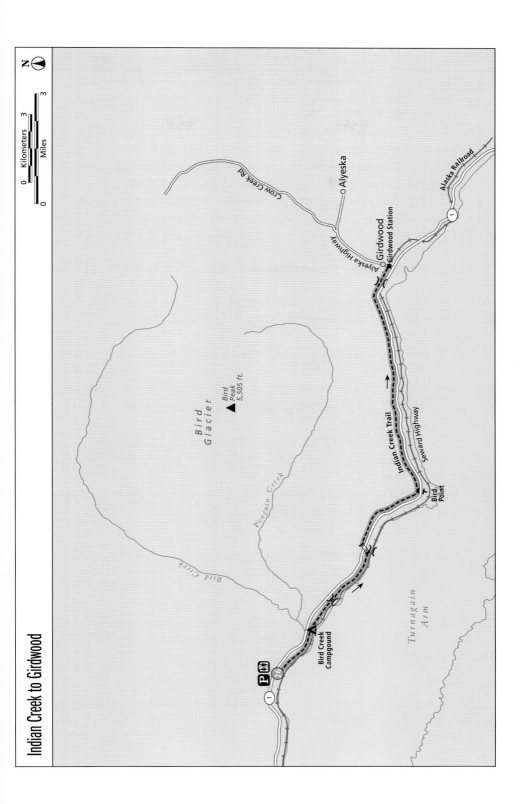

# Miles and Directions

**0.0** Start the paved trail at the south end of the parking lot. N61 10.108 / W149 50.494

**1.4** Cross Bird Creek on a bridge (N60 58.385 / W149 28.065) and reach a viewing platform. N60 58.391 / W149 27.994

**1.7** Pass Bird Creek Campground. N60 58.315 / W149 27.641

**2.5** Turn right at the T and cross a bridge. N60 57.971 / W149 26.584

**4.2** Cross under Seward Highway through a culvert. N60 57.096 W149 24.368

**7.0** Reach Bird Point with parking and facilities. N60 55.803 / W149 20.853

**8.2** Come to a picnic area with a shelter, grills, and toilets. N60 56.149 / W149 18.892

**8.9** Reach a lookout site with viewing scopes. N60 56.216 / W149 17.700

**11.1** Come to another picnic area with a shelter, grills, and toilets. N60 56.414 / W149 13.752

**12.7** Cross a wooden bridge with mountain views and salt slough. N60 56.802 / W149 11.115

**12.8** Leave state park boundaries. N60 56.786 / W149 10.946

**13.4** End the hike at Girdwood Station Mall. N60 56.477 / W149 10.301

# Hike Information

## Local information

Anchorage Visitor Information Center, 546 West Fourth Avenue, Anchorage 99501; (907) 274-3531; www.anchorage.net

Alaska Department of Natural Resources Public Information Center, Atwood Building, 550 West Seventh Avenue, Suite 1260, Anchorage 99501; (907) 269-8400; www.dnr.state.ak.us/parks

Alaska Public Lands Information Center, 605 West Fourth Avenue, Suite 105, Anchorage 99501; (907) 271-2737; www.nps.gov/aplic

## Camping

Bird Creek Campground; (907) 345-5014; located southeast of Anchorage at Mile Marker 101 on Seward Highway; nightly camping fee

## Local organizations

The Anchorage Adventurers Meetup Group; www.adventurers.meetup.com/109 Mountaineering Club of Alaska, 2633 Spenard Road, Anchorage 99503; (907) 272-1811; www.mcak.org

## Local retailers

Recreational Equipment Inc. (REI), 1200 West Northern Lights Boulevard, Anchorage; (907) 272-4565; www.rei.com

Sportsman's Warehouse, 681 Old Seward Highway, Anchorage; (907) 644-1400; www
.sportsmanswarehouse.com

Alaska Mountaineering and Hiking, 2633 Spenard Road, Anchorage; (907) 272-
1811; www.alaskamountaineering.com

Cabelas, 155 W 104th, Anchorage; (907) 341-3400; www.cabelas.com/Stores/
Anchorage

6th Avenue Outfitters, 520 W 6th Avenue, Anchorage; (907) 276-0233; www.6th
avenueoutfitters.com

Bass Pro Shops, 3046 Mountain View Drive, Anchorage; (907) 330-5200; www
.basspro.com/Anchorage

*Local events / attractions*

Girdwood Forest Fair, Girdwood; July

Alyeska Blueberry and Mountain Arts Festival, Alyeska Ski Resort; August

An Anchorage calendar of events can be found at www.anchorage.net/events.html.

## GREEN TIP

Stay on the trail.
Cutting through from one part of a switchback to another
can destroy fragile plant life.

# 27 Falls Creek Trail

If you like cascading waterfalls, a great stream, and exceptional views of Turnagain Arm, you don't want to miss this hike. The rumbling stream with gradual cascading falls and mountain views provides a picturesque valley setting unique to this trail. The trail is rough and steep and climbs high enough that you're likely to see Dall sheep, golden eagles, and Arctic ground squirrels in the higher elevations. Spruce grouse can also be spotted along the heavily forested path at the beginning of the hike.

**Start:** Trailhead at Seward Highway Mile Marker 105.5
**Distance:** 5.5 miles out and back
**Approximate hiking time:** 7–8 hours
**Difficulty:** Moderate to difficult due to steepness and loose stone
**Elevation gain:** 1,450 feet
**Trail surface:** Dirt and stone
**Seasons:** Summer and fall
**Other trail users:** None
**Canine compatibility:** Leashed dogs permitted; under voice control after trailhead
**Land status:** State park

**Nearest town:** Anchorage
**Fees and permits:** No fees or permits required
**Maps:** Imus Geographics Chugach State Park map (www.imusgeographics.com); USGS Anchorage and Seward
**Trail contacts:** Chugach State Park Headquarters, located at the Potter Section House State Historic Site, Mile 115 Seward Highway (mailing address: HC 52 Box 8999, Indian 99540); (907) 345-5014; e-mail: csp@dnr.state.ak.us; open Monday through Friday 10:00 a.m. to 4:30 p.m.
**Special considerations:** None

**Finding the trailhead:** Head south on the Seward Highway from Anchorage. At Mile Marker 115 you will pass Potters Marsh on your left and then the state park headquarters on your right. The trailhead is located on your left at Mile Marker 105.5. There is a waterfall at the trailhead and a small parking area.

## The Hike

Just to the left of the trailhead is a picturesque waterfall coming off the side of the mountain—a harbinger of more to follow. This trail, like most Seward Highway trails, makes an immediate steep ascent into the forest. Proceed up the small, narrow path into a spruce–hardwood forest closely following along Falls Creek. There are many photo opportunities along the trail of small cascading falls that accompany the trail's beautiful Alaskan setting.

The trail is mainly a dirt path through the forest and eventually becomes steeper and rougher. Portions of the trail tend to be wet, muddy, and slick. After the first 0.2 mile, the trail forks. Take the path uphill and away from the creek. The path continues to climb steeply for another 0.2 mile until you arrive at a huge boulder on the right side of the trail in a relatively level area. At this point the trail turns left and briefly heads downhill toward the creek.

*Top: Boulder is prominent marker on Falls Creek Trail.*
*Bottom: Falls Creek Trail is a haven for wildflowers.*

As the trail leaves the forest, the vegetation becomes thick and plentiful. Be cautious of the abundant growth of cow parsnip and devil's club along the trail. The oils from the cow parsnip leaves can cause irritation, itching, and blistering on your skin simply from brushing up against the plant, and the brittle spines of the devil's club can tear both clothes and skin and cause infections. There is also an abundance of poisonous baneberry, not to be confused with the low-bush cranberries along the path.

After about another 0.5 mile you come to a small stream. There is no bridge, but it is an easy crossing. The vegetation eventually thins out and the view opens up above the tree line as the trail continues to follow Falls Creek. Expect some rough traveling as you follow the creek. Plan on climbing over large rocks and uneven wet terrain as you work your way upward.

When you arrive on the first ridge after a total of 1.5 miles, the trail forks once again. The path straight ahead will dead-end taking you toward Indianhouse Mountain. Take the narrow path to the left that dips slightly downhill. Continue along the trail in the valley for approximately another 0.75 mile into a large cirque, or bowl. Head uphill to your right to the hidden tarn called Falls Lake. Many hikers stop here. However, you can safely hike another 1.5 miles up the pass to the ridge above that heads northwest to view Rabbit and McHugh Lakes below.

## Miles and Directions

**0.0**  Start at the trailhead at Seward Highway Mile Marker 105.5. N60 59.061 / W149 34.552

**0.2**  Turn right at the fork in the trail and head steeply uphill. N60 59.243 / W149 34.768

**0.4**  Turn left at the large boulder and head downhill toward the creek. N60 59.414 / W149 34.740

**0.9**  Cross a small stream. N61 00.220 / W149 34.325

**1.5**  Turn left at the fork in the trail and head downhill. N61 00.360 / W149 33.971

**2.25**  Arrive at Falls Lake. Retrace your steps. N61 00.876 / W149 33.838 (Option: Continue hiking 1.5 miles up the pass to views of Rabbit and McHugh Lakes from the ridge.)

**5.5**  Arrive back at the trailhead. N60 59.061 / W149 34.552

## Hike Information

*Local information*

Anchorage Visitor Information Center, 546 West Fourth Avenue, Anchorage 99501; (907) 274-3531; www.anchorage.net

Alaska Department of Natural Resources Public Information Center, Atwood Building, 550 West Seventh Avenue, Suite 1260, Anchorage 99501; (907) 269-8400; www.dnr.state.ak.us/parks

Alaska Public Lands Information Center, 605 West Fourth Avenue, Suite 105, Anchorage 99501; (907) 271-2737; www.nps.gov/aplic

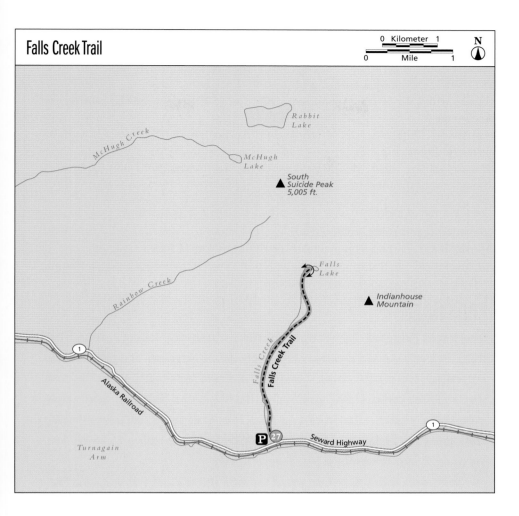

## Falls Creek Trail

*Camping*

Bird Creek Campground; (907) 345-5014; located southeast of Anchorage at Mile Marker 101 on Seward Highway; nightly camping fee

*Local organizations*

The Anchorage Adventurers Meetup Group; www.adventurers.meetup.com/109
Mountaineering Club of Alaska, 2633 Spenard Road, Anchorage 99503; (907) 272-1811; www.mcak.org

*Local retailers*

Recreational Equipment Inc. (REI), 1200 West Northern Lights Boulevard, Anchorage; (907) 272-4565; www.rei.com

Sportsman's Warehouse, 681 Old Seward Highway, Anchorage; (907) 644-1400; www
.sportsmanswarehouse.com

Alaska Mountaineering and Hiking, 2633 Spenard Road, Anchorage; (907) 272-
1811; www.alaskamountaineering.com

Cabelas, 155 W 104th, Anchorage; (907) 341-3400; www.cabelas.com/Stores/
Anchorage

6th Avenue Outfitters, 520 W 6th Avenue, Anchorage; (907) 276-0233; www.6th
avenueoutfitters.com

Bass Pro Shops, 3046 Mountain View Drive, Anchorage; (907) 330-5200; www
.basspro.com/Anchorage

*Local events/attractions*

Girdwood Forest Fair, Girdwood; July
Alyeska Blueberry and Mountain Arts Festival, Alyeska Ski Resort; August
An Anchorage calendar of events can be found at www.anchorage.net/events.html.

# COOK INLET

Several trails throughout Chugach State Park afford extraordinary views of Cook Inlet. But these views only give you a glimpse of its beauty, not the magnitude of significance this extraordinary body of water carries. Coined the "Gateway to South-central Alaska," the Cook Inlet watershed covers 47,000 square miles. This phenomenal ecosystem encompasses alpine tundra, wetlands, estuarine bays and coves, coastal rain forests, and salmon streams. These diverse habitats support a diverse web of wildlife, from brown bears to Steller sea lions and whales to migratory birds and five species of salmon.

Nearly one million visitors from around the world visit this area each year. Cook Inlet supports the tourism and recreation industry, commercial fishing, and the oil industry. Cook Inlet was home to native Alaskan tribes before Europeans arrived in this area, and native subsistence lifestyles still depend on Cook Inlet's waters and surrounding habitats for up to 90 percent of villagers' diets. Even though many things have changed over the years, efforts are continually being made to preserve and revitalize the many traditions of the Alaskan native culture.

The environmentally sound inlet you see today is the result of many organizations working together to sustain the future for the many visitors who will come here to visit and for the future generations of Alaskans who will depend on it.

# 28  McHugh Lake–Rabbit Lake Trail

The McHugh Lake Trail traverses in a northeasterly direction along the McHugh Creek Valley and parallel with McHugh Creek, finally ending at two pristine alpine lakes—Rabbit and McHugh. This excellent full-day hike guarantees outstanding scenic views of Turnagain Arm and Cook Inlet, mountain peaks, glacially carved valleys, mature forests, wildflowers, and Alaskan wildlife.

**Start:** McHugh Creek Picnic Area on Seward Highway
**Distance:** 14.2 miles out and back
**Approximate hiking time:** 8–10 hours
**Difficulty:** Moderate
**Elevation gain:** 2,750 feet
**Trail surface:** Dirt
**Seasons:** June through September
**Other trail users:** None
**Canine compatibility:** Leashed dogs permitted; under voice control after trailhead
**Land status:** State park
**Nearest town:** Anchorage

**Fees and permits:** $5 daily parking fee
**Maps:** Imus Geographics Chugach State Park map (www.imusgeographics.com); USGS Anchorage
**Trail contacts:** Chugach State Park Headquarters, located at the Potter Section House State Historic Site, Mile 115 Seward Highway (mailing address: HC 52 Box 8999, Indian 99540); (907) 345-5014; e-mail: csp@dnr.state.ak .us; open Monday through Friday 10:00 a.m. to 4:30 p.m.
**Special considerations:** None

**Finding the trailhead:** From Anchorage head south on Seward Highway to Mile Marker 112 and a sign labeled MCHUGH CREEK PICNIC AREA. The large parking lot is located on the left (mountain) side of the highway. There are three levels of parking at this popular wayside and scenic overlook. The trailhead access point is located next to the restrooms in the upper lot. It is recommended that you park in the lower level lot when hiking this trail, since the park hours are from 9:00 a.m. to 9:00 p.m. and access to the upper lots is limited when the gate is closed.

## The Hike

Pick up the trail for this hike at the McHugh Creek Picnic Area on Seward Highway. This is a very popular stopping place with a large paved parking area, picnic facilities, restrooms, and a scenic overlook. In addition to hiking the trails, many people stop here to view Turnagain Arm, bore tides, beluga whales, and a large picturesque waterfall near the road. There is also a short-paved trail located on the second level parking lot directly behind the kiosk and latrine that leads to two different viewing platforms of Turnagain Arm and Knik Arm. This is a great vantage point for spotting beluga whales. The facility also has a seasonal park host on site.

Begin the hike next to the restrooms in the upper-level lot. Follow the dirt path into the woods for about 200 feet. Turn left onto the Turnagain Arm Trail and head in a northwesterly direction. You will cross a couple of boardwalks in a rather low,

*View of North and South Suicide Peak*

wet area. After 0.25 mile the McHugh Lake trailhead is evident. Turn right and head uphill into the mature hardwood forest. The first mile, measured from the parking lot, goes through a low wet area, and you are very likely to encounter a healthy population of mosquitoes. Be prepared with a good repellent.

Reach another marker post at 0.8 mile. Continue straight ahead to stay on the McHugh Lake Trail. Most of this trail is a gradual incline and a very enjoyable hike. The first couple of miles take you through stands of large cottonwoods and a mature forest, with several switchbacks as you gain elevation. You will notice an area of charred cottonwood trees to the south from a wildfire in 2016. As with most of Chugach State Park, be attentive on the trail as you hike, since this is good bear and moose habitat.

The 1.0-mile marker provides you with an open view of Turnagain Arm below. Within another 0.8 mile the trail conditions begin to change, and you head steeply uphill over a loose dirt-and-gravel path. Going up the hill is not nearly as challenging as coming down it. Use caution on the return route, since the loose stone and fine dirt make it very slick on the descent. At the top of the incline, you come to an open meadow area and then head back into the woods again.

The trail is marked at the 2.0-mile point, which is the beginning of many open alpine meadows, wildflowers, and great views of Suicide Peaks, McHugh Peak, and McHugh Creek Valley. The path leads in and out of brushy vegetation that nearly covers the path at times. At approximately 2.8 miles descend a slope, cross a small stream, and climb abruptly uphill. Passing the 3.0-mile marker, the trail switches to all stone and heads uphill into the rocks with several switchbacks. At 3.6 miles (from the parking lot) the stone trail forks. Do not proceed straight ahead; instead make a sharp right-hand turn uphill heading toward your destination. This is an easy turn to miss. If you miss it, you'll end up going in the opposite direction from your goal.

Travel through intermittent meadows and brushy vegetation and down and up a couple more ravines. After approximately 5.75 miles pass a small tarn on your left and soon another larger tarn on your right. The main trail heads slightly north away from the creek and uphill to the larger Rabbit Lake. Continuing to follow McHugh Creek will take you to the smaller McHugh Lake.

## Miles and Directions

**0.0**  Start from the upper parking lot at McHugh Creek. N61 01.103 / W149 43.988

**0.2**  Turn left at signpost onto Turnagain Arm Trail. N61 01.188 / W149 43.948

**0.25** Reach the McHugh Lake trailhead and turn right. N61 01.316 / W149 44.263

**0.8**  Continue straight ahead at a signpost. N61 01.396 / W149 43.885

**1.0**  Enjoy the open view of Turnagain Arm from Mile Marker 1. N61 01.445 / W149 43.754

**2.0**  Reach Mile Marker 2 and the beginning of meadow, mountain, and valley views. N61 01.525 / W149 42.024

**2.8**  Cross a stream and begin an abrupt uphill climb. N61 01.649 / W149 41.193

**3.0**  Pass Mile Marker 3; the trail becomes all stone. N61 01.692 / W149 40.713

**3.6**  Make a hard right and head uphill; do not go down and straight ahead. N61 01.708 / W149 40.528

**4.0**  Reach the trail's 4.0-mile mark. N61 02.030 / W149 39.100

**5.75** Pass a small tarn on your left. N61 02.308 / W149 37.213

**6.4**  Pass a larger tarn on your right. N61 02.210 / W149 36.208

**7.1**  Reach Rabbit Lake. N61 02.355 / W149 35.168. (Option: Continue following McHugh Creek 0.5 mile to McHugh Lake. N61 02.071 / W149 35.344)

**14.2** Arrive back at the parking lot. N61 01.103 / W149 43.988

## Hike Information

*Local information*

Anchorage Visitor Information Center, 546 West Fourth Avenue, Anchorage 99501; (907) 274-3531; www.anchorage.net

Alaska Department of Natural Resources Public Information Center, Atwood Building, 550 West Seventh Avenue, Suite 1260, Anchorage 99501; (907) 269-8400; www.dnr.state.ak.us/parks

Alaska Public Lands Information Center, 605 West Fourth Avenue, Suite 105, Anchorage 99501; (907) 271-2737; www.nps.gov/aplic

# McHugh Lake-Rabbit Lake Trail

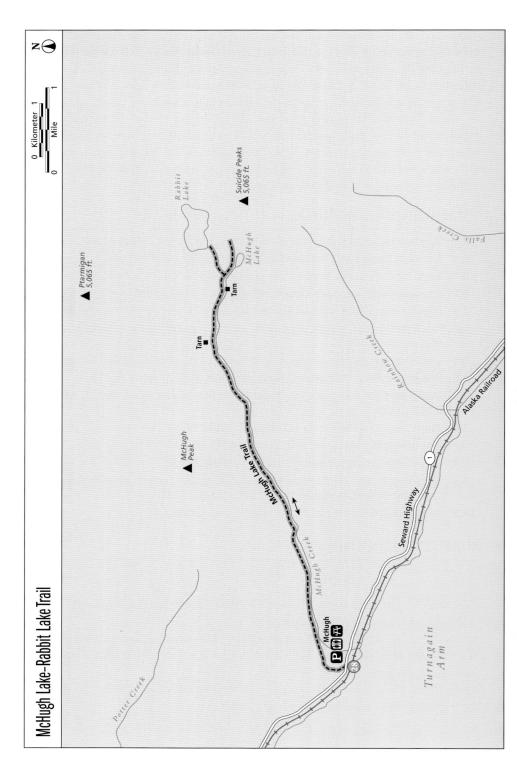

*Meadow on McHugh Lake Trail*

## Camping

Bird Creek Campground; (907) 345-5014; located southeast of Anchorage at Mile Marker 101 on Seward Highway; nightly camping fee

## Local organizations

The Anchorage Adventurers Meetup Group; www.adventurers.meetup.com/109
Mountaineering Club of Alaska, 2633 Spenard Road, Anchorage 99503; (907) 272-1811; www.mcak.org

## Local retailers

Recreational Equipment Inc. (REI), 1200 West Northern Lights Boulevard, Anchorage; (907) 272-4565; www.rei.com
Sportsman's Warehouse, 681 Old Seward Highway, Anchorage; (907) 644-1400; www.sportsmanswarehouse.com
Alaska Mountaineering and Hiking, 2633 Spenard Road, Anchorage; (907) 272-1811; www.alaskamountaineering.com
Cabelas, 155 W 104th, Anchorage; (907) 341-3400; www.cabelas.com/Stores/Anchorage
6th Avenue Outfitters, 520 W 6th Avenue, Anchorage; (907) 276-0233; www.6th avenueoutfitters.com
Bass Pro Shops, 3046 Mountain View Drive, Anchorage; (907) 330-5200; www.basspro.com/Anchorage

## Local events/attractions

Girdwood Forest Fair, Girdwood; July
Alyeska Blueberry and Mountain Arts Festival, Alyeska Ski Resort; August
An Anchorage calendar of events can be found at www.anchorage.net/events.html.

# 29 Bird Ridge Trail

The Bird Ridge Trail is a relatively short trail to the ridge, yet it is challenging and has amazing views of Turnagain Arm. The views alone make this hike worth putting on your to-do list. The very steep yet easy-to-follow trail requires some hiking over rock and loose stone and along the sheer, steep edges of the mountainside. The trail passes through a spruce forest and climbs to the alpine tundra above the tree line. Be prepared for changes in temperature, weather, and windy conditions. This is one of the first spring hikes of the season, combining the first spring wildflowers with winter snow remaining near the ridgetop and surrounding mountain peaks.

**Start:** Mile 101.5 on the Seward Highway
**Distance:** 3.0 miles out and back to ridge
**Approximate hiking time:** 4–5 hours
**Difficulty:** Moderate due to steep trail
**Elevation gain:** 2,500 feet
**Trail surface:** Dirt, mud, gravel, and rock
**Seasons:** Spring, summer, and fall
**Other trail users:** Trail runners
**Canine compatibility:** Leashed dogs permitted; under voice control after trailhead
**Land status:** State park
**Nearest town:** Anchorage

**Fees and permits:** $5 parking fee
**Maps:** Imus Geographics Chugach State Park map (www.imusgeographics.com); USGS Seward
**Trail contacts:** Chugach State Park Headquarters, located at the Potter Section House State Historic Site, Mile 115 Seward Highway (mailing address: HC 52 Box 8999, Indian 99540); (907) 345-5014; e-mail: csp@dnr.state.ak.us; open Monday through Friday 10:00 a.m. to 4:30 p.m.
**Special considerations:** None

**Finding the trailhead:** From Anchorage head south on Seward Highway to Mile Marker 101.5. The trailhead parking lot is on the mountain side of the highway. The small paved lot has a 0.25-mile paved path and long boardwalk leading to restroom facilities, a scenic overlook, and the trailhead.

## The Hike

Begin the trail by following the paved path located on the north side of the parking lot. The path heads east to a long boardwalk and continues up to the restrooms and an overlook. The overlook viewpoint is located about 200 feet slightly to your right. The pavement continues straight ahead and heads down to the Bird Creek parking lot. This is a large lot, which can be used to access this trail as well as Bird Creek, a popular salmon-fishing destination. Turn left just prior to the restrooms to pick up the Bird Ridge Trail. This is where the pavement ends and the real hiking begins.

Head up the dirt path into the spruce forest. The trail immediately starts out steep but is wide and easy to follow. Come to a trail marker post at approximately 0.4 mile. Turn right at the post and continue up the hill. Pass several signs pointing out a natural gas line. About 0.6 mile from the trailhead, come to a flat, open area with a fence

*Upward to Bird Ridge*

along the mountain edge and views of Bird Creek and Turnagain Arm below. The trail heads uphill on your left. The climb is steep, and the trail becomes considerably narrower, with loose stone.

The views of Turnagain Arm below get better and better as you continue to climb. As you hike through towering strands of Sitka spruce trees, you will probably notice the wind pick up as you continue to gain elevation. Around 0.9 mile the vegetation becomes noticeably shorter as you approach the top of the tree line and the biotic communities begin to change.

The trail becomes increasingly rockier and a little more difficult to follow, requiring some scrambling and use of hands around the 1.25-mile mark. Use caution as you climb the trail as it follows the mountain edge. The trail leaves the edge and gradually heads up toward the top of the ridge. The vastness and solitude of the open tundra from Bird Ridge is amazing. Many hikers end their hike on this ridge, which is 1.5 miles from the parking lot.

▶ If you encounter moose along the trail, wait until they move off to the side, or give them plenty of room if you decide to go around them. If a moose charges, run and seek cover behind a tree. Moose injure more people than bears each year in Alaska.

The trail continues, much like a narrow sheep path. The trail is nearly level from here on, inviting further exploring as it continues for almost another 4.0 miles to Bird Ridge Overlook.

# Miles and Directions

**0.0** Start on the paved path at the parking lot at Seward Highway Mile Marker 101.5. N60 58.739 / W149 28.785

**0.2** Cross a long boardwalk. N60 58.631 / W149 28.635

**0.25** Reach the Bird Ridge trailhead and head up the dirt path. N60 58.569 / W149 28.555

**0.4** Turn right at the trailpost and continue uphill. N60 58.642 / W149 28.484

**0.6** The trail veers left. N60 58.556 / W149 28.232

**1.25** Enter an area with rocks and climbing. N60 59.026 / W149 28.126

**1.5** Reach the top of the ridge. Enjoy the view before retracing your steps. N60 59.396 / W149 28.008 (Option: Continue on the narrow, now nearly level path for approximately 4.0 miles to the Bird Ridge Overlook.)

**3.0** Arrive back at the parking lot. N60 58.739 / W149 28.785

# Hike Information

## *Local information*

Anchorage Visitor Information Center, 546 West Fourth Avenue, Anchorage 99501; (907) 274-3531; www.anchorage.net

Alaska Department of Natural Resources Public Information Center, Atwood Building, 550 West Seventh Avenue, Suite 1260, Anchorage 99501; (907) 269-8400; www .dnr.state.ak.us/parks

Alaska Public Lands Information Center, 605 West Fourth Avenue, Suite 105, Anchorage 99501; (907) 271-2737; www.nps.gov/aplic

## *Camping*

Bird Creek Campground; (907) 345-5014; located southeast of Anchorage at Seward Highway Mile Marker 101; nightly camping fee

## *Local organizations*

The Anchorage Adventurers Meetup Group; www.adventurers.meetup.com/109
Mountaineering Club of Alaska, 2633 Spenard Road, Anchorage 99503; (907) 272-1811; www.mcak.org

## *Local retailers*

Recreational Equipment Inc. (REI), 1200 West Northern Lights Boulevard, Anchorage; (907) 272-4565; www.rei.com

Sportsman's Warehouse, 681 Old Seward Highway, Anchorage; (907) 644-1400; www .sportsmanswarehouse.com

Alaska Mountaineering and Hiking, 2633 Spenard Road, Anchorage; (907) 272-1811; www.alaskamountaineering.com

Cabelas, 155 W 104th, Anchorage; (907) 341-3400; www.cabelas.com/Stores/ Anchorage

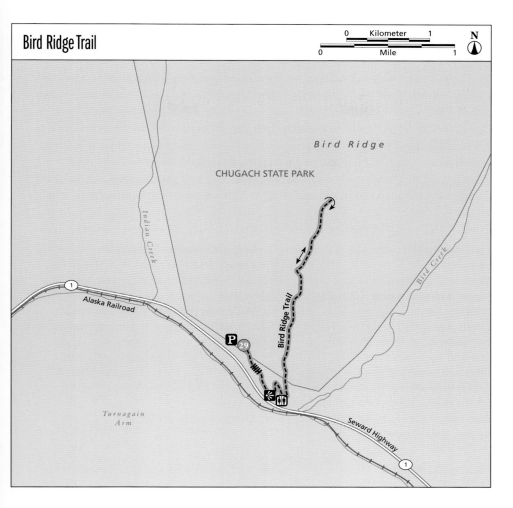

6th Avenue Outfitters, 520 W 6th Avenue, Anchorage; (907) 276-0233; www.6th avenueoutfitters.com

Bass Pro Shops, 3046 Mountain View Drive, Anchorage; (907) 330-5200; www .basspro.com/Anchorage

*Local events/attractions*

Girdwood Forest Fair, Girdwood; July

Alyeska Blueberry and Mountain Arts Festival, Alyeska Ski Resort; August

An Anchorage calendar of events can be found at www.anchorage.net/events.html.

# 30 Bird Creek Trail

Bird Creek takes you through some of the most amazing mature spruce forests in Chugach State Park. The tall, mature trees create a shadowed, somewhat spooky atmosphere, which emphasizes the damp forest floor that's heavily carpeted with mosses and ferns. The trail is very wet and muddy in spring and during wet periods, is often rutted from ATV use, and has one stream crossing; so plan for wet feet. It begins as a wide, easy trail and quickly becomes part of a maze of old roads and ATV trails, making it a bit difficult and confusing to follow. The trail parallels Penguin and Bird Creeks below, which accompany your hike with an acoustical symphony of falling water.

**Start:** Old roadbed by the gate at the corner of the parking lot
**Distance:** 8.6 miles out and back
**Approximate hiking time:** 6–8 hours
**Difficulty:** Easy
**Elevation gain:** 500 feet
**Trail surface:** Dirt, rocks, and mud
**Seasons:** Summer and fall
**Other trail users:** Bikes, horses, ATVs
**Canine compatibility:** Leashed dogs permitted; under voice control after trailhead
**Land status:** State park; regional park
**Nearest town:** Girdwood

**Fees and permits:** $5 parking fee
**Maps:** Imus Geographics Chugach State Park map (www.imusgeographics.com); USGS Seward
**Trail contacts:** Chugach State Park Headquarters, located at the Potter Section House State Historic Site, Mile 115 Seward Highway (mailing address: HC 52 Box 8999, Indian 99540); (907) 345-5014; e-mail: csp@dnr.state.ak.us; open Monday through Friday 10:00 a.m. to 4:30 p.m.
**Special considerations:** None

**Finding the trailhead:** Coming from Anchorage, head south on Seward Highway to Mile Marker 101. Travel 0.3 mile past this marker and turn left toward the mountains on the second road after you pass the Essential 1 gas station. This is Konikson Road; travel 0.6 mile to the park gate and trailhead.

## The Hike

Part of this land is designated as Bird Creek Valley Regional Park. It is owned by the municipality of Anchorage but managed as part of Chugach State Park by the Alaska Division of Parks and Outdoor Recreation. The area is rich in wildlife, and the muddy paths make animal tracking relatively easy. Look for brown bear, moose, fox, lynx, and wolf tracks in the soft mud along the way. Birding is excellent in a climax forest such as this and is also good along some of the wet areas you'll encounter on the hike. Gold panning in Bird Creek is allowed March 16 through July 14.

This is a good trail to bring your topo map with you to help keep you on course because of the numerous old roads in the first part of the hike and forks in the trail.

*Bird Creek popular fishing site*

The hike begins on the old roadbed by the gate at the corner of the parking lot. At about 0.7 mile turn right at a fork in the road to stay on the main trail. (If you want to explore the creek before continuing on the hike, going straight ahead on this path will take you down to the water.)

After turning at the fork in the road, come to a bridged stream crossing in about another 0.7 mile. Immediately after crossing the bridge, the trail forks again. Take the fork to the left. After a short distance the trail forks once again. Both paths loop and join together, but the path to the right is slightly shorter. At the point where the two trails finally meet again, veer to the right. All the way along, you will be slowly ascending above the creek below.

At 3.1 miles the vegetation opens up and affords an outstanding view of Bird Creek and the opposite mountainside, as well as giving you a chance to see how high you've climbed. The trail narrows even more from this point. If it wasn't wet yet, you will probably find standing water somewhere along the trail during the next couple miles.

You will continue to encounter many small ATV trails veering off in different directions. Keep the sound of the creek to your left, or venture on by taking the left forks in the trail. After approximately the 4.2-mile point on the trail, veer left and go down a steep hill, winding toward the creek below. Ford the creek to continue on the narrow, steep trail on the other side. From here on, the trail climbs into the trees. It is overgrown and nonmaintained but continues for another 10.0 miles to Bird Point.

# Miles and Directions

**0.0** Start at the trailhead by the gate at the corner of the parking lot. N60 58.444 / W149 26.000

**0.7** Turn right at the fork to stay on the main trail. N60 58.898 / W 149 25.268

**1.4** Cross a stream on a bridge and immediately take the left fork in the trail. N60 59.315 / W149 24.720

**1.8** Turn right at the fork. N60 59.585 / W149 25.033

**2.0** Turn right at the T in the trail. N60 59.705 / W149 25.271

**3.1** Come to a scenic view of Bird Creek. N61 00.623 / W149 25.063

**4.2** Veer left and head downhill toward the creek. N61 01.419 / W149 24.261

**4.3** The hike ends at the stream crossing. Retrace your steps. N61 01.472 / W149 24.222 (Option: Ford the stream and hike the unmaintained trail another 10.0 miles to Bird Point.)

**8.6** Arrive back at the trailhead and parking lot. N60 58.444 / W149 26.000

# Hike Information

## Local information

Anchorage Visitor Information Center, 546 West Fourth Avenue, Anchorage 99501; (907) 274-3531; www.anchorage.net

Alaska Department of Natural Resources Public Information Center, Atwood Building, 550 West Seventh Avenue, Suite 1260, Anchorage 99501; (907) 269-8400; www.dnr.state.ak.us/parks

Alaska Public Lands Information Center, 605 West Fourth Avenue, Suite 105, Anchorage 99501; (907) 271-2737; www.nps.gov/aplic

## Camping

Bird Creek Campground; (907) 345-5014; located southeast of Anchorage at Seward Highway Mile Marker 101; nightly camping fee

## Local organizations

The Anchorage Adventurers Meetup Group; www.adventurers.meetup.com/109

Mountaineering Club of Alaska, 2633 Spenard Road, Anchorage 99503; (907) 272-1811; www.mcak.org

## Local retailers

Recreational Equipment Inc. (REI), 1200 West Northern Lights Boulevard, Anchorage; (907) 272-4565; www.rei.com

Sportsman's Warehouse, 681 Old Seward Highway, Anchorage; (907) 644-1400; www.sportsmanswarehouse.com

Alaska Mountaineering and Hiking, 2633 Spenard Road, Anchorage; (907) 272-1811; www.alaskamountaineering.com

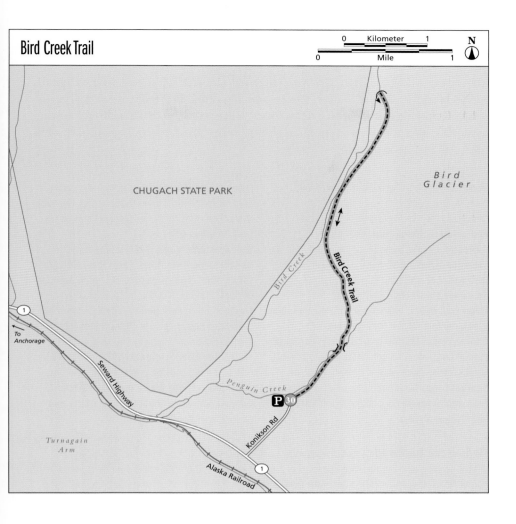

Cabelas, 155 W 104th, Anchorage; (907) 341-3400; www.cabelas.com/Stores/Anchorage

6th Avenue Outfitters, 520 W 6th Avenue, Anchorage; (907) 276-0233; www.6th avenueoutfitters.com

Bass Pro Shops, 3046 Mountain View Drive, Anchorage; (907) 330-5200; www.basspro.com/Anchorage

*Local events/attractions*

Girdwood Forest Fair, Girdwood; July

Alyeska Blueberry and Mountain Arts Festival, Alyeska Ski Resort; August

An Anchorage calendar of events can be found at www.anchorage.net/events.html.

# 31 Historic Iditarod (Crow Pass) Trail

The Historic Iditarod Trail, also known as the Crow Pass Trail, has something for everyone and is rich in wildlife, history, and adventure. The trail is very well maintained and marked and offers extraordinary scenic views with glaciers, fast-moving mountain streams and rivers, numerous large waterfalls, deep gorges, and mountain lakes—all in a 23-mile span.

**Start:** Girdwood (reverse start point, Eagle River Nature Center)
**Distance:** 23.1 miles one-way
**Approximate hiking time:** 2–3 days
**Difficulty:** Easy to difficult
**Elevation gain:** 2,080 feet
**Trail surface:** Dirt, gravel, and stone
**Seasons:** July through September
**Other trail users:** Trail runners in July; bear and sheep hunters August through March
**Canine compatibility:** Leashed dogs permitted at trailhead; under voice control after trailhead
**Land status:** State park
**Nearest town:** Girdwood
**Fees and permits:** $5 parking fee at Eagle River Nature Center

**Maps:** Eagle River Nature Center map (available at the center); Imus Geographics Chugach State Park map (www.imusgeographics.com); USGS Anchorage
**Trail contacts:** Eagle River Nature Center, 32750 Eagle River Road, Eagle River 99577; (907) 694-2108; www.ernc.org; open Tuesday through Sunday 10:00 a.m. to 5:00 p.m. Chugach State Park Headquarters, located at the Potter Section House State Historic Site, Mile 115 Seward Highway (mailing address: HC 52 Box 8999, Indian 99540); (907) 345-5014; e-mail: csp@dnr.state.ak.us; open Monday through Friday 10:00 a.m. to 4:30 p.m.
**Special considerations:** Portions of the trail are avalanche prone in winter.

**Finding the trailhead:** Eagle River Nature Center trailhead: Coming from Anchorage, follow the Glenn Highway north toward the town of Eagle River. After about 10 miles veer right onto the Hiland Road/Eagle River Loop exit. Turn right onto Eagle River Loop Road and continue for 2.5 miles. Turn right at the Lighthouse Church onto Eagle River Road and drive 10 miles to the Eagle River Nature Center parking lot. The trailhead is located behind the nature center.

Crow Pass trailhead: Coming from Anchorage, head south on the Seward Highway toward Girdwood to Mile Marker 90. Turn left toward the mountains onto the Alyeska Highway. Follow this road for 2 miles to Crow Creek Road. Turn left onto Crow Creek and travel 6 miles. The road passes signs for the Iditarod National Historic Trail and Crow Creek Mine. Ignore these signs and continue until you cross a bridge and the road forks. The fork to the left is a private drive. Continue on the fork straight ahead onto a narrow one-lane road. This road winds its way up about 1 more mile to a large parking lot where the trailhead is located.

## The Hike

You can start this hike at either the Eagle River Nature Center or in Girdwood at the Crow Pass trailhead. Most people begin the hike from Girdwood, and that is the route presented here. From this direction, the hike begins with a steep climb for the first 3.0

*Echo Bend on the historic Iditarod Trail*

miles and gradually heads downhill for the remaining 20.0 miles. It is far more convenient to finish up at the nature center, where they sell snacks and drinks and have restroom facilities, a place to sit and relax, and a telephone for contacting your ride.

Before beginning the trail, be sure to familiarize yourself with the path. In addition, bring a map and all the obvious essential items for overnight trips and be well prepared for changes in temperature and weather, as well as windy conditions. You should also know how to ford a river. The Eagle River, the midpoint of the trail, is a wide river with a swift current, and crossing it safely requires serious consideration. Injuries and fatalities have occurred. The water level is lower in the early morning hours. If possible, it is recommended that you check the weather forecast for several days prior to your hike and "bracket" your starting time. If it is raining, the river crossing will be difficult for several days after the rain. If it has been hot, the river will run high for several days after the heat wave. You will also be trekking through an area where bears are likely to be seen. You should know how to avoid bear encounters while hiking, preparing and caching your food, and camping—and know how to react if you encounter a bear along the trail.

From the Girdwood direction, begin the path on the wooden steps next to the restrooms. The trail immediately heads uphill and makes several switchbacks until it gets above the tree line. The trail forks after about 2.2 miles. The fork to the right heads up along the mountainside directly to Crow Pass.

Take the lower fork straight ahead, which heads to the old Monarch gold mine ruins from the late 1800s, with many steel artifacts still decorating the hillside. This fork also takes you past a tall, scenic waterfall as you head steeply uphill, cross Crow Creek, and head up to Crystal Lake at the top of the plateau. Also on this pass is the USDA Forest Service cabin, located just opposite of the lake, which is available to rent for overnight stays. This area receives large amounts of snow, and snow is likely to be evident all through the summer months.

As you head across to the far side of the plateau, follow the cairns that start to appear, passing many areas of open water and small tarns. You will have arrived at the high elevation point of the hike when you see the Raven Glacier to the east. There is also a signpost indicating that you are at Crow Pass and an elevation of 3,500 feet.

Head downhill across the often snow-covered rocky terrain and rockslide areas for about 1.0 mile. The trail can be difficult to stay on because of snow. There are some rocky ledges that you should avoid; try to stay on the trail that safely descends into the valley. Use caution when it is wet and snow covered because of slick conditions. Continuing to descend, come to the confluence of Clear and Raven Creeks. You will need to ford Clear Creek to continue the trail on the opposite side. This entire area for the next several miles is ideal bear and moose habitat, so be sure to make some noise as you proceed. After about 0.5 mile come to the deep Raven Gorge and a bridge crossing the roaring waters below. Cross the bridge and continue a slow descent in and out of the thick vegetation of tall grasses and shrubs for about 3.0 miles. The next bridged stream crossing is Turbid Creek at Mile 7.8.

As you get closer to the Eagle River, the vegetation changes and you head through a nearly perfect mature spruce forest. The path abruptly turns in an easterly direction and goes through a spread of birch and alder trees toward Glacier Lake as it descends down toward the river and fording point. Be sure to ford the river exactly between the two posts located on each bank of the river.

After fording the river, continue straight ahead and ford the smaller branch. After crossing this branch, head along the riverbank to continue on the trail. There are several level camping places available along the gravel bars of the river in this immediate area. At Mile 14.0 Thunder Gorge campsites offer additional choices, the first of several more to follow. Here you will find level places and fire rings.

Just prior to the campsites, cross the fast-moving Thunder Creek. Several logs and a rope will help you get to the other side. The trail between here and the next closest campsite, Twin Falls (Mile 15.0), is mainly up and down rocky ledges closely following the bank of the Eagle River. At Mile 15.6 encounter a wooden ladder that you need to climb to get up and over a boulder; the trail continues at the top. There are two more bridge crossings near the Twin Falls camping sites. Other optional campsites along the river are Icicle Creek Camp (Mile 20.3), Heritage Falls Camp (Mile 21.0), and Echo Bend (Mile 23.0).

Mount Yukla, along the northeast side of the trail, provides perfect habitat for mountain goats, which are often spotted along the way. The dense vegetation and berry plants along this part of the trail are also good habitat for bears, as evidenced by

*Hikers on historic Iditarod Trail from Eagle River Nature Center*

the frequent scat on the trail. It is also possible to spot moose throughout this last part of the hike. At Mile 15.0 a fork in the trail offers either a low-water or high-water route. The low-water route requires you to ford a small lake or pond. The high-water route briefly leaves the river and follows a rockslide along the mountainside, crosses several small footbridges, and rejoins the main trail at the riverbank.

At Mile 17.3 cross Yakety Yak Creek, pass through a spruce forest, and walk onto an old riverbed. Follow the cairns through this area. When you arrive at swift Icicle Creek, an easy walk on a log will get you to the other side. Note beautiful Heritage Falls on the opposite side of the river. Just after a high point called the Knob, the vegetation begins to change to a mix of birch, hemlock, spruce, and aspen before the last bridged creek crossing, Dishwater Creek. A short distance from here you will come to a series of switchbacks and steps that lead to a very prominent lookout called The Perch with great views of the Eagle River valley below. After leaving here, head down hill and on around the corner to Echo Bend, which is also a designated campsite area.

The path changes to roots and rock and heads steadily uphill. You are very likely to see a substantial increase in other hikers from here on. Many people frequently hike to this point from the nature center. The trail passes turnoffs to the Yukla Yurt, Rapids Camp Yurt, Dew Mound Trail, Four Corners, Rodak Nature Trail, and Albert Loop Trail before ending at the Eagle River Nature Center.

# Historic Iditarod (Crow Pass) Trail

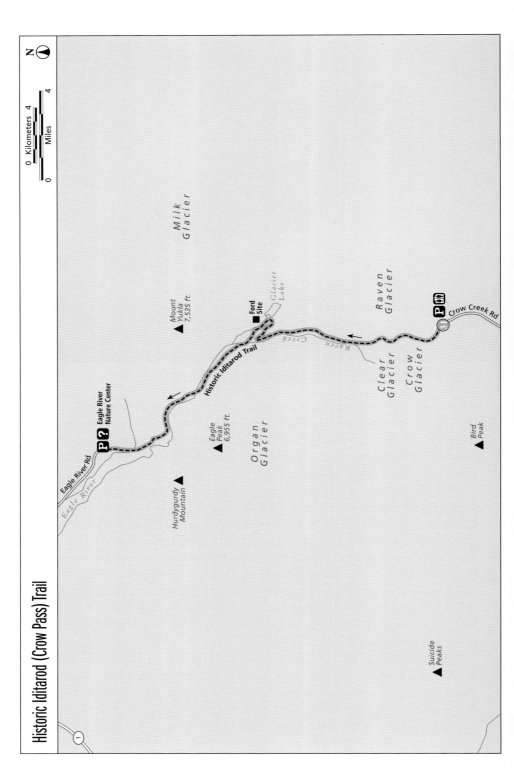

# Miles and Directions

**0.0** Start on the wooden steps next to the restrooms. N61 01.692 / W149 06.969

**2.0** Stay straight at the fork and head toward the ruins of a gold mine. N61 02.559 / W149 06.964 (Option: The trail to the right heads directly to Crow Pass.)

**2.5** Reach the gold mine ruins. N61 02.800 / W149 06.913

**3.0** Pass the USDA Forest Service cabin. N61 03.217 / W149 07.009

**5.5** Ford Clear Creek. N61 05.010 / W149 07.406

**6.2** Raven Gorge. N61 05.367 / W149 07.242

**7.8** Reach Turbid Creek, a bridged stream crossing. N61 06.414 / W149 06.479

**11.8** Arrive at the Eagle River ford sites, north south. This is the midpoint of the hike. N61 08.154 / W149 05.658

**13.0** Thunder Gorge campsites. N61 08.937 / W149 06.290

**15.0** Come to a bridged stream crossing and Twin Falls campsites. N61 10.158 / W149 08.435

**17.3** Cross Yakety Yak Creek on a bridge. N61 11.040 / W149 11.574

**17.8** Cross Icicle Creek. N61 11.161 / W149 12.011

**18.8** Cross a bridge over Dishwater Creek. N61 11.860 / W149 12.753

**19.1** Reach The Perch. N61 11.941/W149 13.345

**20.0** Reach Echo Bend, a designated campsite area. N61 11.797 / W149 14.931

**23.1** End the hike at Eagle River Nature Center. N61 14.037 / W149 16.255

# Hike Information

*Local information*

Anchorage Visitor Information Center, 546 West Fourth Avenue, Anchorage 99501; (907) 274-3531; www.anchorage.net

Alaska Department of Natural Resources Public Information Center, Atwood Building, 550 West Seventh Avenue, Suite 1260, Anchorage 99501; (907) 269-8400; www.dnr.state.ak.us/parks

Alaska Public Lands Information Center, 605 West Fourth Avenue, Suite 105, Anchorage 99501; (907) 271-2737; www.nps.gov/aplic

*Camping*

North: Eagle River Campground (907-345-5014); 10 miles from Anchorage on Glenn Highway at the Eagle River Loop/Hiland Road exit; nightly camping fee
South: Bird Creek Campground; (907) 345-5014; located southeast of Anchorage at Seward Highway Mile Marker 101; nightly camping fee

*Hike tours*

Friends of Eagle River (operators of Eagle River Nature Center); (907) 694-2108; e-mail: ERNC@alaska.net

# CROSSING STREAMS AND RIVERS

Many trails in Chugach State Park may lead you to unbridged streams or rivers. Cold, silty water can make crossing difficult and uncomfortable. There are several things you can do to make stream crossings safer, less stressful, and more comfortable.

- Study your route before you begin so that you know ahead of time that you will be crossing a stream.
- Bring spare clothing with you. Wear synthetics or quick-drying wool to cover your legs; avoid wearing cotton. Having warm and dry clothing on the other side can be a lifesaver. Cold water temperatures can cause numbness, misplaced steps, and falls.
- Don't try to cross without shoes or boots. Bring along an extra pair of old sneakers or sandals for crossing the stream.

Here are a few more tips to help you cross safely:

- Loosen your backpack straps and undo the waistband before you cross in case you need to drop your pack. Protect anything that could get wet.
- Choose your crossing site carefully. Some trails have designated crossing points between posts. At unmarked sites, choose the widest and most shallow place. Use a walking stick or hiking pole to test the water depth in front of you as you cross. A walking stick and poles will also provide extra stability.
- Walk slowly, concentrate on what you are doing while facing the far shore, and let your feet feel their way along the bottom as you cross. If there is more than one of you, cross together by linking arms, or link your arms around a walking stick and put the strongest person on the upstream side.
- Don't look down at the rushing water as you move across. Doing so can cause vertigo. Keep your eyes fixed on the exit point.
- Choose your time to cross, particularly when a river looks full or threatening. Glacial rivers are highest during midday when the sun is hottest. If possible, cross early in the day, when the water level is substantially lower.
- Fuel up ahead of time with snacks and liquids to stay well hydrated and help prevent hypothermia.

*Local organizations*

The Anchorage Adventurers Meetup Group; www.adventurers.meetup.com/109
Mountaineering Club of Alaska, 2633 Spenard Road, Anchorage 99503; (907) 272-1811; www.mcak.org

*North side of Crow Pass Trail at 3,500 feet*

## Local retailers

Recreational Equipment Inc. (REI), 1200 West Northern Lights Boulevard, Anchorage; (907) 272-4565; www.rei.com

Sportsman's Warehouse, 681 Old Seward Highway, Anchorage; (907) 644-1400; www.sportsmanswarehouse.com

Alaska Mountaineering and Hiking, 2633 Spenard Road, Anchorage; (907) 272-1811; www.alaskamountaineering.com

Cabelas, 155 W 104th, Anchorage; (907) 341-3400; www.cabelas.com/Stores/Anchorage

6th Avenue Outfitters, 520 W 6th Avenue, Anchorage; (907) 276-0233; www.6th avenueoutfitters.com

Bass Pro Shops, 3046 Mountain View Drive, Anchorage; (907) 330-5200; www.basspro.com/Anchorage

## Local events / attractions:

South: Girdwood Forest Fair, Girdwood; July
Alyeska Blueberry and Mountain Arts Festival, Alyeska Ski Resort; August
North: Alaskan Scottish Highland Games, Eagle River Lions Park, Anchorage; June
Bear Paw Festival, Eagle River; July
Alaska State Fair, Palmer; August and September
An Anchorage calendar of events can be found at www.anchorage.net/events.html.

# 32 Winner Creek Trail

The Winner Creek Trail is a favorite of many hikers. For one thing, it is different from most every other trail in Chugach State Park and the Anchorage area. Located about 40 miles south of Anchorage near Girdwood, the trail is actually the beginning of the northern tip of the temperate rain forest. The path goes through beautiful boreal forest composed of towering moss-covered Sitka spruce. The forest floor is also lined with moss, moss-covered decaying logs, and ferns. The highlights are two impressive gorges, one with a hand tram suspended by ropes and pulleys 100 feet or so above Glacier Creek.

**Start:** Behind Hotel Alyeska
**Distance:** 5.0 miles out and back
**Approximate hiking time:** 2–3 hours
**Difficulty:** Easy to moderate
**Elevation gain:** 400 feet
**Trail surface:** Paved and dirt
**Seasons:** Year-round
**Other trail users:** Walkers, runners, and cyclists; cross-country skiers in winter
**Canine compatibility:** Leashed dogs permitted

**Land status:** Chugach National Forest
**Nearest town:** Girdwood
**Fees and permits:** No fees or permits required
**Maps:** Imus Geographics Chugach State Park map (www.imusgeographics.com); USGS Anchorage
**Trail contacts:** Chugach National Forest, 3301 'C' Street, Suite 300, Anchorage 99503; (909) 743-9500; www.fs.fed.us/r10/chugach
**Special considerations:** None

**Finding the trailhead:** Heading south on the Seward Highway from Anchorage, travel approximately 40 miles to Mile Marker 90. Turn left onto the Alyeska Highway and head toward Girdwood. Travel 3 miles and turn left at the stop sign onto Arlberg Road. Follow Arlberg to its end at the Hotel Alyeska; park in visitor parking at the national forest signs.

## The Hike

Start the trail behind Hotel Alyeska; the main path is obvious. On this hike, like many others in the area, be sure to pack rain gear and mosquito repellent. It can very well be sunny in downtown Anchorage with intermittent or steady light rain here. Because of the rain forest conditions, portions of the path can be wet in addition to slippery boards on the trail. However, many parts of the trail are heavily graveled, making it easy traveling.

Don't let wet conditions discourage you from making this hike. This is a great scenic trail with a lot to offer, including a glimpse of Alaskan nature not seen on typical mountain trails. It is extremely well maintained and suitable for all levels of hikers.

You will immediately be amazed at the rain forest flora as you proceed up the trail from the hotel. At approximately the 1.5-mile point a sign indicates that you are 1.0 mile from the gorge. At about 2.1 miles the trail turns to the left. Straight ahead or slightly to the right, an old bridge crosses a creek. This is not the trail to the tram. Instead veer to the left, following the creek.

As you approach Winner Creek Gorge, you will hear the creek well in advance. The footbridge crossing the deep, narrow gorge with overhanging trees is impressive and dramatic, with the rock formations and pounding water on the rocks below. After crossing the gorge, the trail turns left, allowing you to look back at the gorge from a different perspective. Use caution at the edges of the trail if you are trying to photograph the bridge.

The hand tram is the next stop—and the final destination for most hikers. The tram consists of a steel cage that can hold two adults. You pull your way across Glacier Creek by means of a pulley system. It starts out with a slight downward dip toward the center of the creek with gravity on your side to get you in motion. It requires some substantial effort to pull you and your partner to the other side as the tram path heads slightly upward. If the trail is busy, you will need to wait your turn to use the tram for both your initial creek crossing and your return journey. The trail continues on the other side of Glacier Creek for 0.8 mile, providing access to Crow Creek Mine and to a small parking lot for an alternative approach to the tram.

*Winner Creek's temperate rainforest vegetation*

# Winner Creek Trail

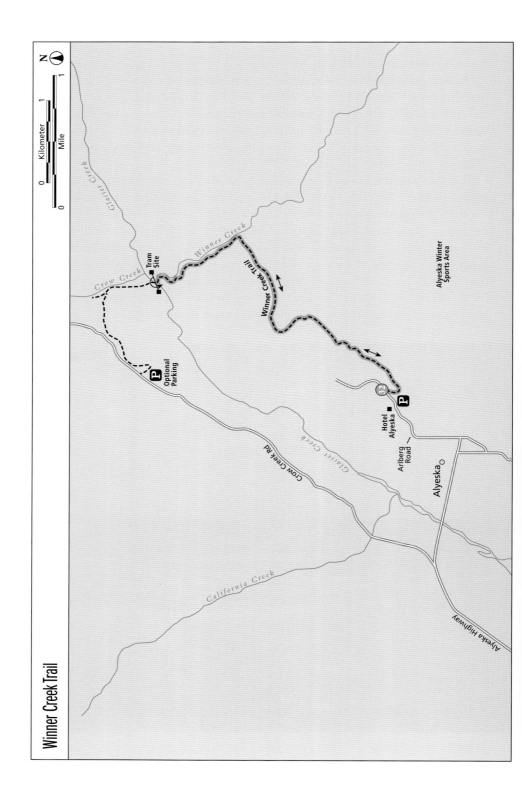

# Miles and Directions

**0.0**  Start the trail behind Hotel Alyeska. N60 58.191 / W149 05.706

**0.5**  Cross a small bridge over a creek. N60 58.258 / W149 05.526

**0.8**  Bikes stop at this point. N60 58.603 / W149 05.136

**1.5**  Reach a sign that notes you are 1.0 mile from the tram and first gorge. N60 58.966 / W149 04.065

**2.1**  Turn left at the fork. Ignore the path that slants right to an old bridge. N60 59.355 / W149 04.589

**2.3**  Cross a footbridge over Winner Creek Gorge. N60 59.469 / W149 04.587

**2.5**  Arrive at the hand tram over Glacier Creek. This is your turnaround point. N60 59.500 / W149 04.674 (Option: Use the hand tram to cross the creek and continue 0.8 mile to the alternative parking lot on Crow Creek Road. N60 59.565 / W149 05.946)

**5.0**  Arrive back at the trailhead behind Hotel Alyeska. N60 58.191/W149 05.706

# Hike Information

## Local information

Anchorage Visitor Information Center, 546 West Fourth Avenue, Anchorage 99501; (907) 274-3531; www.anchorage.net

Alaska Department of Natural Resources Public Information Center, Atwood Building, 550 West Seventh Avenue, Suite 1260, Anchorage 99501; (907) 269-8400; www.dnr.state.ak.us/parks

Alaska Public Lands Information Center, 605 West Fourth Avenue, Suite 105, Anchorage 99501; (907) 271-2737; www.nps.gov/aplic

## Camping

North: Eagle River Campground (907-345-5014); 10 miles from Anchorage on Glenn Highway at the Eagle River Loop/Hiland Road exit; nightly camping fee

South: Bird Creek Campground; (907) 345-5014; located southeast of Anchorage at Seward Highway Mile Marker 101; nightly camping fee

Hike tours: Friends of Eagle River (operators of Eagle River Nature Center); (907) 694-2108; e-mail: ERNC@alaska.net

## Local organizations

The Anchorage Adventurers Meetup Group; www.adventurers.meetup.com/109

Mountaineering Club of Alaska, 2633 Spenard Road, Anchorage 99503; (907) 272-1811; www.mcak.org

## Local retailers

Recreational Equipment Inc. (REI), 1200 West Northern Lights Boulevard, Anchorage; (907) 272-4565; www.rei.com

Sportsman's Warehouse, 681 Old Seward Highway, Anchorage; (907) 644-1400; www
.sportsmanswarehouse.com

Alaska Mountaineering and Hiking, 2633 Spenard Road, Anchorage; (907) 272-
1811; www.alaskamountaineering.com

Cabelas, 155 W 104th, Anchorage; (907) 341-3400; www.cabelas.com/Stores/
Anchorage

6th Avenue Outfitters, 520 W 6th Avenue, Anchorage; (907) 276-0233; www.6th
avenueoutfitters.com

Bass Pro Shops, 3046 Mountain View Drive, Anchorage; (907) 330-5200; www
.basspro.com/Anchorage

*Local events/attractions:*

South: Girdwood Forest Fair, Girdwood; July
Alyeska Blueberry and Mountain Arts Festival, Alyeska Ski Resort; August
North: Alaskan Scottish Highland Games, Eagle River Lions Park, Anchorage; June
Bear Paw Festival, Eagle River; July
Alaska State Fair, Palmer; August and September
An Anchorage calendar of events can be found at www.anchorage.net/events.html.

◀  *Winner Creek tram across gorge*

# 33 Potter Marsh Wildlife Viewing Boardwalk Trail

The Potter Marsh Wildlife Viewing Boardwalk Trail is a must-do stop for photography, wildlife and wild bird viewing in south Anchorage. The 534-acre marsh is located at the south end of the Anchorage Coastal Wildlife Refuge. It is one of the most accessible and scenic wildlife viewing areas in Anchorage. Moose, black and brown bear, bald eagles, songbirds, waterfowl, shorebirds and salmon are common sightings throughout the year. The boardwalk sits next to the scenic Turnagain Arm upon a beautiful mountain backdrop. Upon arrival, you will find a large paved parking area, restroom facilities and easily traveled wooden boardwalk with benches, several viewing platforms and spotting scopes for your use. Bring your binoculars.

**Start:** Trailhead kiosk is located at the edge of parking lot
**Distance:** 1.1-mile out and back
**Approximate hiking time:** 1 hour
**Difficulty:** Easy
**Elevation gain:** 75 feet
**Trail surface:** Wooden boardwalk
**Seasons:** Year-round.
**Other trail users:** Birders, nature trips, school classrooms
**Canine compatibility:** no dogs allowed on boardwalk, parking lot only

**Land status:** Anchorage Coastal Wildlife Refuge
**Nearest town:** Anchorage
**Fees and permits:** No fees required
**Maps:** Imus Geographics, Chugach State Park Hillside Trail System: Alaska Department of Natural Resources
**Trail contacts:** Alaska Department of Fish and Game, Division of Wildlife Conservation, 333 Raspberry Road, Anchorage, AK 99518-1599, 907-267-2189
**Special considerations:** Wheel chair friendly, good wildlife viewing area, bathrooms on site

**Finding the trailhead:** The Potter Marsh Wildlife Viewing Boardwalk Trail trailhead is conveniently located south of Anchorage on the New Seward Highway. Coming from downtown Anchorage, head east on 6th Avenue. Turn right onto Gambell Street and travel 4.0 miles. Gambell Street will join AK-1. Continue on for 5.6 miles. Turn left onto East 154th Avenue across from the Rabbit Creek Shooting Park. Continue 0.03 miles to destination and the large paved parking area.

## The Hike

The Potter Marsh Wildlife Viewing Boardwalk Trail begins at the trailhead at the east side of the parking area with an option to travel either left or right. Left will take you to an observation deck with an optional loop trail back to the parking lot about halfway to the end. The opposite direction parallels the New Seward Highway and overlooks the marsh and the Chugach Mountains. This side along the highway can be very windy on some days, so dressing accordingly will be helpful. The Alaska

*Chugach Mountain Backdrop*

Department of Fish and Game maintains this site and will generally have a volunteer host available to answer questions during the summer months.

The site is open year-around, however during certain seasons you will view different types of wildlife. Starting in late April running through September, Canada geese, canvasback ducks, red-necked pharlopes, horned and red-necked grebes, northern pintails, and northern harriers will be found using the marsh area.

The summer months of late May through August when the spring and fall migrations occur, gulls, arctic terns and shorebirds are very prevalent. Trumpeter swans will also be seen.

When you walk the boardwalk to the left toward the mountain side, you will come to Rabbit Creek which flows directly underneath the boardwalk into the marsh. This is a good location to see several species of salmon such as chinook, coho and humpbacks from May to August. Continue on the boardwalk and take in the views, read the various interpretive panels along the way and look for other species of wildlife as you proceed to the end. Moose and an occasional bear are often seen. At the far end of the boardwalk, a pair of binoculars will help you to spot eagle nests in the tops of the large cottonwood along the bluff. Look for the white heads up in the treetops. Continue to look for various birds and wildlife as you head back toward the trailhead, as the wildlife sightings change rapidly. When you have finished the boardwalk, you can drive south on the New Seward Highway for about one quarter of a mile. There is a small pull-over on the marsh side of the road. This is another good location for waterfowl viewing, nesting birds and photography. Once again, keep your binoculars handy.

## Miles and Directions

**0.0**  Start at the large kiosk trailhead in parking lot and turn left. N61° 04.670' W149° 49.631'

**0.2**  Arrive at end of boardwalk and large viewing platform. N61° 04.676' W149° 49.323'

**0.3**  End of boardwalk along Seward Highway. N61° 04.460' W149° 49.704'

**0.4**  Arrive back at trailhead and continue on boardwalk toward Seward Highway.

**1.1**  Arrive back at parking lot. N61° 04.670' W149° 49.631'

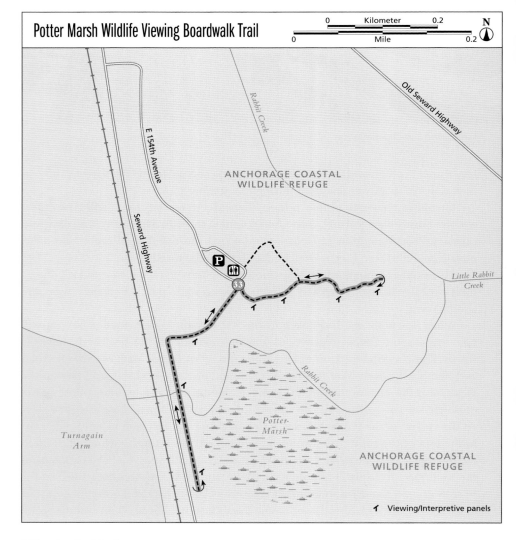

Potter Marsh Wildlife Viewing Boardwalk Trail

# Hike Information

*Local information*

Anchorage Visitor Information Center, 546 West Fourth Avenue, Anchorage 99501; (907) 274-3531; www.anchorage.net

Alaska Department of Natural Resources Public Information Center, Atwood Building, 550 West Seventh Avenue, Suite 1260, Anchorage 99501; (907) 269-8400; www.dnr.state.ak.us/parks

Alaska Public Lands Information Center, 605 West Fourth Avenue, Suite 105, Anchorage 99501; (907) 271-2737; www.nps.gov/aplic

Alaska Department of Fish and Game, Division of Wildlife Conservation, 333 Raspberry Road, Anchorage, AK 99518; (907)267-2189. www. http://www.adfg.alaska.gov/index.cfm?adfg=anchoragecoastal.contacts

*Camping*

Bird Creek Campground; (907) 345-5014; located southeast of Anchorage at Mile Marker 101 on Seward Highway; nightly camping fee

*Local organizations*

The Anchorage Adventurers Meetup Group; www.adventurers.meetup.com/109

Mountaineering Club of Alaska, 2633 Spenard Road, Anchorage 99503; (907) 272-1811; www.mcak.org

*Local retailers*

Recreational Equipment Inc. (REI), 1200 West Northern Lights Boulevard, Anchorage; (907) 272-4565; www.rei.com

Sportsman's Warehouse, 681 Old Seward Highway, Anchorage; (907) 644-1400; www.sportsmanswarehouse.com

Alaska Mountaineering and Hiking, 2633 Spenard Road, Anchorage; (907) 272-1811; www.alaskamountaineering.com

Cabelas, 155 W 104th, Anchorage; (907) 341-3400; www.cabelas.com/Stores/Anchorage

6th Avenue Outfitters, 520 W 6th Avenue, Anchorage; (907) 276-0233; www.6thavenueoutfitters.com

Bass Pro Shops, 3046 Mountain View Drive, Anchorage; (907) 330-5200; www.basspro.com/Anchorage

*Local events/attractions*

Girdwood Forest Fair, Girdwood; July

Alyeska Blueberry and Mountain Arts Festival, Alyeska Ski Resort; August

An Anchorage calendar of events can be found at www.anchorage.net/events.html.

# Anchorage Urban Trails

The trail system within the city limits of Anchorage is nationally recognized for its excellence. More than 120 miles of paved trails connect city parks and greenways that include salmon-rich streams and prime habitat for moose, bears, and other Alaskan wildlife. Because of its lower elevation, this trail system is enjoyed by locals all year long.

▶ **More than 120 miles of paved trails connect city parks and greenways that include salmon-rich streams and prime habitat for moose, bears, and other Alaskan wildlife.**

These trails are mostly level, connecting the north side of Anchorage to the south side and the east side to the west. There are numerous access points on all the trails, allowing Anchorage residents to use them for commuting to work, school, and community events.

However, don't let the fact that you are within the Anchorage city limits fool you into thinking you won't encounter wildlife. Many of the trails follow salmon creeks that provide food for bears. Always be "bear aware" on the trails around Anchorage—and keep an eye out for the many moose that also make Anchorage their home..

*Moose will commonly use Alaska trails*
Caitlin Romm-Tyson

# 34 Earthquake Park/Inside the Slide Trail

On Good Friday March 27, 1964, an earthquake with a magnitude of 9.2 lasting 4 minutes and 38 seconds hit the Anchorage region. It was recorded as the largest earthquake to shake North America and the second most powerful earthquake in the world. This park shows the after-effect of that Great Alaskan Earthquake and how it permanently damaged Anchorage and Southcentral Alaska. The interpretive panels along the trail tell the story about this earthquake and provide some astounding facts and figures of what happened in 1964.

Within Earthquake Park is a short loop dirt trail called Inside the Slide. At the intersection of the Earthquake Park Trail and the Tony Knowles Coastal Trail, head north about 0.2 miles. Here you will find the well-marked trailhead on your right. The topography of this area shows how the land moved and was permanently altered during this historic earthquake. Both short hikes are fun and easy and deliver some unforgettable Alaskan and national history—in addition to the occasional Anchorage moose that might be sharing the trail.

**Start:** Paved parking lot on W. Northern Lights Blvd/Point Woronzof Drive

**Distance:** 0.75 miles out and back. Inside the Slide: 0.5 mile loop

**Approximate hiking time:** 45 minutes to 1 hour

**Difficulty:** Easy

**Elevation gain:** 321 feet

**Trail surface:** Paved, dirt

**Seasons:** Year-round

**Other trail users:** Hikers, bicycles

**Canine compatibility:** Leashed dogs permitted

**Land status:** Anchorage Municipality

**Nearest town:** Anchorage

**Fees and permits:** No parking fees or permits required

**Maps:** Anchorage Trail and Parks Map; http://munimaps.muni.org/trails/reference.htm

**Trail contacts:** Anchorage Parks Foundation; www.anchorageparks.org

**Special considerations:** None

**Finding the trailhead:** Coming from downtown Anchorage, head west on West 5th Avenue. Turn left onto L Street and continue onto Minnesota Drive for 1.0 mile. Turn right onto Northern Lights Boulevard and travel for 2.1 miles. Destination will be on your right.

## The Hike

This is a popular stop for hikers, runners, walkers and visitors. Upon arrival to the large paved parking lot, you will find a large visible trailhead at the far end of the lot. This short-paved easy trail has several interpretive panels along the way and ends at a spacious open area with an exhibit and viewing deck at the water's edge of Turnagain Arm. There is a very short loop trail going around the monument. From there, head

*Inside the Slide Trail lined with horsetail vegetation*

back out to the Coastal trail, turn left and hike about 0.2 miles. The large open area off the paved trail to your right is the Inside the Slide trailhead.

Inside the Slide is an impressive area of land that was moved by the earthquake of 1964. This mass of land literally slid more than 100 feet and the elevation was 25 to 40 feet higher. Within this immediate area is a series of hidden ponds and rolling hills. Be sure to follow the well-marked signs along the way. There are numerous side trails in this area and it is easy to get off course if you don't. The rolling and meandering trail is easy with ten interpretive panels along the path. This area is a natural attractant for waterfowl and other types of wildlife because of the vegetation and numerous low wet areas.

Begin the trail at the trailhead. Follow the orange blazes and be sure to make an immediate left turn that goes up a short steep hill. This immediate turn is just before a small boardwalk and a very prominent trail that continues forward. You do not want to travel on this trail beyond the bridge. If you crossed the bridge you missed your turn and you'll miss the entire trail.

After going over the hill, continue onward and watch for the interpretive panels and orange trail markers throughout the hike. The trail is easy to follow at this point. You will cross a series of small bridges every several hundred feet throughout the entire trail. The trail, being wetland and a series of small ponds, is a haven for mosquitos. You will want to prepare for this accordingly.

# Miles and Directions

**0.0** Start at Earthquake Park trailhead in parking lot. N61° 11.780' W149° 58.653'

**0.3** Cross intersection of Coastal Trail and follow short loop back to Coastal Trail. N61° 11.880' W149° 58.780'

**0.4** Turn left onto Coastal Trail. N61° 11.880' W149° 58.780'

**0.6** Arrive at Into the Slide Trailhead. N61° 11.838' W149° 58.460

**0.7** Cross small bridge. N61° 11.799' W149° 58.300'

**0.8** Bridge crossing. N61° 11.818' W149° 58.245'

**0.9** Overlook of area. N61° 11.825' W149° 58.099'0

**1.0** Cross another small bridge. N61° 11.846' W149° 58.272'

**1.1** Small bridge crossing over wet area. N61° 11.829' W149° 58.408'

**1.2** End back at trailhead. N61° 11.835' W149° 58.448'

# Hike Information

## Local information

Anchorage Visitor Information Center, 546 West Fourth Avenue, Anchorage 99501; (907) 274-3531; www.anchorage.net

Alaska Department of Natural Resources Public Information Center, Atwood Building, 550 West Seventh Avenue, Suite 1260, Anchorage 99501; (907) 269-8400; www.dnr.state.ak.us/parks

Alaska Public Lands Information Center, 605 West Fourth Avenue, Suite 105, Anchorage 99501; (907) 271-2737; www.nps.gov/aplic

## Camping

North: Eagle River Campground (907-345-5014); 10 miles from Anchorage on Glenn Highway at the Eagle River Loop/Hiland Road exit; nightly camping fee

South: Bird Creek Campground; (907) 345-5014; located southeast of Anchorage at Seward Highway Mile Marker 101; nightly camping fee

## Local organizations

The Anchorage Adventurers Meetup Group; www.adventurers.meetup.com/109

Mountaineering Club of Alaska, 2633 Spenard Road, Anchorage 99503; (907) 272-1811; www.mcak.org

## Local retailers

Recreational Equipment Inc. (REI), 1200 West Northern Lights Boulevard, Anchorage; (907) 272-4565; www.rei.com

Sportsman's Warehouse, 681 Old Seward Highway, Anchorage; (907) 644-1400; www.sportsmanswarehouse.com

# Earthquake Park / Inside The Slide Trail

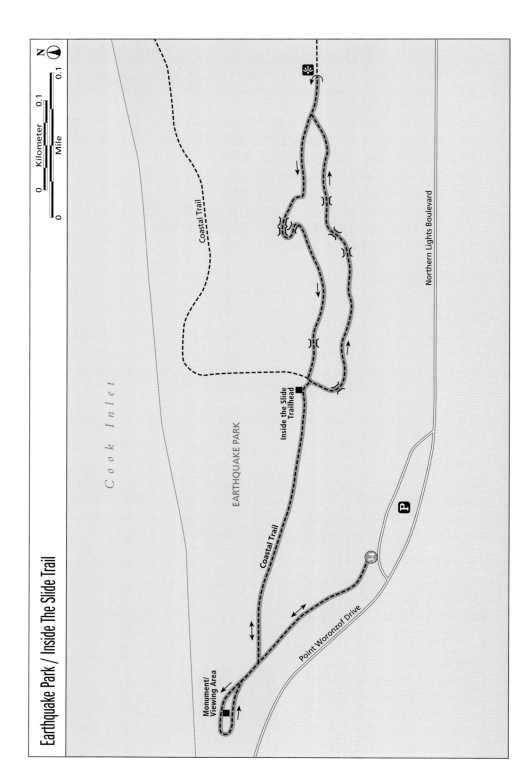

Cook Inlet

EARTHQUAKE PARK

Coastal Trail

Coastal Trail

Inside the Slide
Trailhead

Monument/
Viewing Area

Point Woronzof Drive

Northern Lights Boulevard

N

Kilometer
0        0.1

Mile
0        0.1

*Historical stop in Earthquake Park*

Alaska Mountaineering and Hiking, 2633 Spenard Road, Anchorage; (907) 272-1811; www.alaskamountaineering.com

Cabelas, 155 W 104th, Anchorage; (907) 341-3400; www.cabelas.com/Stores/Anchorage

6th Avenue Outfitters, 520 W 6th Avenue, Anchorage; (907) 276-0233; www.6th avenueoutfitters.com

Bass Pro Shops, 3046 Mountain View Drive, Anchorage; (907) 330-5200; www .basspro.com/Anchorage

*Local events/attractions*

South: Girdwood Forest Fair, Girdwood; July

Alyeska Blueberry and Mountain Arts Festival, Alyeska Ski Resort; August

North: Alaskan Scottish Highland Games, Eagle River Lions Park, Anchorage; June

Bear Paw Festival, Eagle River; July

Alaska State Fair, Palmer; August and September

An Anchorage calendar of events can be found at www.anchorage.net/events.html.

# 35 Tony Knowles Coastal Trail

The Tony Knowles Coastal Trail was named for former Alaska governor Tony Knowles, who served from 1981 to 1987. One of four greenbelt trails located in Anchorage, the trail connects the north part of downtown to Kincaid Park in the south.

The multipurpose trail engages various users including cyclists, hikers, dog walkers, roller skaters, runners, and winter skiers and is a crowded trail, particularly during the summer months. The trail spans 11.0 miles one-way and provides extraordinary views of downtown Anchorage, the Chugach Mountains, Denali (Mount McKinley), Mount Susitna (Sleeping Lady), and Fire Island. You are also very likely to encounter moose on the trail. The entire trail is paved and mostly easy, other than the last mile, which has a steady hill to climb as you approach Kincaid Park.

**Start:** Intersection of Second Avenue and H Street in downtown Anchorage
**Distance:** 22.0 miles out and back
**Approximate hiking time:** 10–12 hours
**Difficulty:** Easy to moderate over both flat and hilly terrain
**Elevation gain:** 117 feet
**Trail surface:** Paved
**Seasons:** Year-round
**Other trail users:** Walkers, runners, and cyclists; cross-country skiers in winter

**Canine compatibility:** Leashed dogs permitted
**Land status:** Anchorage municipality
**Nearest town:** Anchorage
**Fees and permits:** No fees or permits required
**Maps:** Anchorage Trail and Parks Map; http://munimaps.muni.org/trails/reference.htm
**Trail contacts:** Anchorage Parks Foundation; www.anchorageparks.org
**Special considerations:** None

**Finding the trailhead:** The Tony Knowles Coastal Trail technically begins in downtown Anchorage at the intersection of Second Avenue and H Street. However, more people begin the trail at Elderberry Park at Fifth Avenue and N Street because parking is more readily available at this location. To find Second and H Street, follow Fifth Avenue west through downtown Anchorage. Turn north onto H Street, which becomes Christiansen Drive. Head downhill and turn left at the next intersection, which is Second Avenue; the trailhead is just ahead. To go to Elderberry Park, continue west on Fifth Avenue toward Cook Inlet. Continue across L Street and head down a steep hill. Parking is on your right.

## The Hike

The Tony Knowles Coastal Trail is probably the best-known multipurpose trail in the Anchorage area and is considered a gem when it comes to trails. It basically follows along Cook Inlet in a north-south direction and connects downtown Anchorage and Kincaid Park. Expect to encounter various types of wildlife along the trail. Moose in particular are very common and should be taken very seriously when they are on or

*View of Westchester Lagoon from Coastal Trail*

near the trail. Be sure to slow down, stop, and even wait until the trail is clear. Moose are not tame and can be very dangerous.

The trail is easy to follow, and most people who want to complete the entire trail out and back travel by bike. If you're ambitious, though, it can be done as a long day hike.

Beginning the trail at Second Avenue and H Street, the Alaska Railroad and the Port of Anchorage are on your right. Cross a wooden bridge and follow the path toward the water. You quickly come to Elderberry Park on your right and the historic Oscar Anderson House. The trail heads slightly downhill and through a tunnel. This is a busy trail, and it is important to stay on your side and use caution in blind spots.

As you ascend slightly up and wind to the left, there are good views of the mud-flats and Point McKenzie across the water. The trail goes through two tunnels and passes the west side of Westchester Lagoon. It turns and crosses a bridge over a wet-land area and then winds along the water's edge, with some good opportunities to view various species of wading birds and waterfowl.

During the next several miles, you will have several opportunities to see some of Anchorage's best parks. Earthquake Park is just before the 4.0-mile point. This area dropped more than 30 feet during the famous 9.2-scale Good Friday earthquake of March 1964. The trail winds through the park, which has several reader boards and a monument. Just beyond Earthquake Park is Airport Park, with extraordinary views of the downtown Anchorage skyline and mountain views across Knik Arm.

Point Woronzof is a bit more than a mile up the trail. This is a popular family stop-ping place with a beach and bluffs to explore and great views of Sleeping Lady and,

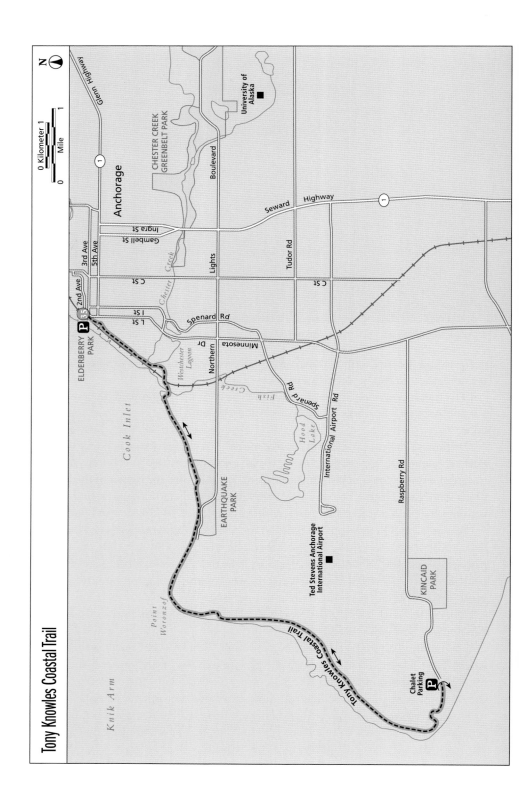

# Tony Knowles Coastal Trail

Knik Arm

Cook Inlet

Point Woronzof

EARTHQUAKE PARK

Tony Knowles Coastal Trail

Chalet Parking

KINCAID PARK

Ted Stevens Anchorage International Airport

Hood Lake

Fish Creek

Westchester Lagoon

ELDERBERRY PARK

2nd Ave

3rd Ave

5th Ave

Anchorage

Chester Creek

Gambell St

Ingra St

Lights

L St

C St

Spenard Rd

Northern Dr

Minnesota Dr

Spenard Rd

International Airport Rd

Raspberry Rd

Tudor Rd

C St

Seward Highway

CHESTER CREEK GREENBELT PARK

Boulevard

University of Alaska

Glenn Highway

N

0 Kilometer 1
0 Mile 1

on clear days, Mount McKinley. From this point on, as you approach Kincaid Park, the trail is heavily forested. About 2.6 miles beyond Point Woronzof, you will come to a bridge crossing over a small gorge. All along, you can't help but notice the airline jets and Ted Stevens International Airport. For approximately the last mile follow a steep, steady incline as you come to trail's end at the chalet at Kincaid Park.

## Miles and Directions

**0.0** Start at Second Avenue and H Street in downtown Anchorage. N61 13.234 / W149 53.851

**0.3** Pass Elderberry Park on your right and the historic Oscar Anderson House and go through a tunnel. N61 12.615 / W149 55.370

**1.1** Pass under the Alaska Railroad and cross a bridge; turn right to stay on the trail. N61 12.529 / W149 55.370 (Option: Turn left to pick up the Chester Creek Trail.)

**1.5** Cross a bridge over a marshy area, go through a tunnel, and head toward Fish Creek. N61 12.340 / W149 55.951

**2.5** Arrive at Lyn Ary Park. N61 12.176 / W149 56.890

**3.6** Reach a large four-way intersection and archway at Earthquake Park. N61 11.878 / W149 58.768 (Option: Turn left to reach the Earthquake Park parking lot. N61 11.778 / W149 58.653)

**4.1** Pass Airport Park and a large gravel parking lot with views of the Anchorage skyline. N61 11.930 / W149 59.567

**5.2** Arrive at Point Woronzof. N61 12.064 / W150 01.196

**7.8** Cross a bridge over a small gorge. N61 10.372 / W150 02.952

**11.0** Reach trail's end at Kincaid Park. Unless you have arranged for a shuttle, retrace your steps. N61 09.213 / W150 03.319

**22.0** Arrive back at the Second Avenue and H Street trailhead. N61 13.234 / W149 53.851

## Hike Information

### Local information

Anchorage Visitor Information Center, 546 West Fourth Avenue, Anchorage 99501; (907) 274-3531; www.anchorage.net

Alaska Department of Natural Resources Public Information Center, Atwood Building, 550 West Seventh Avenue, Suite 1260, Anchorage 99501; (907) 269-8400; www.dnr.state.ak.us/parks

Alaska Public Lands Information Center, 605 West Fourth Avenue, Suite 105, Anchorage 99501; (907) 271-2737; www.nps.gov/aplic

### Camping

North: Eagle River Campground (907-345-5014); 10 miles from Anchorage on Glenn Highway at the Eagle River Loop/Hiland Road exit; nightly camping fee

South: Bird Creek Campground; (907) 345-5014; located southeast of Anchorage at Seward Highway Mile Marker 101; nightly camping fee

Hike tours: Friends of Eagle River (operators of Eagle River Nature Center); (907) 694-2108; e-mail: ERNC@alaska.net

### Local organizations

The Anchorage Adventurers Meetup Group; www.adventurers.meetup.com/109

Mountaineering Club of Alaska, 2633 Spenard Road, Anchorage 99503; (907) 272-1811; www.mcak.org

### Local retailers

Recreational Equipment Inc. (REI), 1200 West Northern Lights Boulevard, Anchorage; (907) 272-4565; www.rei.com

Sportsman's Warehouse, 681 Old Seward Highway, Anchorage; (907) 644-1400; www.sportsmanswarehouse.com

Alaska Mountaineering and Hiking, 2633 Spenard Road, Anchorage; (907) 272-1811; www.alaskamountaineering.com

Cabelas, 155 W 104th, Anchorage; (907) 341-3400; www.cabelas.com/Stores/Anchorage

6th Avenue Outfitters, 520 W 6th Avenue, Anchorage; (907) 276-0233; www.6thavenueoutfitters.com

Bass Pro Shops, 3046 Mountain View Drive, Anchorage; (907) 330-5200; www.basspro.com/Anchorage

### Local events/attractions

South: Girdwood Forest Fair, Girdwood; July

Alyeska Blueberry and Mountain Arts Festival, Alyeska Ski Resort; August

North: Alaskan Scottish Highland Games, Eagle River Lions Park, Anchorage; June

Bear Paw Festival, Eagle River; July

Alaska State Fair, Palmer; August and September

An Anchorage calendar of events can be found at www.anchorage.net/events.html.

*Multi-use trail*

# 36 Lanie Fleischer Chester Creek Trail

Four main trails in the Anchorage area are considered part of the Anchorage Green-belt: the Tony Knowles Coastal Trail, the Campbell Creek Trail, the Lanie Fleischer Chester Creek Trail and the Ship Creek Trail. This is another multipurpose trail that is heavily used throughout the year. The trail begins at the popular Westchester Lagoon and traverses toward the Chugach Mountains in the east. The easy paved path affords great scenery and a variety of wildlife-viewing opportunities along the way as it connects many major sectors of the city.

**Start:** Margaret Eagan Sullivan Park
**Distance:** 10.2 miles out and back
**Approximate hiking time:** 5-6 hours
**Difficulty:** Easy
**Elevation gain:** Negligible
**Trail surface:** Paved
**Seasons:** Year-round
**Other trail users:** Walkers, runners, and cyclists; cross-country skiers in winter

**Canine compatibility:** Leashed dogs permitted
**Land status:** Anchorage municipality
**Nearest town:** Anchorage
**Fees and permits:** No fees or permits required
**Maps:** Anchorage Trail and Parks Map; http://munimaps.muni.org/trails/reference.htm
**Trail contacts:** Anchorage Parks Foundation; www.anchorageparks.org.
**Special considerations:** None

**Finding the trailhead:** Coming from downtown Anchorage, head south on L Street, which becomes Minnesota Drive. Turn right onto 15th Avenue; Westchester Lagoon is straight ahead. There is plenty of parking, with two lots along the street side of the lagoon, as well as restroom facilities. The lots do fill up during the summer months, though. The trailhead is located on the north side of Westchester Lagoon at Margaret Eagan Sullivan Park. The trail begins at the intersection with the Tony Knowles Coastal Trail at the northwest side of the lagoon, next to a set of benches.

## The Hike

You can expect plenty of company on any given day on the Chester Creek Trail. It begins at the Westchester Lagoon, bordering the Knik Arm—a popular recreational area for picnicking, playing Frisbee, walking the dog, bird-watching, running, biking, and just getting out and enjoying the outdoors. Because the easterly bound trail connects to many of the parks in Anchorage, the University of Alaska and Pacific University, and medical centers along the way, it is used by many local commuters.

The trail starts at the intersection with the Tony Knowles Coastal Trail. Turn left at the intersection and head eastward along the paved path, following the shoreline of the lagoon. Veer left at the first fork and head through the tunnel that takes you under Minnesota Drive. (If you continue straight ahead, you will arrive at a parking lot and the Westchester Waterfowl Sanctuary.) Veer left again and go through another tunnel taking you under Spenard Road. Continue for slightly less than 0.3 mile and pass under Arctic Boulevard; Valley of the Moon Park is on your right. Just before

*Trail closely follows Chester Creek*

going under C Street, you will see the community gardens on your right. Pass under C Street, veer right to cross a small bridge, and immediately on your right is the small park commonly known as Gorilla Park.

At approximately 1.5 miles pass under A Street and by several access points to the Sullivan Arena on your left. The trail heads through a birch-spruce forest and crosses a bridge at approximately 1.9 miles. About 0.25 mile beyond the bridge, pass under the Seward Highway, cross another bridge, pass Woodside Park, and traverse through stands of birch and spruce and a wetland area.

Follow the signs pointing toward Goose Lake. At approximately the 3.0-mile point, there's a resting bench where you can sit and appreciate the natural area and flowing waters of Chester Creek. Just beyond the rest area, arrive at a small pond on your right and then cross the creek again.

Follow the trail under the Lake Otis Parkway and pass Davenport Field. Travel another 0.5 mile and go left at the fork toward Tikishla Park. This is approximately 3.75 miles from the trailhead. Turn right just beyond the park and head over the bridge toward Goose Lake. Cross another bridge, take the fork to the right, and climb slightly uphill and over Northern Lights Boulevard. The trail T's after approximately another 0.2 mile. Turn right at this intersection. (Turning left will take you to Russian Jack Park.) Continue downhill to arrive at Goose Lake and the pavilion. Travel past the pavilion and lake and into the birch-spruce forest at a slight incline.

After approximately 0.75 mile come to the University of Alaska parking garage and then to the intersection of Alumni Loop and UAA Drive. Turn left onto UAA Drive and then left again onto Providence Drive. The trail continues into the forest and past Mosquito Lake on your left. Cross Providence/University Drive onto Elmore Road. Follow the sidewalk and, just before reaching Tudor Road, turn left uphill to the crosswalk that will take you safely across Tudor. Follow the trail downhill, where it turns to the right and brings you to the Campbell Creek Trail trailhead.

# Lanie Fleischer Chester Creek Trail

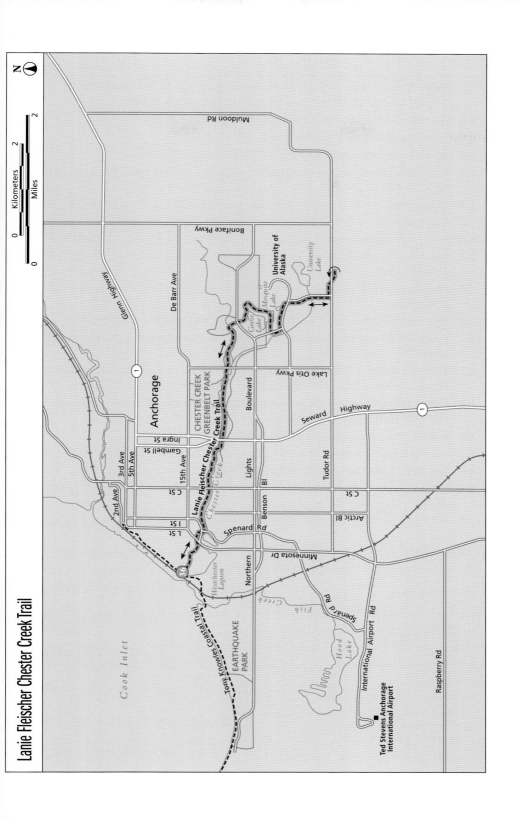

# Miles and Directions

**0.0** Start in Margaret Eagan Sullivan Park at the intersection with the Tony Knowles Coastal Trail. Turn left onto the Chester Creek Trail. N61 12.516 / W149 55.339

**0.4** Veer left at the trail fork. N61 12.348 / W149 54.783

**0.7** Pass under Minnesota Drive. N61 12.288 / W149 54.240

**1.0** The trail travels under Arctic Boulevard. N61 12.304 / W149 53.885

**1.3** Pass under C Street. The community gardens are on your right just before the tunnel. N61 12.211 / W49 53.244

**1.4** Cross a bridge and travel past Gorilla Park on your right. N61 12.204 / W149 53.171

**1.5** Pass under A Street; Sullivan Arena is on your left. N61 12.198 / W149 53.001

**1.9** Cross a bridge after walking through a birch-spruce forest. N61 12.153 / W149 52.536

**2.2** Pass under the Seward Highway, cross a bridge, and go past Woodside Park. N61 12.096 / W149 52.106

**3.0** Come to a bench on the left by Chester Creek, where you can sit and rest. N61 12.067 / W149 50.873

**3.1** Pass a small pond and cross a bridge over the creek. N61 12.030 / W149 50.542

**3.2** Pass under the Lake Otis Parkway; Davenport Field is on your right. N61 12.035 / W 149 50.254

**3.75** Turn left at the fork and travel past Tikishla Park. Shortly after the park, turn right toward Goose Lake. N61 11.955 / W149 49.524

**3.8** Cross a bridge. Turn right at the trail fork and head uphill and over Northern Lights Boulevard. N61 11.978 / W149 49.460

**4.0** When the trail T's, turn right. (Option: Turn left to go to Russian Jack Park.)

**4.1** Arrive at Goose Lake and pavilion. N61 11.814 / W149 49.183

**4.9** Turn left onto UAA Drive. N61 11.487 / W149 49.394

**5.1** Reach the trailhead for Campbell Creek Trail, your turnaround point. N61 10.812 / W149 48.046

**10.2** Arrive back at the trailhead. N61 12.516 / W149 55.339

# Hike Information

## Local information

Anchorage Visitor Information Center, 546 West Fourth Avenue, Anchorage 99501; (907) 274-3531; www.anchorage.net

Alaska Department of Natural Resources Public Information Center, Atwood Building, 550 West Seventh Avenue, Suite 1260, Anchorage 99501; (907) 269-8400; www.dnr.state.ak.us/parks

Alaska Public Lands Information Center, 605 West Fourth Avenue, Suite 105, Anchorage 99501; (907) 271-2737; www.nps.gov/aplic

## Camping

North: Eagle River Campground (907-345-5014); 10 miles from Anchorage on Glenn Highway at the Eagle River Loop/Hiland Road exit; nightly camping fee
South: Bird Creek Campground; (907) 345-5014; located southeast of Anchorage at Seward Highway Mile Marker 101; nightly camping fee
Hike tours: Friends of Eagle River (operators of Eagle River Nature Center); (907) 694-2108; e-mail: ERNC@alaska.net

## Local organizations

The Anchorage Adventurers Meetup Group; www.adventurers.meetup.com/109
Mountaineering Club of Alaska, 2633 Spenard Road, Anchorage 99503; (907) 272-1811; www.mcak.org

## Local retailers

Recreational Equipment Inc. (REI), 1200 West Northern Lights Boulevard, Anchorage; (907) 272-4565; www.rei.com
Sportsman's Warehouse, 681 Old Seward Highway, Anchorage; (907) 644-1400; www.sportsmanswarehouse.com
Alaska Mountaineering and Hiking, 2633 Spenard Road, Anchorage; (907) 272-1811; www.alaskamountaineering.com
Cabelas, 155 W 104th, Anchorage; (907) 341-3400; www.cabelas.com/Stores/Anchorage
6th Avenue Outfitters, 520 W 6th Avenue, Anchorage; (907) 276-0233; www.6thavenueoutfitters.com
Bass Pro Shops, 3046 Mountain View Drive, Anchorage; (907) 330-5200; www.basspro.com/Anchorage

## Local events/attractions

South: Girdwood Forest Fair, Girdwood; July
Alyeska Blueberry and Mountain Arts Festival, Alyeska Ski Resort; August
North: Alaskan Scottish Highland Games, Eagle River Lions Park, Anchorage; June
Bear Paw Festival, Eagle River; July
Alaska State Fair, Palmer; August and September
An Anchorage calendar of events can be found at www.anchorage.net/events.html.

# FAR NORTH BICENTENNIAL PARK

Far North Bicentennial Park is another great outdoor option within the Anchorage city limits for hikers and others who want to get out and enjoy the outdoors. Its 4,000 acres, situated at the foothills of the Chugach Mountains, hold more than 18 miles of trails with streams and abundant wildlife. This area is heavy with moose and both black and brown bears, so use caution when exploring the trails.

# 37 Campbell Creek Trail

The Campbell Creek Trail stretches from south Anchorage near Minnesota Drive and Dimond Boulevard and heads northeast toward Tudor Road. This popular multipurpose trail follows the scenic Campbell Creek, making it an excellent year-round recreational trail for fishing, picnicking, kids, families, hikers, bicycling, dog walkers, and winter skiers. Numerous access points along the entire trail make it easily accessible from many Anchorage neighborhoods. Campbell Creek is an important watershed and provides excellent salmon viewing, wildlife habitat, and natural flood control.

**Start:** Campbell Creek Greenbelt parking lot
**Distance:** 7.4 miles one-way; 14.8 miles out and back
**Approximate hiking time:** 3–4 hours one-way; 7–9 hours out and back
**Difficulty:** Easy
**Elevation gain:** Negligible
**Trail surface:** Paved
**Seasons:** Year-round
**Other trail users:** Walkers, runners, and cyclists; cross-country skiers in winter

**Canine compatibility:** Leashed dogs permitted
**Land status:** Anchorage municipality
**Nearest town:** Anchorage
**Fees and permits:** No fees or permits required
**Maps:** Anchorage Trail and Parks Map; http://munimaps.muni.org/trails/reference.htm
**Trail contacts:** Anchorage Parks Foundation; www.anchorageparks.org
**Special considerations:** None

**Finding the trailhead:** Coming from downtown Anchorage, head south on the Seward Highway. Exit on Dimond Boulevard and head west, traveling approximately 2 miles. Cross over Minnesota Drive and go through the stoplight at the intersection of Dimond Boulevard, Victor Road, and Northwood Street. The parking lot is immediately on your right; a sign reads Campbell Creek Greenbelt. Walk back across the bridge on Dimond and turn left onto Northwood Street, where the paved trail begins.

## The Hike

The Campbell Creek Trail is easily accessible from numerous points in the many neighborhoods that skirt the trail's 7.4-mile run, making it heavily used and well populated. The multipurpose paved trail stretches from south Anchorage to the northeast side. Start the trail by parking in the main parking lot, located on the north side of Dimond Boulevard just past Minnesota Drive, where there is ample parking. Another parking area, large enough for a couple of cars, is located on Northwood Street right at the beginning of the paved trail.

The trail heads slightly downhill and quickly comes to one of many bridge crossings that safely take you over the meandering and winding Campbell Creek. After approximately 0.9 mile cross under Minnesota Drive as you start heading in a northeasterly direction across town. Almost the entire trail follows the creek and runs

*Gorgeous white birch lining trail*

through beautiful stands of birch-spruce trees. Moose, waterfowl, and other birds are common along the trail. About 0.6 mile after Minnesota Drive, you will cross under Arctic Boulevard, and 0.3 mile beyond here you will come to a bike sign where you need to turn right and cross a bridge. After 2.0 miles of travel, pass Taku Lake on your right. You will cross Campbell Creek a seemingly endless number of times, pass under the major north-south streets of Anchorage, and also cross under the Alaska Railroad.

After another approximately 0.5 mile, come to a T in the trail with a large sign-post in the center. Turn left and continue on the paved path. Cross the creek a couple more times and reach a street crossing. Proceed across with caution. At approximately 4.1 miles cross under the Old Seward Highway and come to an area with several restaurants and retail businesses you might want to take time to check out. This is a popular stopping area for tour buses.

After approximately 4.4 miles the paved maintained trail ends. Turn left and head across the bridge onto a narrow dirt path. The paved trail begins again on the other side of the Seward Highway. The dirt path follows directly along the shoreline of the creek and under the highway. The path is wet and head clearance is quite low, so be cautious as you work your way to the other side of the highway. Once on the other side, hike out onto Rakof Street and travel 2 blocks east. The paved trail begins again on your right at approximately 4.7 miles.

You pass one more lake, Waldron Lake, on your left. This lake provides some good opportunities for viewing different types of waterfowl. The trail follows around and comes out on East 47th Street and heads directly into Lake Otis Boulevard. Follow the crossing signs that take you under Lake Otis Boulevard rather than trying to cross the roadway at this point, where crossing is very dangerous. The Waldron Drive underpass is slightly out of your way, but is a much safer choice.

Once on the other side, the trail goes through a scenic park, crosses a couple more bridges, and passes the Chuck Albrecht Softball Complex. After another approximately 0.5 mile, Campbell Creek Trail ends at Tudor Road. Cross Tudor and the trail will join the Lanie Fleischer Chester Creek Trail.

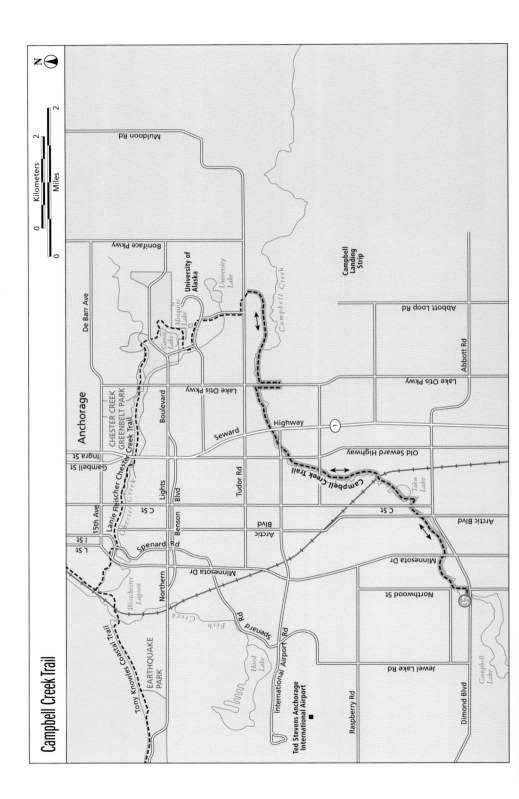

# Campbell Creek Trail

# Miles and Directions

**0.0** Begin at the trailhead and main parking lot. N61 08.269 / W149 55.581 (Option: Use the small parking area on Northwood Street. N61 08.290 / W149 55.327)

**0.3** Reach one of many bridge crossings over Campbell Creek. N61 08.404 / W149 55.272

**0.9** Cross under Minnesota Drive. N61 08.519 / W149 54.523

**1.5** Cross under Arctic Boulevard. N61 08.784 / W149 53.557

**1.8** Turn right at a bike sign and cross a bridge. N61 08.898 / W149 53.289 Soon cross under C Street.

**2.0** Pass Taku Lake on your right. N61 08.976 / W149 53.089

**2.5** Cross under the Alaska Railroad and over Little Campbell Creek. N61 09.331 / W149 52.620

**3.3** Cross a bridge. N61 09.912 / W149 52.621

**4.1** Cross under Old Seward Highway. N61 10.337 / W149 52.061

**4.25** Cross under International Airport Road. N61 10.423 / W149 51.846

**4.4** The paved trail ends at the Seward Highway. Turn left and cross a bridge onto a dirt path. N61 10.494 / W149 51.631

**4.7** The paved trail begins again. N61 10.555 / W149 51.326

**5.9** Travel past Waldron Lake on your left. N61 10.655 / W149 50.996

**7.4** The trail ends at the Tudor Road trailhead. N61 10.812 / W149 48.046 (Option: Cross Tudor Road to connect with the Lanie Fleischer Chester Creek Trail.)

**14.8** Return to the trailhead if hiking out and back. N61 08.269/ W149 55.581

# Hike Information

## Local information

Anchorage Visitor Information Center, 546 West Fourth Avenue, Anchorage 99501; (907) 274-3531; www.anchorage.net

Alaska Department of Natural Resources Public Information Center, Atwood Building, 550 West Seventh Avenue, Suite 1260, Anchorage 99501; (907) 269-8400; www.dnr.state.ak.us/parks

Alaska Public Lands Information Center, 605 West Fourth Avenue, Suite 105, Anchorage 99501; (907) 271-2737; www.nps.gov/aplic

## Camping

To the north is the Eagle River Campground (907-345-5014), 10 miles from Anchorage on Glenn Highway at the Eagle River Loop/Hiland Road exit; nightly camping fee. To the south is the Bird Creek Campground (907-345-5014), located southeast of Anchorage at Seward Highway Mile Marker 101; nightly camping fee.

Hike tours: Friends of Eagle River (operators of Eagle River Nature Center); (907) 694-2108; e-mail: ERNC@alaska.net

## Local organizations

The Anchorage Adventurers Meetup Group; www.adventurers.meetup.com/109
Mountaineering Club of Alaska, 2633 Spenard Road, Anchorage 99503; (907) 272-1811; www.mcak.org

## Local retailers

Recreational Equipment Inc. (REI), 1200 West Northern Lights Boulevard, Anchorage; (907) 272-4565; www.rei.com

Sportsman's Warehouse, 681 Old Seward Highway, Anchorage; (907) 644-1400; www.sportsmanswarehouse.com

Alaska Mountaineering and Hiking, 2633 Spenard Road, Anchorage; (907) 272-1811; www.alaskamountaineering.com

Cabelas, 155 W 104th, Anchorage; (907) 341-3400; www.cabelas.com/Stores/Anchorage

6th Avenue Outfitters, 520 W 6th Avenue, Anchorage; (907) 276-0233; www.6thavenueoutfitters.com

Bass Pro Shops, 3046 Mountain View Drive, Anchorage; (907) 330-5200; www.basspro.com/Anchorage

## Local events/attractions:

South: Girdwood Forest Fair, Girdwood; July
Alyeska Blueberry and Mountain Arts Festival, Alyeska Ski Resort; August
North: Alaskan Scottish Highland Games, Eagle River Lions Park, Anchorage; June
Bear Paw Festival, Eagle River; July
Alaska State Fair, Palmer; August and September
An Anchorage calendar of events can be found at www.anchorage.net/events.html.

## CAMPBELL TRACT FACILITY

The U.S. Department of the Interior Bureau of Land Management operates the 730-acre Campbell Tract Facility. It is commonly used by outdoor enthusiasts from hikers to horseback riders and is connected to the Chugach Mountains to the east. Wildlife such as lynx, moose, foxes, coyotes, and both black and brown bears are evident in the area. Campbell Creek meanders through the north part of the tract and provides habitat for trout and salmon—as well as food for bears—so be bear-aware when exploring the area. The Campbell Creek Science Center, an outdoor education facility, is also part of the Campbell Tract Facility.

Drive south on Lake Otis Parkway to 68th Street, and turn left onto 68th Street toward the mountains. This street ends at Elmore Road. Turn right and then immediately left into the facility.

# 38 Ship Creek Trail

Ship Creek Trail is not one of the most well-known trails in the area, but it is a great trail to check out and not to be missed. It is an important part of the Anchorage greenbelt trail system and can also be accessed from the popular Tony Knowles Coastal Trail. The easy to follow paved path follows Ship Creek for the entire length of the trail. The trail presents views of the Chugach Mountains and downtown Anchorage, white birch, berry picking, birding opportunities and wildflowers along the trail's edge on the north and an industrial setting to the south. If you want to see salmon when they are running, this is the trail to do so. From July through September salmon are easily spotted swimming upstream.

**Start:** Ship Creek Trailhead located by N. C Street bridge crossing Ship Creek
**Distance:** 5.2 miles out and back
**Approximate hiking time:** 2-3 hours
**Difficulty:** Easy
**Elevation gain:** Negligible
**Trail surface:** Paved
**Seasons:** Year-round
**Other trail users:** Walkers, runners, and cyclists; cross-country skiers in winter

**Canine compatibility:** Leashed dogs permitted
**Land status:** Anchorage municipality
**Nearest town:** Anchorage
**Fees and permits:** Parking fees in public lots
**Maps:** Anchorage Trail and Parks Map; http://munimaps.muni.org/trails/reference.htm
**Trail contacts:** Anchorage Parks Foundation; www.anchorageparks.org
**Special considerations:** None

**Finding the trailhead:** Coming from downtown Anchorage from 5th Avenue, head north on E. Street, veer right onto W. 2nd Avenue, which becomes N. C Street. This will go past the Alaska Railroad depot and the Alaska Railroad corporate office building. Turn right onto E. ship Creek Avenue to parking lot. The start of the trailhead is located at North C Street bridge which is behind Alaska Geographic Association and the Ulu Factory. This trail can also be accessed from the Tony Knowles Coastal Trail.

## The Hike

The city of Anchorage has one of the best urban trail systems found anywhere throughout the entire United States. Ship Creek Trail is one of four trails that are part of this greenbelt system. It is located on the north side of Anchorage and follows directly along Ship Creek and ends at Tyson Elementary School. The illuminated paved trail is also a popular biking trail.

Begin at the trailhead located at the North C Street bridge. As you head eastward on the trail, you will pass by a popular salmon fishing area. Here you can see the salmon, generally July through September, swimming upstream to spawn. The banks of the creek will be lined with anglers working the waters. The depth of this stream is directly related to the tide; and during low tide you will see shore birds flitting along

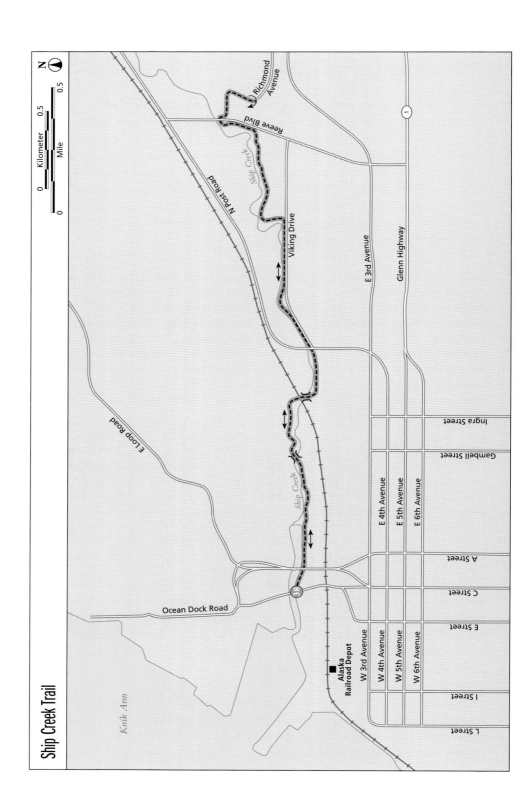

# Ship Creek Trail

*Ship Creek Trail*

the mudflats in the area. Various ducks, geese, godwit, turnstones and several species of sandpipers are common particularly during the spring and fall. Another ¼ mile up the trail you will pass by the Knik Arm Power Plant dam on your left. This is a good stopping point to view up stream and look for salmon and wild birds.

Throughout the trail you will cross several bridges. At approximately mile 1.5 the trail will loop up and over the Alaska Railroad train trestle and Ship Creek. This is a large bridge with equally big views.

The trail concludes next to Tyson Elementary School. As with all Anchorage trails, always use caution and be aware of wildlife such as bears and moose that frequently use the same trails that people do. Even in downtown Anchorage wildlife abounds. From here, head back on the same path to the parking area.

## Miles and Directions

**0.0**  Start at Ship Creek Trailhead, N61° 13.411' W149° 53.269'

**0.6**  Bridge crossing, N61° 13.423' W149° 52.312'

**0.8**  Bridge crossing, N61° 13.409' W149° 51.879'

**1.5**  Bridge crossing, N61° 13.457' W149° 50.948'

**2.2**  Bridge crossing, N61° 13.590' W149° 49.930'

**2.6**  Turn around at Tyson Elementary School, N61° 13.574' W149° 49.749'

**5.2**  Arrive back at the trailhead.

# Hike Information

## Local information

Anchorage Visitor Information Center, 546 West Fourth Avenue, Anchorage 99501; (907) 274-3531; www.anchorage.net

Alaska Department of Natural Resources Public Information Center, Atwood Building, 550 West Seventh Avenue, Suite 1260, Anchorage 99501; (907) 269-8400; www.dnr.state.ak.us/parks

Alaska Public Lands Information Center, 605 West Fourth Avenue, Suite 105, Anchorage 99501; (907) 271-2737; www.nps.gov/aplic

## Camping

To the north is the Eagle River Campground (907-345-5014), 10 miles from Anchorage on Glenn Highway at the Eagle River Loop/Hiland Road exit; nightly camping fee. To the south is the Bird Creek Campground (907-345-5014), located southeast of Anchorage at Seward Highway Mile Marker 101; nightly camping fee.

Hike tours: Friends of Eagle River (operators of Eagle River Nature Center); (907) 694-2108; e-mail: ERNC@alaska.net

*Anglers fishing Ship Creek*

## Local organizations

The Anchorage Adventurers Meetup Group; www.adventurers.meetup.com/109
Mountaineering Club of Alaska, 2633 Spenard Road, Anchorage 99503; (907) 272-1811; www.mcak.org

## Local retailers

Recreational Equipment Inc. (REI), 1200 West Northern Lights Boulevard, Anchorage; (907) 272-4565; www.rei.com

Sportsman's Warehouse, 681 Old Seward Highway, Anchorage; (907) 644-1400; www.sportsmanswarehouse.com

Alaska Mountaineering and Hiking, 2633 Spenard Road, Anchorage; (907) 272-1811; www.alaskamountaineering.com

Cabelas, 155 W 104th, Anchorage; (907) 341-3400; www.cabelas.com/Stores/Anchorage

6th Avenue Outfitters, 520 W 6th Avenue, Anchorage; (907) 276-0233; www.6thavenueoutfitters.com

Bass Pro Shops, 3046 Mountain View Drive, Anchorage; (907) 330-5200; www.basspro.com/Anchorage

## Local events/attractions:

South: Girdwood Forest Fair, Girdwood; July
Alyeska Blueberry and Mountain Arts Festival, Alyeska Ski Resort; August
North: Alaskan Scottish Highland Games, Eagle River Lions Park, Anchorage; June
Bear Paw Festival, Eagle River; July
Alaska State Fair, Palmer; August and September
An Anchorage calendar of events can be found at www.anchorage.net/events.html.

# The Art of Hiking

The following section will help you understand better what it means to "do what you can" while still making the most of your hiking experience. Anyone can take a hike, but hiking safely and well is an art requiring preparation and proper equipment.

## Trail Etiquette

The following guidelines will help preserve our natural areas for generations to come.

**Zero impact.** Always leave an area just like you found it—if not better than you found it. Avoid camping in fragile alpine meadows and along the banks of streams and lakes. Use a camp stove versus building a wood fire. Pack up all your trash and extra food. Bury human waste at least 100 feet from water sources under 6 to 8 inches of topsoil. Don't bathe with soap in a lake or stream. Use prepackaged moistened towelettes to wipe off sweat and dirt, or bathe in the water without soap.

**Stay on the trail.** It's true, a path anywhere leads nowhere new, but purists will just have to get over it. Paths serve an important purpose; they limit impact on natural areas. Straying from a designated trail may seem innocent, but it can cause damage to sensitive areas—damage that may take years to recover, if it can recover at all. Even simple shortcuts can be destructive. So, please, stay on the trail.

**Leave no weeds.** Noxious weeds tend to overtake other plants, which affects animals and birds that depend on them for food. To minimize the spread of noxious weeds, regularly clean your boots, tents, packs, and hiking poles of mud and seeds. Also brush your dog to remove any weed seeds before heading off into a new area.

**Keep your dog under control.** You can buy a flexi-lead that allows your dog to go exploring along the trail while enabling you to reel him in should another hiker approach or should he decide to chase a rabbit. Always obey leash laws, and be sure to bury your dog's waste or pack it out in resealable plastic bags.

**Respect other trail users.** Often you're not the only one on the trail. With the rise in popularity of multiuse trails, you'll have to learn a new kind of respect, beyond the nod and "hello" approach you may be used to. First determine whether you're on a multiuse trail, and then assume the appropriate precautions.

When you encounter motorized vehicles (ATVs, motorcycles, and four-wheel drives), be alert. Though they should always yield to the hiker, often they're going too fast or are too lost in the buzz of their engine to react to your presence. If you hear activity ahead, step off the trail just to be safe.

You're not likely to hear a mountain biker coming, so be prepared and know ahead of time whether you share the trail with cyclists. Cyclists should always yield to hikers, but that's little comfort to the hiker if they don't. So be aware.

When you approach horses or pack animals on the trail, always step quietly off-trail, preferably on the downhill side, and let them pass. If you're wearing a large backpack, it's often a good idea to sit down. To some animals, a hiker wearing a large backpack might appear threatening.

## Getting into Shape

Unless you want to be sore—and possibly have to shorten your trip or vacation—be sure to get in shape before a big hike. If you're terribly out of shape, start a walking program early, preferably eight weeks in advance. Start with a fifteen-minute walk during your lunch hour or after work, and gradually increase your walking time to an hour. You should also increase your elevation gain. Walking briskly up hills really strengthens your leg muscles and gets your heart rate up. If you work in a storied office building, take the stairs instead of the elevator. If you prefer going to a gym, walk the treadmill or use a stair machine. You can further increase your strength and endurance by walking with a loaded backpack. Stationary exercises you might consider are squats, leg lifts, sit-ups, and push-ups. Other good ways to get in shape include biking, running, aerobics, and of course, short hikes. Stretching before and after a hike keeps muscles flexible and helps avoid injuries.

## Preparedness

It's been said that failing to plan means planning to fail. So do take the necessary time to plan your trip. Whether going on a short day hike or an extended backpack trip, always prepare for the worst. Simply remembering to pack a copy of the U.S. Army Survival Manual is not preparedness. Although carrying the manual is not a bad idea if you plan on entering truly wild places, it's merely the tourniquet answer to a problem. You need to do your best to prevent the problem from arising in the first place. In order to survive—and to stay reasonably comfortable—you need to concern yourself with the basics: water, food, and shelter. Don't go on a hike without having these bases covered. And don't go on a hike expecting to find these items in the woods or mountains.

**Water.** Even in frigid conditions, you need at least two quarts of water a day to function efficiently. Add heat and taxing terrain, and you can bump that figure up to one gallon. That's simply a base to work from—your metabolism and your level of conditioning can raise or lower that amount. Unless you know your level, assume that you need one gallon of water a day. Now, where do you plan on getting the water?

Preferably not from natural water sources. These sources can be loaded with intestinal disturbers, such as bacteria, viruses, and fertilizers. *Giardia lamblia,* the most common of these disturbers, is a protozoan parasite that lives part of its life cycle as a cyst in water sources. The parasite spreads when mammals defecate in water sources. Once ingested, giardia can induce cramping, diarrhea, vomiting, and fatigue within two days to two weeks after ingestion. Giardiasis is treatable with prescription drugs. If you believe you've contracted giardiasis, see a doctor immediately.

**Food.** If we're talking about survival, you can go days without food, as long as you have water. But we're also talking about comfort. Try to avoid foods that are high in sugar and fat like candy bars and potato chips. These food types are harder to digest and are low in nutritional value. Instead bring along foods that are easy to pack, nutritious, and high in energy (e.g., bagels, nutrition bars, dehydrated fruit, gorp, and jerky). If you are on an overnight trip, easy-to-fix dinners include rice mixes with dehydrated potatoes, corn, pasta with cheese sauce, and soup mixes. For a tasty breakfast, you can fix hot oatmeal with brown sugar and reconstituted milk powder topped off with banana chips. If you like a hot drink in the morning, bring along herbal tea bags or hot chocolate. If you are a coffee junkie, you can purchase coffee that is packaged like tea bags. You can prepackage all of your meals in heavy-duty resealable plastic bags to keep food from spilling in your pack. These bags can be reused to pack out trash.

**Shelter.** The type of shelter you choose depends less on the conditions than on your tolerance for discomfort. Shelter comes in many forms—tent, tarp, lean-to, bivy sack, cabin, cave, etc. If you're camping in the desert, a bivy sack may suffice, but if you're above the tree line and a storm is approaching, a better choice is a three- or four-season tent. Tents are the logical and most popular choice for most backpackers—they're lightweight and packable, and you can rest assured that you always have shelter from the elements. Before leaving on your trip, anticipate what the weather and terrain will be like, and plan for the type of shelter that will work best for your comfort level. In Alaska the weather will change often and will be different at different elevations and within different locations. It is always best to be prepared for everything from sunshine and rain to even snow at higher elevations. (See "Equipment" later in this section.)

**Finding a campsite.** If there are established campsites, stick to those. If not, start looking for a campsite early—around 3:30 or 4:00 p.m. Stop at the first decent site you see. Depending on the area, it could be a long time before you find another suitable location. Pitch your camp in an area that's level. Make sure the area is at least 200 feet from fragile areas like lakeshores, meadows, and stream banks. And try to avoid areas thick in underbrush; they can harbor insects and provide cover for approaching animals.

If you are camping in stormy, rainy weather, look for a rock outcrop or a shelter in the trees to keep the wind from blowing your tent all night. Be sure that you don't camp under trees with dead limbs that might break off on top of you. Also, try to find an area that has an absorbent surface, such as sandy soil or forest duff. This, in addition to camping on a surface with a slight angle, will provide better drainage. By all means, don't dig trenches to provide drainage around your tent—remember, you're practicing zero-impact camping.

Every trail in the Anchorage area is in bear country. Steer clear of creekbeds, animal paths, and the main trail for establishing your campsite. If you see any signs of a bear's presence (i.e., scat, footprints, carcasses), relocate. You'll need to find a campsite near a tall tree where you can hang your food and other items, such as deodorant, toothpaste, and soap, that may attract bears.

Carry a lightweight nylon rope for hanging your food. Hang your food in a tree at least 20 feet from the ground and 5 feet away from the tree trunk. You can put food and other items in a waterproof stuff sack and tie one end of the rope to the stuff sack. To get the other end of the rope over the tree branch, tie a good-size rock to it, and gently toss the rock over the tree branch. Pull the stuff sack up until it reaches the top of the branch and tie it off securely. Don't hang your food near your tent—and don't cook near your tent! Always hang your food at least 100 feet away from your campsite and cook downwind. Alternatives to hanging your food are bear-proof plastic tubes and metal bear boxes, which also should be located away from the tent site.

Lastly, think of comfort. Lie down on the ground where you intend to sleep and see if it's a good fit. For morning warmth (and a nice view to wake up to), have your tent face east.

## First Aid

You may think you're tough, but get 10 miles into the mountains and develop a blister, and you'll wish you had carried that first-aid kit. Many companies produce lightweight, compact first-aid kits. Just make sure yours contains at least the following:

- ❏ adhesive bandages
- ❏ moleskin or duct tape
- ❏ various sizes of sterile gauze and dressings
- ❏ white surgical tape
- ❏ an Ace bandage
- ❏ an antihistamine
- ❏ aspirin
- ❏ Betadine solution
- ❏ a first-aid book
- ❏ antacid tablets
- ❏ tweezers
- ❏ scissors
- ❏ antibacterial wipes
- ❏ triple-antibiotic ointment
- ❏ plastic gloves
- ❏ sterile cotton-tip applicators
- ❏ syrup of ipecac (to induce vomiting)
- ❏ thermometer
- ❏ wire splint

Here are a few tips for dealing with, and hopefully preventing, certain ailments.

**Sunburn.** Take along sunscreen or sunblock, protective clothing, and a wide-brimmed hat. If you do get sunburned, treat the area with aloe vera gel and protect it from further sun exposure. At higher elevations, the sun's radiation can be particularly damaging to skin. Remember that your eyes are vulnerable to this radiation as well. Sunglasses can be a good way to prevent headaches and permanent eye damage from the sun, especially in places where light-colored rock or patches of snow reflect light up in your face.

**Blisters.** Be prepared to take care of these hike-spoilers by carrying moleskin (a lightly padded adhesive), gauze and tape, or adhesive bandages. An effective way to apply moleskin is to cut out a circle of moleskin, remove the center—like a dough-nut—and place it over the blistered area. Cutting the center out will reduce the pressure applied to the sensitive skin. Other products can help you combat blisters. Some are applied to suspicious hotspots before a blister forms to help decrease friction to that area; others are applied to the blister after it has popped to help prevent further irritation.

**Insect bites and stings.** You can treat most insect bites and stings by applying 1 percent hydrocortisone cream topically and taking ibuprofen or acetaminophen to reduce swelling. If you forgot to pack these items, a cold compress or a paste of mud and ashes can sometimes assuage the itching and discomfort. Remove any stingers by using tweezers or scraping the area with your fingernail or a knife blade. Don't pinch the area—you'll only spread the venom.

Some people are highly sensitive to bites and stings and may have a serious allergic reaction that can be life threatening. Symptoms of a serious allergic reaction can include wheezing, an asthmatic attack, and shock. The treatment for this severe type of reaction is epinephrine. If you know that you are sensitive to bites and stings, carry a prepackaged epinephrine kit or an EpiPen, which can be obtained only by prescription from your doctor.

**Plants.** There are two common plants on Alaska trails you need to pay attention to: devil's club and cow parsnip. The name devil's club alone sounds as though you should avoid it—and with good reason. This tall plant grows in moist, shaded areas, often along stream banks, and is full of thorns—even on the leaves. As painful as the thorns can be, the plant has been used for ages by Alaskan natives for curing such ailments as stomach ulcers, arthritis, hypoglycemia, and headaches.

Cow parsnip is another common, tall-growing plant found along the edges of many trails and is often referred to as "Alaskan poison ivy." It belongs to the same family as parsley and carrots. In contrast to devil's club, cow parsnip likes sunny areas and is often hiked through by many trail users. The chemicals from the plant react very slowly with bare skin and can cause rashes and painful second-degree blistering. Avoidance is the best treatment. However, if you're exposed, wash the areas with soap and avoid sun exposure for the next twenty-four hours.

*Top: Poisonous bane berry*
*Bottom: Devil's club has large serrated leaves and thorns.*

**Dehydration.** Have you ever hiked in hot weather and had a roaring headache and felt fatigued after only a few miles? More than likely you were dehydrated. Symptoms of dehydration include fatigue, headache, and decreased coordination and judgment. When you are hiking, your body's rate of fluid loss depends on the outside temperature, humidity, altitude, and your activity level. On average, a hiker walking in warm weather loses four liters of fluid a day. That fluid loss is easily replaced by normal consumption of liquids and food. However, if you are walking briskly in hot, dry weather and hauling a heavy pack, you can lose one to three liters of water an hour. It's important to always carry plenty of water and to stop often and drink fluids regularly, even if you aren't thirsty.

**Heat exhaustion** is the result of a loss of large amounts of electrolytes and often occurs if a hiker is dehydrated and has been under heavy exertion. Common symptoms of heat exhaustion include cramping, exhaustion, fatigue, lightheadedness, and nausea. You can treat heat exhaustion by getting out of the sun and drinking an electrolyte solution made up of one teaspoon of salt and one tablespoon of sugar dissolved in a liter of water. Drink this solution slowly over a period of one hour. Drinking plenty of fluids (preferably an electrolyte solution/sports drink) can prevent heat exhaustion. Avoid hiking during the hottest parts of the day and wear "breathable" clothing, a wide-brimmed hat, and sunglasses.

**Hypothermia** is one of the biggest dangers in the backcountry, especially for day hikers in the summertime. That may sound strange, but even in Alaska in midsummer, when it is sunny and 65 degrees, there is a risk of hypothermia. You're clad in nylon shorts and a cotton T-shirt. About halfway through your hike, the sky begins to cloud up, and in the next hour a light drizzle begins to fall and the wind starts to pick up. Before you know it, you are soaking wet and shivering—the perfect recipe for hypothermia. More-advanced signs include decreased coordination, slurred speech, and blurred vision. When a victim's temperature falls below 92 degrees, blood pressure and pulse plummet, possibly leading to coma and death.

To avoid hypothermia, always bring a windproof/rainproof shell, a fleece jacket, tights made of a breathable synthetic fiber, gloves, and a hat when you are hiking in the mountains. Learn to adjust your clothing layers based on the temperature. If you are climbing uphill at a moderate pace, you will stay warm; but when you stop for a break, you'll become cold quickly unless you add more layers of clothing.

If a hiker is showing advanced signs of hypothermia, dress the person in dry clothes and make sure he or she is wearing a hat and gloves. Place the person in a sleeping bag in a tent or shelter that will provide protection from the wind and other elements. Give warm fluids to drink and keep the person awake.

**Frostbite.** When the mercury dips below 32 degrees, your extremities begin to chill. If a persistent chill attacks a localized area—say, your hands or your toes—the circulatory system reacts by cutting off blood flow to the affected area. The idea is to protect and preserve the body's overall temperature, and so it's death by attrition for the affected area. Ice crystals start to form from the water in the cells of the neglected tissue. Deprived of heat, nourishment, and now water, the tissue literally starves. This is frostbite.

Prevention is your best defense against this condition. Most prone to frostbite are your face, hands, and feet, so protect these areas well. Wool is the material of choice because it provides ample air space for insulation and draws moisture away from the skin. Synthetic fabrics, however, have recently made great strides in the cold-weather clothing market. Do your research. Wearing a pair of light silk liners under your regular gloves is a good trick for keeping warm. They afford some additional warmth, but more importantly they'll allow you to remove your mitts for precision work without exposing the skin.

If your feet or hands start to feel cold or numb due to the elements, warm them as quickly as possible. Place cold hands under your armpits or bury them in your crotch. If your feet are cold, change your socks. If there's plenty of room in your boots, add another pair of socks. Remember, though, that constricting your feet in tight boots can restrict blood flow and actually make your feet colder more quickly. Your socks need to have breathing room if they're going to be effective. Dead air provides insulation. If your face is cold, place your warm hands over your face, or simply wear a head stocking.

Should your skin go numb and start to appear white and waxy, chances are you've got or are developing frostbite. Don't try to thaw the area unless you can maintain the warmth. In other words, don't stop to warm up your frostbitten feet only to head back on the trail. You'll do more damage than good. Tests have shown that hikers who walked on thawed feet did more harm, and endured more pain, than hikers who left the affected areas alone. Do your best to get out of the cold entirely and seek medical attention—which usually consists of performing a rapid rewarming in water for twenty to thirty minutes.

The overall objective in preventing both hypothermia and frostbite is to keep the body's core warm. Protect key areas where heat escapes, like the top of the head, and maintain the proper nutrition level. Foods that are high in calories aid the body in producing heat. Never smoke or drink alcohol when you're in situations where the cold is threatening. By affecting blood flow, these activities ultimately cool the body's core temperature.

## Natural Hazards

**Bears.** Anchorage has a grizzly bear population, and they need to be taken very seriously. Bear maulings and attacks occur every year. It is important to know how to identify a black bear from a grizzly and how to react if you encounter a bear. Color alone is not enough, since black bears can vary in color. How to react can also differ according to the circumstances and if the bear is acting defensively or thinks you are food. Black bears also live in the Anchorage area. (See "The Bears of Chugach" sidebar in this book's introduction for more bear facts.)

Always be bear-aware and watch for bear tracks, fresh droppings, and carcasses. Hike with a companion (or several), and talk or sing where visibility or hearing is limited—particularly around salmon rivers and streams, which are major food sources. Most of all, avoid surprising a bear. Keep a clean camp, prepare and hang food away from your tent site, and don't sleep in the clothes you wore while cooking.

Be especially careful in spring to avoid getting between a mother and her cubs. In late summer and fall, bears are busy eating berries and salmon to fatten up for winter, so be extra careful around berry bushes and salmon rivers and streams. Unleashed dogs have been known to come running back to their owners with a bear close behind. Keep your dog on a leash or leave it at home when hiking in bear country.

**Moose.** Because moose have very few natural predators other than the grizzly bears and wolves in our area, they don't fear humans like other animals do. You are likely to find moose anywhere in the Anchorage area, including downtown on Fifth Street as well as on every trail. Do not approach moose as if they are tame—they are not. Mothers with calves, as well as bulls during mating season, can be particularly aggressive. Always walk around moose or wait for the trail to clear and give them plenty of space. If a moose charges you, head for the nearest tree or structure for safety.

## Navigation

Whether you are going on a short hike in a familiar area or planning a weeklong backpack trip, you should always be equipped with the proper navigational equipment—at the very least a detailed map and a sturdy compass. It is important not only to have them but also to know how to use them.

**Maps.** There are many different types of maps available to help you find your way on the trail. Easiest to find are USDA Forest Service maps and BLM (Bureau of Land Management) maps. These maps tend to cover large areas, so be sure they are detailed enough for your particular trip. You can also obtain specific national park maps as well as high-quality maps from private companies and trail groups. These maps can be obtained from outdoor stores or ranger stations.

U.S. Geological Survey (USGS) topographic maps are particularly popular with hikers—especially serious backcountry hikers. These maps contain the standard map elements such as roads, lakes, and rivers, as well as contour lines that show the details of the trail terrain like ridges, valleys, passes, and mountain peaks. The 7.5-minute series (1 inch on the map equals approximately ⅔ mile on the ground) provides the closest inspection available. USGS maps are available by mail (U.S. Geological Survey, Map Distribution Branch, P.O. Box 25286, Denver, CO 80225) or online at mapping .usgs.gov/esic/to_order.html.

If you want to check out the high-tech world of maps there are a variety of resources online.

Map reading is a skill that you can develop by first practicing in an area you are familiar with. To begin, orient the map so that it is lined up in the correct direction (i.e., north on the map is lined up with true north). Next familiarize yourself with the map symbols and try to match them up with terrain features around you such as a high ridge, mountain peak, river, or lake. If you are practicing with a USGS map, notice the contour lines. On gentler terrain these contour lines are spaced farther apart; on steeper terrain they are closer together. Pick a short loop trail, and stop frequently to check your position on the map. As you practice map reading, you'll learn how to anticipate a steep section on the trail, a good place to take a rest break, and so on.

**Compasses.** First off, the sun is not a substitute for a compass. So what kind of compass should you have? Here are some characteristics you should look for: a rectangular base with detailed scales, a liquid-filled and protective housing, a sighting line on the mirror, luminous alignment and back-bearing arrows, a luminous north-seeking arrow, and a well-defined bezel ring.

You can learn compass basics by reading the detailed instructions included with your compass. If you want to fine-tune your compass skills, sign up for an orienteering class or purchase a book on compass reading. Once you've learned the basic skills of using a compass, be sure to practice them before you head into the backcountry.

**GPS (Global Positioning System).** If you are a klutz at using a compass, you may be interested in checking out the technical wizardry of a GPS device. GPS was developed by the Pentagon and works off twenty-four NAVSTAR satellites, which were designed to guide missiles to their targets. A GPS device is a handheld unit that calculates your latitude and longitude with the easy press of a button. The Department of Defense used to scramble the satellite signals a bit to prevent civilians (and spies!) from getting extremely accurate readings, but that practice was discontinued in May 2000. GPS units now provide nearly pinpoint accuracy (within 30 to 60 feet).

There are many different types of GPS units available, ranging in price from $100 to $400. In general, all GPS units have a display screen and keypad where you input information. In addition to acting as a compass, the unit allows you to plot your route, easily retrace your path, track your traveling speed, find the mileage between waypoints, and calculate the total mileage of your route.

Before you purchase a GPS unit, keep in mind that these devices don't pick up signals indoors, in heavily wooded areas, on mountain peaks, or in deep valleys.

**Pedometers.** A pedometer is a small, clip-on unit with a digital display that calculates your hiking distance in miles or kilometers based on your walking stride. Some units also calculate the calories you burn and your total hiking time. Pedometers are available at most large outdoor stores and range in price from $20 to $40.

## Trip Planning

Planning your hiking adventure begins with letting a friend or relative know your trip itinerary so that they can call for help if you don't return at your scheduled time. Your next task is to make sure you are outfitted to experience the risks as well as rewards of the trail. This section highlights gear and clothing you may want to take with you to get the most out of your hike.

## Day Hikes

- ❑ camera/film/flash cards/spare batteries
- ❑ compass/GPS unit
- ❑ pedometer
- ❑ day pack
- ❑ first-aid kit
- ❑ food
- ❑ guidebook
- ❑ headlamp/flashlight with extra batteries and bulbs
- ❑ hat
- ❑ insect repellent
- ❑ knife/multipurpose tool
- ❑ map
- ❑ matches in waterproof container and fire starter
- ❑ fleece jacket
- ❑ rain gear
- ❑ space blanket
- ❑ sunglasses
- ❑ sunscreen
- ❑ watch
- ❑ water
- ❑ water bottles/water hydration system

## Overnight Trip

- ❑ backpack and waterproof rain cover
- ❑ backpacker's trowel
- ❑ bandanna
- ❑ bear repellent spray
- ❑ bear bells
- ❑ biodegradable soap
- ❑ pot scrubber
- ❑ collapsible water container (2- to 3-gallon capacity)
- ❑ clothing—extra wool socks, shirt, and shorts
- ❑ cook set/utensils
- ❑ ditty bags to store gear

- ❑ extra plastic resealable bags
- ❑ gaiters
- ❑ garbage bag
- ❑ ground cloth
- ❑ journal/pen
- ❑ nylon rope for hanging food
- ❑ long underwear
- ❑ permit (if required)
- ❑ rain jacket and pants
- ❑ sandals to wear around camp and to ford streams
- ❑ sleeping bag
- ❑ waterproof stuff sack
- ❑ sleeping pad
- ❑ small bath towel
- ❑ camp stove and fuel
- ❑ tent
- ❑ toiletry items
- ❑ water filter/purification system
- ❑ whistle

## Equipment

With the outdoor market currently flooded with products, many of which are pure gimmickry, it seems impossible to both differentiate and choose the necessary from the unnecessary. Do I really need a tropical fish–lined collapsible shower? (No, you don't.) The only defense against the maddening quantity of items thrust in your face is to think practically—and to do so before you go shopping. The worst buys are impulsive buys. Since most name brands will differ only slightly in quality, it's best to know what you're looking for in terms of function. Buy only what you need. Don't forget that you will be carrying what you've bought on your back. Here are some things to keep in mind before you go shopping.

**Clothes.** Clothing is your armor against Mother Nature's little surprises. Hikers should be prepared for any possibility, especially when hiking in mountainous areas. Adequate rain protection and extra layers of clothing are a good idea. In summer, a wide-brimmed hat can help keep the sun at bay. In winter, the first layer you'll want to wear is a "wicking" layer of long underwear that keeps perspiration away from your skin. Wear long underwear made from synthetic fibers that wick moisture away from the skin and draw it toward the next layer of clothing, where it then evaporates. Avoid wearing long underwear made of cotton, which is slow to dry and keeps moisture next to your skin.

The second layer you'll wear is the "insulating" layer. Aside from keeping you warm, this layer needs to "breathe" so that you stay dry while hiking. One fabric that provides insulation and dries quickly is fleece. It's interesting to note that this one-of-a-kind fabric is often made out of recycled plastic. Purchasing a zip-up jacket made of this material is highly recommended.

The last line of layering defense is the "shell" layer. You'll need some type of waterproof, windproof, breathable jacket that fits over all your other layers. It should have a large hood that fits over a hat. You'll also need a good pair of rain pants made from a similar waterproof, breathable fabric. Some Gore-Tex jackets cost as much as $500, but there are more affordable fabrics out there that work just as well.

Now that you've learned the basics of layering, don't forget to protect your hands and face. In cold, windy, or rainy weather, you'll need a hat made of wool or fleece and insulated, waterproof gloves that will keep your hands warm and toasty. As mentioned earlier in this section, buying an additional pair of light silk liners to wear under your regular gloves is a good idea.

**Footwear.** If you have any extra money to spend on your trip, put that money into boots or trail shoes. Poor shoes will bring a hike to a halt faster than anything else. Buy shoes that provide support and are lightweight and flexible. A lightweight hiking boot is better than a heavy leather mountaineering boot for most day hikes and backpacking. Trail-running shoes provide a little extra cushion and are made in a high-top style that many people like to wear for hiking. These running shoes are lighter, more flexible, and more breathable than hiking boots. If you know you'll be hiking in wet weather often, purchase boots or shoes with a Gore-Tex liner, which will help keep your feet dry.

When buying your boots, be sure to wear the same type of socks you'll be wearing on the trail. If the boots you're buying are for cold-weather hiking, try the boots on while wearing two pairs of socks. Speaking of socks, a good cold-weather sock combination is to wear a thinner sock made of wool or polypropylene covered by a heavier outer sock made of wool. The inner sock protects the foot from the rubbing effects of the outer sock and prevents blisters. Many outdoor stores have some type of ramp to simulate hiking uphill and downhill. Be sure to take advantage of this test—toe-jamming boot fronts can be very painful and debilitating on the downhill trek.

Once you've purchased your footwear, be sure to break them in before you hit the trail. New footwear is often stiff and needs to be stretched and molded to your foot.

**Hiking poles.** Hiking poles help with balance and, more importantly, take pressure off your knees. Poles with shock absorbers are easier on your elbows and knees. Poles are also helpful tools when fording streams and rivers. Some poles even come with a camera attachment to be used as a monopod.

**Backpacks.** No matter what type of hiking you do, you'll need a pack of some sort to carry the basic trail essentials. There are a variety of backpacks on the market, but let's first discuss what you intend to use it for: day hikes or overnight trips.

If you plan on doing a day hike, a day pack should have some of the following characteristics: a padded hip belt that's at least 2 inches wide (avoid packs with only a small nylon piece of webbing for a hip belt); a chest strap (the chest strap helps stabilize the pack against your body); external pockets to carry water and other items that you want easy access to; an internal pocket to hold keys, a knife, a wallet, and other miscellaneous items; an external lashing system to hold a jacket; and a hydration pocket for carrying a hydration system (a water bladder with an attachable drinking hose).

For short hikes, some hikers like to use a fanny pack to store just a camera, food, a compass, a map, and other trail essentials. Most fanny packs have pockets for two water bottles and a padded hip belt.

If you intend to do an extended overnight trip, there are multiple considerations. First off, you need to decide what kind of framed pack you want. There are two basic pack types for backpacking: internal frame and external frame. An internal-frame pack rests closer to your body, making it more stable and easier to balance when hiking over rough terrain. An external frame pack is an aluminum frame attached to the exterior of the pack. An external-frame pack is better for long backpack trips because it distributes the pack weight better and you can carry heavier loads. It's easier to pack, and your gear is more accessible. It also offers better back ventilation in hot weather.

The most critical measurement for fitting a pack is torso length. The pack needs to rest evenly on your hips without sagging. A good pack will come in two or three sizes and have straps and hip belts that are adjustable according to your body size and characteristics.

When you purchase a backpack, go to an outdoor store with salespeople who are knowledgeable in how to properly fit a pack. Once the pack is fitted for you, load the pack with the amount of weight you plan on taking on the trail. The weight of the pack should be distributed evenly, and you should be able to swing your arms and walk briskly without feeling out of balance. Another good technique for evaluating a pack is to walk up and down stairs and make quick turns to the right and to the left to be sure the pack doesn't feel out of balance. Other features that are nice to have on a backpack include a removable day pack or fanny pack, external pockets for extra water, and extra lash points to attach a jacket or other items.

**Sleeping bags and pads.** Sleeping bags are rated by temperature. You can purchase a bag made of synthetic fiber, or you can buy a goosedown bag. Goosedown bags are more expensive, but they have a higher insulating capacity by weight and will keep their loft longer. You'll want to purchase a bag with a temperature rating that fits the time of year and conditions you are most likely to camp in.

One caveat: The techno-standard for temperature ratings is far from perfect. Ratings vary from manufacturer to manufacturer, so to protect yourself you should purchase a bag rated 10 to 15 degrees below the temperature you expect to be camping in. Synthetic bags are more resistant to water than down bags, but many down bags are now made with a Gore-Tex shell that helps to repel water. Down bags are also more compressible than synthetic bags and take up less room in your pack, which is an important consideration if you are planning a multiday backpack trip.

Features to look for in a sleeping bag include a mummy-style bag, a hood you can cinch down around your head in cold weather, and draft tubes along the zippers that help keep heat in and drafts out. You'll also want a sleeping pad to provide insulation and padding from the cold ground. There are different types of sleeping pads available, from the more expensive self-inflating air mattresses to the less expensive closed-cell foam pads. Self-inflating air mattresses are usually heavier than closed-cell foam mattresses and are prone to punctures.

**Tents.** The tent is your home away from home while on the trail. It provides protection from wind, snow, rain, and insects. A three-season tent is a good choice for backpacking and can range in price from $100 to $500. These lightweight and versatile tents provide protection in all types of weather, except heavy snowstorms or high winds, and range in weight from four to eight pounds. Look for a tent that's easy to set up and will easily fit two people with gear.

Dome-type tents usually offer more headroom and places to store gear. Other tent designs include a vestibule where you can store wet boots and backpacks. Some nice-to-have items in a tent include interior pockets to store small items and lashing points to hang a clothesline. Most three-season tents also come with stakes so you can secure the tent in high winds. Before you purchase a tent, set it up and take it down a few times to be sure it is easy to handle. Also, sit inside the tent and make sure it has enough room for you and your gear.

**Cell phones.** Many hikers are carrying their cell phones into the backcountry these days in case of emergency. That's fine and good, but please know that cell phone coverage is usually nonexistent on most Alaskan trails, other than within the city limits. Let's go back to being prepared. You are responsible for yourself in the backcountry. There is no substitute for proper preparation on a hike and knowing what to do in emergency situations. Your cell phone probably won't help you.

## Hiking with Children

Hiking with children isn't a matter of how many miles you can cover or how much elevation gain you make in a day; it's about seeing and experiencing nature through their eyes.

Kids like to explore and have fun. They like to stop and point out bugs and plants, look under rocks, jump in puddles, and throw sticks. If you're taking a toddler or young child on a hike, start with a trail that you're familiar with. Trails that have interesting things for kids, like piles of leaves to play in or a small stream to wade through during summer, will make the hike much more enjoyable for them and help keep them from getting bored.

You can keep your child's attention if you have a strategy before starting on the trail. Using games is not only an effective way to keep a child's attention but also a great way to teach him or her about nature. Play hide-and-seek, where your child is the mouse and you are the hawk. Quiz children on the names of plants and animals. If your children are old enough, let them carry their own day pack filled with snacks and water. So that you are sure to travel at their pace and not yours, let them lead the way. Playing follow the leader works particularly well when you have a group of children. Have each child take a turn at being the leader.

With children, a lot of clothing is key. The only thing predictable about weather is that it will change. Especially in mountainous areas, weather can change dramatically in a very short time. Always bring extra clothing for children, regardless of the season. In winter have your children wear wool socks and warm layers such as long underwear, a fleece jacket and hat, wool mittens, and good rain gear. It's not a bad idea to have these items along in late fall and early spring as well. Good footwear is also important. The best bet for little ones is a sturdy pair of high-top tennis shoes or lightweight hiking boots. If you're hiking in summer near a lake or stream, bring along a pair of old sneakers that your child can put on when he wants to go exploring in the water. Remember: When you're near any type of water, watch your child at all times. Also keep a close eye on teething toddlers, who may decide a rock or a leaf of poison oak is an interesting item to put in their mouth.

From spring through fall you'll want your kids to wear a wide-brimmed hat to keep their face, head, and ears protected from the hot sun. Make sure your children wear sunscreen at all times. Choose a brand without para-aminobenzoic acid, or PABA. Children have sensitive skin and may have an allergic reaction to sunscreen that contains PABA. If you are hiking with a child younger than six months, don't use sunscreen or insect repellent. Instead, be sure that the child's head, face, neck, and ears are protected from the sun with a wide-brimmed hat and that all other skin exposed to the sun is protected with the appropriate clothing.

Remember that food is fun. Kids like snacks, so it's important to bring a lot of munchies for the trail. Stopping often for snack breaks is a fun way to keep the trail interesting. Raisins, apples, granola bars, crackers and cheese, cereal, and trail mix all make great snacks. If your child is old enough to carry his or her own backpack, fill it with treats before you leave. If your kids don't like drinking water, you can bring boxes of fruit juice.

Avoid poorly designed child-carrying packs—you don't want to break your back carrying your child. Most child-carrying backpacks designed to hold a forty-pound child will have a large pocket to hold diapers and other items. Some have an optional rain/sun hood.

## Hiking with Your Dog

Bringing your furry friend with you is always more fun than leaving him behind. Our canine pals make great trail buddies because they never complain and always are good company. Hiking with your dog can be a rewarding experience, especially if you plan ahead. In Alaska, many hikers hike with their dogs. However, because of the many natural dangers in this state, complete control is vitally important for his safety and for yours.

**Getting your dog in shape.** Before you plan outdoor adventures with your dog, make sure he's in shape for the trail. Getting your dog into shape takes the same discipline as getting yourself into shape, but luckily your dog can get in shape with you. Take your dog with you on your daily runs or walks. If there is a park near your house, throw a tennis ball or play Frisbee with your dog.

Swimming is also an excellent way to get your dog into shape. If there is a lake or river near where you live and your dog likes the water, have him retrieve a tennis ball or stick. Gradually build your dog's stamina over a two- to three-month period. A good rule of thumb is to assume that your dog will travel twice as far as you will on the trail. If you plan on doing a 5-mile hike, be sure your dog is in shape for a 10-mile hike.

**Training your dog for the trail.** Before you go on your first hiking adventure with your dog, be sure he has a firm grasp on the basics of canine etiquette and behavior. Make sure he can sit, lie down, stay, and come. One of the most important commands you can teach your canine pal is to "come" under any situation. It's easy for your friend's nose to lead him astray or possibly get him lost. Another helpful command is the "get behind" command. When you're on a hiking trail that's narrow, you can have your dog follow behind you when other trail users approach. Nothing is more bothersome than an enthusiastic dog that runs back and forth on the trail and disrupts the peace of the trail for others. When you see other trail users approaching you on the trail, give them the right-of-way by quietly stepping off the trail and making your dog lie down and stay until they pass.

**Equipment.** The most critical pieces of equipment you can invest in for your dog are proper identification and a sturdy leash. Flexi-leads work well for hiking because they give your dog more freedom to explore but still leave you in control. Make sure your dog has identification that includes your name and address and a number for your veterinarian. Other forms of identification for your dog include a tattoo or a microchip. Consult your veterinarian for more information on these last two options.

The next piece of equipment you'll want to consider is a pack for your dog. Instead of holding all your dog's essentials in your pack, give him a job and let him carry his own gear! Dogs that are in good shape can carry 30 to 40 percent of their own weight.

Most packs are fitted by a dog's weight and girth measurement. Companies that make dog packs generally include guidelines to help you pick out the size that's right for your dog. Some characteristics to look for when purchasing a pack for your dog include a harness that has two padded girth straps, a padded chest strap, leash attachments, removable saddlebags, internal water bladders, and external gear cords.

You can introduce your dog to the pack by first placing the empty pack on his back and letting him wear it around the yard. Keep an eye on him during this first

*An unleashed dog encountering a bear can be a danger to its owner and others.*

introduction. He may decide to chew through the straps if you aren't watching him closely. Once he learns to treat the pack as an object of fun and not a foreign enemy, fill the pack evenly on both sides with a few ounces of dog food in resealable plastic bags. Have your dog wear his pack on your daily walks for a period of two to three weeks. Each week add a little more weight to the pack until your dog will accept the maximum amount of weight he can carry.

You can also purchase collapsible water and dog food bowls for your dog. These bowls are lightweight and can easily be stashed into your pack or your dog's. If you are hiking on rocky terrain or in the snow, you can purchase footwear for your dog that will protect his feet from cuts and bruises.

Always carry plastic bags to remove feces from the trail. It is a courtesy to other trail users and helps protect local wildlife and water sources.

Here are some additional items to bring when you take your dog hiking: a comb, a collar and a leash, dog food, flea/tick powder, paw protection, water, and a first-aid kit that contains eye ointment, tweezers, scissors, stretchy foot wrap, gauze, antibacterial wash, sterile cotton-tip applicators, antibiotic ointment, and cotton wrap.

**First aid for your dog.** Your dog is just as prone—if not more prone—to getting in trouble on the trail as you are, so be prepared. Here's a rundown of the more likely misfortunes that might befall your canine companion.

**Bees and wasps.** If a bee or wasp stings your dog, remove the stinger with a pair of tweezers and place a mudpack or a cloth dipped in cold water over the affected area.

**Porcupines, bears, and moose.** Three more good reasons to keep your dog on a leash: to prevent him from getting a nose full of porcupine quills, leading a charging bear back to you, and getting trampled by a moose.

**Heat stroke.** Avoid hiking with your dog in really hot weather. Dogs with heat stroke will pant excessively, lie down and refuse to get up, and become lethargic and disoriented. If your dog shows any of these signs on the trail, have him lie down in the shade. If you are near a stream, pour cool water over your dog's entire body to help bring his body temperature back to normal.

**Paw injuries.** Be sure to keep your dog's nails trimmed to avoid soft-tissue or joint injuries. If your dog slows and refuses to go on, check to see that his paws aren't torn or worn. You can protect your dog's paws from trail hazards such as sharp gravel, rock, lava scree, and thorns by having him wear dog boots.

**Sunburn.** Dogs with light-colored skin are susceptible to sunburn on their nose and other exposed skin areas. Applying a nontoxic sunscreen to exposed skin areas will help protect him from overexposure.

**Mosquitoes.** These little flying machines can do a job on your dog's snout and ears. Spray your dog with fly repellent formulated for horses to discourage both flying pests.

**Giardia.** Dogs can get giardia, which results in diarrhea. It is usually not debilitating, but it's definitely messy. A vaccine against giardia is available.

**Mushrooms.** Make sure your dog doesn't sample mushrooms along the trail. They could be poisonous to him, but he doesn't know that.

When you are finally ready to hit the trail with your dog, keep in mind that most national parks and many wilderness areas do not allow dogs on trails. Your best bet is to hike in national forests, BLM lands, and state parks. Always call ahead to see what the restrictions are.

# Hike Index

Albert Loop Trail, 2
Anchorage Overlook Trail, 94
Backside of Flattop Mountain
    Trail, 103
Bird Creek Trail, 152
Bird Ridge Trail, 148
Bold Ridge Trail, 61
Campbell Creek Trail, 190
Dew Mound Trail, 11
Earthquake Park / Inside the Slide
    Trail, 175
East Fork Trail to Tulchina Falls, 66
Eklutna Lakeside Trail, 46
Eydlu Bena Loop Trail, 57
Falls Creek Trail, 138
Flattop Mountain Trail, 97
Hanging Valley Trail, 41
Hillside Trail System (Overview), 83
Historic Iditarod (Crow Pass) Trail, 156
Indian Creek to Girdwood, 132
Lanie Fleischer Chester Creek
    Trail, 185

Lower Eagle River Trail and Barbara
    Falls, 22
McHugh Lake–Rabbit Lake Trail, 143
Mount Baldy, 27
Near Point Trail, 113
Potter Marsh Wildlife Viewing
    Boardwalk Trail, 170
Powerline Trail, 88
Ptarmigan Valley Trail, 77
Rendezvous Peak Trail, 32
River Trail at North Fork Eagle
    River, 18
Rodak Nature Trail, 7
Ship Creek Trail, 195
South Fork Eagle River Valley Trail, 36
Thunderbird Falls Trail, 72
Tony Knowles Coastal Trail, 180
Turnagain Arm Trail, 126
Twin Peaks Trail, 52
Williwaw Lakes Trail, 107
Winner Creek Trail, 164
Wolverine Peak Trail, 119

# About the Author

**John Tyson** has been a freelance photographer since 1996. His lifelong love of nature is evidenced by his work, which has been used by many national magazine, calendar, and book publishers. He is also the author of the books *Homes and Shelters for Backyard Birds* and *Best Easy Day Hikes Anchorage*. John has been hiking internationally and in parks across the country for more than thirty years and also enjoys biking, canoeing and birding.